By the same author

A Gazeteer of British Ghosts
A Gazeteer of Scottish and Irish Ghosts
Ghosts of North West England
Haunted London
A Host of Hauntings
Hauntings – New Light on Ten Famous Cases
The Ghosts of Borley
  (with Dr Paul Tabori)
Into the Occult
Deeper Into the Occult
The Vampire's Bedside Companion
Lives to Remember – A Casebook on Reincarnation
  (with Leonard Wilder)
Dictionary of the Supernatural
Ghosts of Wales
The Ghost Hunter's Companion
  (in preparation)
Horror Man – The Life of Boris Karloff
Life's a Drag – A Life of Danny La Rue

As editor:

Thirteen Famous Ghost Stories
  (Everyman's Library)

The Complete Book of Dowsing and Divining

Peter Underwood
Member of the British Society of Dowsers

Rider & Company
London Melbourne Sydney Auckland Johannesburg

For our good friends Bib and Don Galpin
at whose delightful cottage in Dorset
this book was completed

Rider & Company

An imprint of the Hutchinson Publishing Group

3 Fitzroy Square, London W1P 6JD

Hutchinson Group (Australia) Pty Ltd
30-32 Cremorne Street, Richmond South, Victoria 3121
PO Box 151, Broadway, New South Wales 2007

Hutchinson Group (NZ) Ltd
32-34 View Road, PO Box 40-086, Glenfield, Auckland 10

Hutchinson Group (SA) (Pty) Ltd
PO Box 337, Bergvlei 2012, South Africa

First published 1980
© Peter Underwood 1980

Set in APS Malibu by Brown Knight & Truscott Ltd

Printed in Great Britain by The Anchor Press Ltd
and bound by Wm Brendon & Son Ltd
both of Tiptree, Essex

British Library Cataloguing in Publication Data

Underwood, Peter
    The complete book of dowsing and divining
    1. Divining-rod
    I. Title
    133.3′23   BF1628

ISBN 0 09 141660 4

Contents

List of Illustrations   7
Acknowledgements   9
Introduction   11

1   A Short History of the Divining Rod   14
2   The Authenticity of Dowsing   37
3   Theories of Dowsing and Divining   47
4   Aspects of Dowsing and Divining   63
5   Dowsing Instruments and their Uses   84
6   Dowsers of the Past   109
7   Meet the Dowsers   129
8   Dowsing and Divining in the Modern World   150
9   How to Acquire the Art of Dowsing   168
10   Adventures in Dowsing and Divining   185
11   Dowsing Tests and their Problems   203
12   The British Society of Dowsers   217

Epilogue: a last word on how dowsing works   220
Select Bibliography   222
Index   224

Illustrations

The site of Borley Rectory, 'the most haunted house in England', at the time when dowsing was employed in an attempt to find the missing church plate.

Mrs Parker of Long Melford divining for the Borley church plate.

The author using a traditional hazel twig in a corner of his garden in Hampshire.

The author map dowsing; using a pendulum over a large-scale map.

The author using a dowsing stick or wand, perhaps the most primitive of all divining instruments.

Farmer David Bown with his angle-rods.

The interior of Borley Church, Essex, where dowsers and other sensitives (including Michael Bentine) have encountered a strange force. The Waldegrave tomb is on the left.

A chapel in the catacombs of Rome. It has been suggested that the 'staffs' may be early divining rods.

A typical biblical illustration of what may be a divining wand: 'Ruth and Naomi', after a painting by A. Hopfgarten.

The Divining-rod in mines in the sixteenth century Sebastian Munster, *Cosmographia universalis* (Basel, 1544).

Divining for metals in the sixteenth century. An illustration from the first treatise on divining, Agricola's *De re metallica*, 1571.

Exploration of a mining area by means of the divining-rod in the seventeenth century.
S. E. Lohneyss, *Bericht vom Bergkwerck* (Zellerfeldt, 1617).

A river scene such as some dowsers visualize as they walk across a barren tract of land. Actually the River Severn near Gloucester.

The Tower Lieutenant's official residence. The missing Barkstead treasure is likely to be buried somewhere nearby.

The Tower of London where several dowsers have attempted to locate hidden treasure.

Mr Robert Leftwich.

Treating a patient by radiesthesia.

Herbert Weaver using the Revealer Field Detector; a photographic record of the first attempt at 'resolving the centre of an artificial ray-path joined to a missing person'. 1967.

All photographs are the copyright of the author except for the following: Borley Church (*Peter Le Neve-Foster*); The Tower of London, and the Tower Lieutenant's official residence (*Chris Underwood*); The Revealer Field Detector (*Herbert Weaver*). Radiesthesia (*Radio Times Hulton Picture Library*)

Acknowledgements

The author gratefully acknowledges the help and co-operation of Geoffrey Abbott, Marc Alexander, Ray Armes, Peter G. Booker, David Bown, Tony Broughall, D. Gaskell Brown, Crispin Derby, Forbes Gibb, Michael Godfrey of *New Scientist*, Dr Vernon Harrison, Renée Haynes, A. Henshaw, Peter Le Neve-Foster, Sheila Merritt, Legory H. O'Loughlin, Peter Opie, Les Palmer, Grace and Arthur Peters, James Lee-Richardson, M. D. Rust, Chris Underwood, Herbert Weaver, A. H. Wesencraft; and also of such organizations as the British Society of Dowsers, the Society for Psychical Research, the Royal Aircraft Establishment at Farnborough, Hampshire, the South Californian Chapter of the American Society of Dowsers, *Fate* magazine, Dover Publishing Company, *Los Angeles Times*, the Harry Price Library at University of London, Weidenfeld (Publishers) Ltd, Water Research Centre, National Water Council, Northumbrian Water Authority, North West Water Authority, Severn Trent Water Authority, Southern Water Authority, South West Water Authority, Thames Water Authority, Welsh Water Authority, Wessex Water Authority, Yorkshire Water Authority and Strathclyde Regional Council.

Introduction

Another book on dowsing and divining? That is exactly what I thought when I first began to think about this book, and then I decided that what was needed to make mine a worthwhile book on a subject that seemed to be overladen with books of all kinds, was to take into account the works already written and see what the combined information led to; what the consensus of published opinion was on these matters; what the unpublished opinions and individual beliefs were; what the dowsers themselves thought and what adventures they had had; what some of the lesser known aspects of dowsing were; and how dowsing and dowsers fitted into the modern world.

As I began to research the subject I found that superstition has always dogged the history of dowsing and I recalled discussing this aspect of the subject with the late Robert Leftwich, one of the British Society of Dowsers official practitioners. I remarked on some of the superstitions, such as: the divining rod's affecting particular objects by special and identifiable degrees; the idea that only certain woods made successful divining rods; the part allegedly played by colour; and the importance of the position of the planets. Robert, in common with most modern dowsers, had little time for such beliefs and he agreed with me that, if one were to believe in all the supposed potential influences likely to affect the process, dowsing would not have survived to the present day.

One of the more outlandish ideas concerning dowsing has been the suggestion that a divining rod is an example of unconscious sexual symbolism, and in such a subject as dowsing and divining it is all too easy to be led into such fascinating byways that lead nowhere. I suppose one could even explore the fairy tradition of The Dancing Water in relation to dowsing, and it is an interesting thought that the art might in some way be associated with that magic spring of water which ensured perpetual youth and beauty (according to the Comtesse D'Aulnoy's *Fairy Tales* published in 1682), but I have endeavoured to keep my feet firmly on the ground and explore the phenomenon of dowsing through the eyes of experienced dowsers and investigators.

Yet even among practising dowsers there are widely diverging viewpoints and completely different approaches to a subject that has fascinated mankind and worried official science for centuries. For example, one correspondent (Mr A. Henshaw from Dorset) tells me 'after years of research and countless tests' he discovered that the 'location of underground streams is only a sideline to a far more interesting problem ....' To continue in his own words:

Briefly I discovered that in addition to magnetism and electricity there is a third force similar in many ways to the other two with which it forms a balance of power. This force is present in all active forms of life. It can be controlled the same as the other two and when any object becomes saturated with it, it becomes positive at its centre and negative at its outer edge, and although the dowser's stick reacts to it, the dowser himself is not conscious of any reaction – as he would be if he touched a live electric wire. By controlling this force he can identify almost any object by measuring the resistance of the object to the force. No two objects have the same resistance to the force. Size makes no difference; the only difference is time, and by testing it is possible to identify any object if it is in another room and out of sight of the dowser ... as a means of identification it is superior to any way that I have ever heard of ....

Another correspondent, Mr D. Gaskell Brown of Cornwall, tells me that for some forty-five years he has been interested in various aspects of healing, ranging all the way from herbalism to psychic healing and he feels that this is an important aspect of dowsing. His letter continues:

I usually use the pendulum for making the analysis of a patient's condition. In the majority of cases I never meet the patient but use a signature, a lock of hair, a photograph or a spot of blood as a "contact". From any of these I can make an analysis in some detail and decide whether the trouble is physical, mental or emotional. So far as treatment is concerned it is not suggestion because both animals and babies respond, as do adults who do not know they are being treated. One of the great advantages of this sort of treatment is that no physical contact is necessary and that it is just as effective over great distances as it is when the patient is close at hand . . . .

It seems to me that the time is long overdue for an objective and penetrating look at such a curious and potentially important subject as dowsing and divining.

The Savage Club   PETER UNDERWOOD
Berkeley Square
London W1

1. A Short History of the Divining Rod

A belief in the power and efficiency of the divining rod can be said to have existed from the earliest ages, if we accept the 'wish-rods' of the ancient Greeks and Romans whose writings contain numerous allusions to such objects, and especially the staff of Hermes, sometimes shown as a forked rod.

Viewed from the position of a diviner many classical writers appear to have the divining rod in mind when writing certain passages. Flavius Arrianus, commonly called Arrian, a Greek historian, philosopher and pupil and friend of Epictetus, is credited with writing, '... He had a bad father, but I have a good one, and that is the staff of Hermes. Touch what you will with it, they say, and it turns to gold.' Marcus Tullius Cicero, Roman statesman, orator, philosopher and man of letters wrote in his philosophy of morals *De Officiis* the well-known passage, 'But were all the necessaries of life supplied to us by means of a divine rod [*virgula divina*] then ....' Publius Cornelius Tacitus, the Roman historian and governor of Britain, tells us in his valuable ethnographical work *Germania* that the Germans practised arts of divination by means of rods: 'For the purpose their method is simple. They cut a rod off some fruit-trees into bits, and after having distinguished them by various marks, they cast them into a white cloth ... then the priest thrice draws each piece, and explains the oracle according to the marks.' Other early writers speak of the use of 'an osier rod', i.e. a twig of willow.

The reference to Hermes is particularly interesting.

One of the earliest and most primitive of all the gods of Greece, the rod or wand invariably carried by this herald of the gods, has been thought by some students of rhabdomancy to be a divining rod, and it may be significant that Hermes, the Greek Mercury, is usually represented as a handsome, nude and lively youth with winged sandals, a broad-brimmed traveller's hat and the caduceus, or rod, entwined with two serpents. Now serpents, in addition to being one of the basic symbols of alchemy and of ancient religion, have long been regarded as guardians of mines, and the discovery of mines is frequently the objective of the diviner's art. So we have the messenger of the gods, patron of the quick-witted, the god of good luck, carrying a rod entwined with serpents.

From earliest times, serpents and demons were supposed to guard the mines from intrusion and it may be that the supernatural power of the serpents on Hermes's wand had ascendancy over the guardian serpents, while the holy and sacred associations of the rod itself dealt with the demon guardians.

So estimates of the age of the divining rod vary from one authority[1] suggesting a history of 7000 years, to another[2] supposing an age of 3200 years, to Sir William Barrett and Theodore Besterman, in their classic volume, *The Divining Rod: An Experimental and Psychological Investigation*,[3] estimating the age of the rod as somewhere between 400 and 500 years!

The explanation for such wide differences in the possible age of the divining rod by equally distinguished experts probably lies in the fact that each is viewing the divining rod in a different way. Certainly the divining rod can be regarded as a means of divination since it indicates the presence of water, a mineral or something non-mineral by bending. Thus, it might seem reasonable to look at the divining rod in the same way as one might look at the other forms of divination used by ancient

[1]Solco W. Tromp, *Psychical Physics: A Scientific Analysis of Dowsing, Radiesthesia and Kindred Phenomena* (Elsevier, Houston, 1949).
[2]Gaston Burridge, writing in *Western Folklore* in 1955.
[3]Methuen, 1926.

man who sought for signs and signals in the behaviour of birds, in a cock's picking up of grain, from the position of the stars and planets, from the entrails of animals, from excrement, and from sacrificial ashes – to mention a few.

Depending on what the omens were, ancient man embarked on war, held council meetings, married, divorced or conducted business; but, if the omens told him the time was unfavourable, then he waited. Viewed on this level – when dowsing is one method of divination – the divining rod is indeed of very ancient origin.

But it can be argued that the special use of a rod of some kind that could indicate the presence of minerals is of much more recent date, and the earliest pictorial representation of a dowser at work would appear to be in the first quarter of the sixteenth century: an ancient Latin folio by Sebastian Munster, called *Cosmography*. Yet there are enthusiastic water diviners who point to the biblical Moses as the first water diviner, since he produced water for the Israelites in the wilderness of Zin (between the Red Sea and the Dead Sea) by the use of his rod. It is interesting to note in passing that most biblical scholars agree that the word 'rod' or 'staff' means a shoot or branch of a tree, and that the staff of the Bible was 'like a sceptre, an emblem of dominion.'[1] Many present-day water diviners would not argue with such descriptions of their divining rods.

So, with a little imagination, some of the divining fraternity suggest that a divining rod or forked twig was commonly used by the ancient Persians, Romans, Greeks, Assyrians and Scythians; and there is no denying that the Romans used the term *virgula divina* – the 'divining rod' – although the term was mainly used to distinguish the art of the divining rod from other methods of divination; Georgius Agricola called the rod *virgula furcata* – forked rod – but the term 'divining rod' has persisted, together with some of the superstitious notions associated with the old *virgula divina*.

By the same token the word 'rhabdomancy' is derived

[1] John Eadie, *A Biblical Cyclopaedia* (Richard Griffin, 1855).

from the Greek *rhabdos* for rod and *manteia* for divination, but to the indifferent observer there is no real evidence that either the Romans or the Greeks in ancient times used their rods for the location of water or gold or any other mineral. And, although representations of Mediter-ranean idols carrying forked rods have been discovered, it seems likely that such rods were purely symbols of power rather than divining instruments.

It is significant that the German scholar and man of science Georgius Agricola (1490-1555), who was known as 'the father of mineralogy', quotes early Roman poly-maths such as Pliny the Elder, who wrote a scholarly thirty-seven volume work on natural history in which he dealt with the earth's shape and surface phenomena such as seas, rivers and springs, and included detailed instructions for finding water. Pliny the Elder had a keen eye, but there is no mention of anything remotely resembling a divining rod.

On the other hand Georgius Agricola himself, in his posthumously published *De re metallica*[1] – a complete and systematic treatise on mining and metallurgy – provides an early description of the divining rod in the form of a forked stick. Agricola's famous work was probably writ-ten some years before the author's death, since the dedication is dated 1550; he spent a lot of time visiting mines and studying the various techniques they employed. This is his description of the forked twig and the early method of divining for metal:

There are many great contentions between miners concern-ing the forked twig, for some say that it is of the greatest use in discovering veins, and others deny it. Some of those who manipulate and use the twig, first cut a fork from a hazel bush with a knife, for this bush they consider more efficacious than any other for revealing the veins, especially if the hazel bush grows above a vein. . . . All alike grasp the forks of the twig with their hands, clenching their fists, it being necessary that the clenched fingers should be held toward the sky in order that the twig should be raised at that end where the two branches meet. They then wander hither and thither at random

[1]Translated from the first Latin edition by H. C. and L. H. Hoover – Mr and Mrs Herbert Hoover (Dover, New York, 1950).

through mountainous regions. It is said that the moment they place their feet on a vein the twig immediately turns and twists, and so by its action discloses the vein; when they move their feet again and go away from that spot the twig becomes once more immobile.

The truth is, they assert, the movement of the twig is caused by the power of the veins, and sometimes this is so great that the branches of trees growing near a vein are deflected toward it. On the other hand, those who say the twig is of no use to good and serious men, also deny that the motion is due to the power of the veins, because the twigs will not move for everybody, but only for those who employ incantations and craft.

This is one of the earliest definite references to a divining rod as we know it today. Although there are earlier allusions to the art, many of them leave much to the imagination. The first discussion of the art of the divining rod in English occurs in Robert Fludd's *Philosophia Moysaica* (Gouda, 1638). Sir William Barrett (1844-1925) has referred to a 1430 manuscript that would appear to have been written by a kind of primitive mine surveyor. Barrett was a physicist who carefully and methodically studied most branches of psychical research (he was one of the founders of both the English and the American Societies for Psychical Research), and he conducted detailed examination of rhabdomancy and produced the already referred to *The Divining Rod* (with Theodore Besterman, in 1926), but in his earlier volume, *Psychical Research*,[1] he presents a fascinating, if occasionally inaccurate, survey of the subject, which he entitles 'The So-Called Divining or Dowsing Rod'.

At the end of the sixteenth century the divining rod became a topic of controversy among thinking people. By this time there can be no doubt that rods were being used extensively and successfully in Germany, especially in the Hartz mountains, for the detection of undiscovered minerals and in 1518 Martin Luther (1483-1546), the German religious reformer, declared that the use of the divining rod violated the first commandment, 'Thou shalt have no other gods before me' (Exodus 20:3). One

[1]William Norgate, 1911.

may be tempted to agree with my old friend Dennis Wheatley's caustic comment, 'Luther was obviously a nut',[1] but this proclamation against the rod was reinforced in 1658 when the divining rod was again attacked on theological grounds by the publication of an academic thesis at Wittenberg, the capital of the little duchy of Saxe-Wittenberg with close associations with Martin Luther, who had lived there for a time at the Augustinian monastery, and later the town became the home of Luther and his wife and family.

The 'learned dissertation', as it has been called, concluded that the movements of the divining rod when it indicated the presence of some invisible mineral were due either to fraud or, more ominously, to 'an implicit pact' with the devil. Other declarations and treatises followed similar lines of thought, all associating the divining rod and its users with satanic connections. Typically an early eighteenth-century engraving shows a priest removing a mask from the face of a dowser to reveal a devil! Yet in some respects this attitude continues to this day.

Such aspersions were dealt with by the dowsing fraternity in a subtle way. They disassociated themselves from any accusation of collusion with the devil by gradually saturating the ritual and practicality of divining with reputedly holy influences. Their rods or twigs should be cut, preferably between eleven and twelve o'clock, on St John the Baptist's Day, the midsummer festival celebrated on 24 June, or on Good Friday (probably so-named to distinguish it from the other Fridays of the year, as Friday was considered to be an unlucky day).[2] They should be of special wood: the magical hazel with its reputed power against all enchantments, the rowan with its protection against evil of all kinds, the sacred mistletoe – especially useful in finding treasure – or the magic birch or lucky willow with their powers to repel enchantment. As it was cut (if possible from a tree which had had seven shoots in the year), whatever wood

[1] Dennis Wheatley, *Drink and Ink, 1919-1977* (Hutchinson, 1979).
[2] W. Carew Hazlitt, *Faiths and Folklore* (Reeves and Turner, 1905).

was chosen, the Holy Trinity was invoked and the twig had to be torn from the tree with one quick motion.

The forked branch would either be bound to a child about to be baptized or about to receive the name of John, or it would be placed in the bed of a newly baptized child and afterwards the 'wand' would take the Christian name of the child. Some authorities maintain that only after the twig had been placed on an altar, wrapped in swaddling clothes and laid on a white plate, and had Holy Mass read over it, could it be used by a Protestant. Incantations calling upon the Father, the Son and the Holy Ghost would be used during the act of divination, and gradually the satanic associations with the divining rod and its works retreated and finally almost disappeared, leaving behind the tradition that certain woods make the best divining rods; although still today not all dowsers will admit that any forked twig will act as a divining rod – or indeed any forked article.

In 1692 the activity in France of an inferior mason, Jacques Aymar, brought a new dimension to the practice of divining with a rod.[1] On the morning of 6 July of that year a wine merchant and his wife were both found brutally murdered in the cellar of their establishment at Lyons. They had died the previous evening, robbery having obviously been the motive since every available penny had been taken, and it seemed highly probable that there had been more than one assailant. Beside the corpses lay a large bottle wrapped in straw and a blood-stained bill-hook. At first the authorities were hopeful of an early arrest but they were unable to find any clues to help them and soon they were at a complete loss to know which way to turn to solve the dastardly crime.

Then a neighbour of the victims reminded the authorities of a curious incident following a mysterious theft at Grenoble four years earlier. There, when they were unable to solve the crime, the local magistrate had enlisted the help of a certain Jacques Aymar of Dauphiny, a man who claimed to be able to use a divining rod to trace criminals. At Grenoble, after following where the

[1]See the present author's *Deeper Into the Occult* (Harrap, 1975).

rod led, Aymar found himself, together with representatives of the local authority, outside the gates of a prison.

His method was to hold the divining rod lightly in his hands and to follow wherever the rod led as it rotated in his hands, seemingly without any conscious effort on his part. If he took a wrong turning or started to walk in the wrong direction, the rod ceased to rotate. By this means Aymar laboriously led the way, street by street, to the prison yard. After permission was obtained to enter the prison the diviner succeeded in discovering the culprits who revealed the name of a farmer who had received the stolen goods. When the farmer denied all knowledge of the matter, Aymar again brought his rod into play and located the hidden valuables.

Apparently it all began when Aymar was using his divining rod in an attempt to find water; suddenly the rod dipped sharply in his hands. Thinking that he had found an underground spring or subterranean stream, Aymar arranged for digging to take place at the spot indicated by the rod. Instead of water, the body of a corpse was dug out of the ground, a woman who had been murdered by strangulation and buried in a barrel. The victim was recognized as a local person who had disappeared a few months earlier. Aymar accompanied the authorities to the woman's home and there his divining rod indicated the husband as the perpetrator of the crime. The man attempted to escape and so sealed his own fate.

When the magistrates of Lyons heard of these activities of Jacques Aymar they decided to send for him. First Aymar was taken to the scene and to the house where the atrocity had been committed and there, without any guidance from anyone, he located the scene of the murders, and at the exact spots where each of the bodies had laid the rod in Aymar's hands became very agitated; the diviner's pulse was found to have increased to such a rate that a doctor present asserted that with such a pulse-rate a patient would be described as being in a state of high fever.

With such definite indications to guide him, Aymar left the cellar and, still apparently guided by his rod, set off up the street at a brisk walking pace. Following a devious route for the rest of that day and the day following Aymar eventually led the three officials accompanying him to a cottage where, despite the protestations of the occupants, Aymar indicated that the murderers had visited the cottage and had been given refreshment there.

At this stage the officials decided to test Aymar's powers and with his consent they obtained three more bill-hooks, identical with the one used for the crime, and buried them and the murder weapon, secretly and at different times, in various parts of a garden. Aymar was then brought to the plot of ground and asked to find the blood-stained tool. He demonstrated without difficulty that his rod vibrated over the place where the murder weapon was buried and remained motionless over the burial places of the other bill-hooks.

Still not quite convinced, the officials led Aymar away and re-buried all four bill-hooks in different places and when they brought the diviner back to the testing ground they imposed the additional condition of blindfolding him. Still he had no difficulty in finding the blood-stained bill-hook. Satisfied that he or his rod possessed some unknown power, the authorities allowed Aymar to endeavour to guide them to the murderers.

He led them a long way to the bank of the River Rhône and there pointed out the footprints of three men at the water's edge and said they had taken to the water. A boat was obtained and, although Aymar found some difficulty in following the trail over water, he eventually did so. After some time he indicated where the three men had landed and where they had stopped and rested, and by slow and laborious degrees he made his way to a military camp.

Once inside the camp at Sablon, Aymar again became very agitated and with flushed cheeks and a high pulse-rate he prepared to seek out the men concerned in the murders, but the soldiers became hostile and he and his companions were forced to leave the camp.

Back at Lyons his progress was studied and a special licence was granted to enter the camp and continue 'investigations', but as soon as he returned to Sablon he announced that the men being sought were no longer there. Again Aymar took up the trail and led his companions along the banks of the Rhône as far as Beaucaire and there he announced that the murderers had parted company.

Through the crowded streets (it was the time of the annual town fair) Aymar led the way, still guided by his rod, to the prison. There he declared that inside they would find one of the wanted men. When the necessary permits had been arranged, Aymar and his party were allowed into the prison and were taken to that part of the establishment where the latest prisoners were lodged. There Aymar applied his rod to each man in turn and it showed a positive response when aimed at a hunchback who had recently been admitted, charged with a theft in the town.

Aymar announced that the hunchback was one of three men involved in the robbery and murders at Lyons and he said he would endeavour to find the remaining two. He added that the movements of his rod told him that the two missing criminals had been in Beaucaire but had left by a path that met the Nîmes road. At this point the officials decided that the hunchback, who protested his complete innocence and said he had never visited Lyons, should be taken to that city to face the magistrates on a charge of murder and so the party, including Aymar, returned to Lyons.

Aymar was careful to lead the officials and their prisoner back to Lyons by the exact path which he was convinced the criminals had taken as they fled and although the hunchback repeatedly protested that he had never been that way before, his protestations were of no avail for he was recognized time and again at different houses and inns they passed, where the three men had stopped for rest or refreshment.

At the little town of Bagnols the host and hostess of a tavern recognized him at once and swore that he and two companions had spent the night at the inn and their detailed descriptions of the two missing men corresponded with that of the occupants of cottages where the three men had obtained food and drink.

The hunchback, in the face of all this damning evidence, admitted that he had been with the two wanted men but said he had been their servant and had had no part in the actual murders and robbery; he had been directed to an upper room where he had kept watch while the criminals carried out their evil work.

At Lyons, under examination, he elaborated on this story to the extent that he described how the two thieves had taken a large bottle wrapped in straw to the wine cellar and had persuaded the wine merchant and his wife to accompany them while he had remained upstairs in the shop. After the murders the two men had returned to the shop where they had helped themselves to money and jewellery. Then all three men fled to the courtyard of a large house where they passed the night. (This was a house that Aymar had approached with some hesitation before making his way out of Lyons.) Next day, said the hunchback, they had left Lyons together, stopping at the cottage and elsewhere, as indicated by Aymar; everything the diviner said about the fleeing men appeared to be confirmed.

Aymar was now given authority to see whether he could find the other two men and after many detours he again led the way to the prison at Beaucaire. This time his search for the guilty pair among the prisoners proved fruitless, but the prison authorities were able to confirm that a man answering the description of one of the men sought had in fact called at the prison soon after the hunchback had been taken away and, learning that his friend had been taken to Lyons, he had hurriedly left. Aymar now set out to trace this man and soon he found that the trail of the other missing man joined that of the man he was looking for and he continued his efforts to follow the two men for several days. Eventually Aymar and his companions reached the border of France and it seemed evident that the two criminals had eluded their pursuers by leaving France and entering Switzerland.

Back in Lyons the hunchback, on his way to execution, was taken past the wine shop, where the recorder publicly read out the crime and sentence, which had been decided by thirty judges, and the criminal knelt and begged pardon for the murders in which he had been involved. He was then broken on the wheel in the Place des Terreaux on 30 August 1692.

It is an astonishing story, authenticated by three circumstantial accounts, numerous letters and reports written by one of the magistrates and eye-witness testimony of the whole affair. Aymar became something of a national celebrity and, when he successfully passed several impressive tests imposed on him by the authorities at Lyons, his fame led him to Paris where, strangely enough, his gifts seemed to desert him and he failed test after test devised by the resourceful Prince de Conté and eventually Aymar returned to his home a discredited and disappointed man. But the implications of his activities and his undoubted success on occasions opened the way for later users of the divining rod, and not even a decree issued by the Inquisition in 1701 could effectively halt the use of the divining rod which became more and more popular. That popularity continues to this day after it was realized that the rod could apparently always locate water.

It might be said in passing that from the accounts available it would seem likely that Jacques Aymar possessed clairvoyant powers in addition to the ability to use the divining rod, and it is interesting to note that similar faculties have been enjoyed by many dowsers and users of the divining rod since that time. It may be that clairvoyant and clairaudient powers, which many people believe everyone possesses to a greater or lesser degree, enhance or assist the ability to use a divining rod; it may even be that the act of dowsing is a physical demonstration of extrasensory perception, of which clairvoyance and clairaudience are now considered to be a part. Be that as it may, Jacques Aymar ably demonstrated that in certain hands the divining rod is able to do more than locate water.

A little known early example of water divining is to be found in the life of Saint Teresa of Avila (1515-1582). The 'saint of the flaming heart', revered by Roman

Catholics as the greatest woman writer in Spain, author of *The Castle of the Soul*, experienced visions and is credited with restoring a child to life.

She formed a new order, the Reformed Carmelites, and before opening her new house in 1562, was in process of considering an excellent site for her convent where there was only one drawback: there seemed to be no sign of any water in the area. Then one day, according to a life of the saint,[1] a friar named Antonio was in the church cloister with some fellow friars and he chanced to have in his hand a twig which he waved – some say he made the sign of the cross. At any rate, Teresa reported that he made a movement with the twig and then, spontaneously and without really knowing why he did so, he said, 'Dig just there . . . .' Accordingly the friars set about digging and soon found a plentiful supply of water – a supply that was subsequently used for drinking, washing and all the needs of the convent – a supply which, it is said, never ran dry.

Never having heard of dowsing, Teresa, naturally enough in the circumstances, had no explanation for the event and regarded it as a miracle. In fact it is the first historical reference to dowsing for water, notwithstanding that it was unintentional – presumably. Certainly Saint Teresa ran the convent and lived there for the next twenty years during which time she enjoyed 'glorious revelations' in 'numerous visions' – in addition to a plentiful supply of fresh and sweet water!

Another important early book showing that even in the seventeenth century the French government used the art of the diviner to find water is Baroness de Beausoleil's *La restitution de Pluton*.[2] Both the Baroness and her husband apparently used their ingenuity or art over a substantial period of time to discover, authenticate and develop, mines for the government of the day. Using divining rods to locate the water, they gradually became respected and established as dowsers so that in the book the Baroness was able to rcommend the use of the

[1]Helen Hester Colvill, *Saint Teresa of Spain*, (Dutton, New York, 1909).
[2]1640.

divining rod for discovering unknown springs of water in areas believed to be dry.

It is sad to relate that both the Baroness and the Baron were later apprehended on a charge of sorcery, and indeed the Baron died in the Bastille. His wife breathed her last at Vincennes (a wooded suburb of Paris) about 1645, although she had lived to see the divining rod achieve some degree of general respectability, and certainly the idea of divining for metal spread through western Europe and especially to Cornwall, where German miners had been imported to England during the reign of Elizabeth I.

The Germans took to England their divining rods and by the end of the seventeenth century locating gold, metal and water by means of the divining rod was common practice in practically every part of Europe.

Soon, with exploration and colonization of parts of the continents of Africa, Asia, the Americas, Australasia and the subcontinent of India, the use of the divining rod was virtually worldwide. Only in southern India is there some evidence that the use of some kind of divining rod may have been employed before the arrival of the British, in 1612.

It is interesting to notice that early divination by means of the rod can be found in each colonized region of South Africa – whether the colonizers be British, Dutch or German – and in South America following the arrival of settlers from Portugal and Spain, where the divining rod had been known and used for centuries. In the same way the practice spread to Canada and the United States with the arrival of English and French settlers, and there is certainly no evidence of water divining in the history of the North American Indians whose culture is full of other divination practices.

The miners of Saxony and the Hartz mountain region of Germany are usually regarded as being the first users of the forked rod for divining purposes, certainly to any great extent. Sir William Barrett[1] has pointed out that they were possibly led to its use by the once universal

[1]*Psychical Research* (Williams and Norgate, 1911).

belief that metallic ores attracted certain trees which drooped over the place where those ores were to be found; in fact, of course, the drooping is likely to have been caused by a deficiency in the soil. A branch of the tree would be cut off and held to see where it drooped. Later, a branch was held in each hand and the extremities tied together. Finally, for convenience, a forked branch would be cut and the two ends grasped one in each hand with palms upwards, the arms of the holder being brought to the sides of the body so that the forked twig was held in somewhat unstable equilibrium, 'and the diviner set forth on his quest' with, in olden times, certain solemnities and invocations.

During the reign of Elizabeth I the Cornish mines were developed and exploited by a few 'merchant venturers' and, during their travels to explore the best methods of locating and mining minerals, they visited Saxony and brought back with them stories and accounts of local diviners and their rods and the remarkable results they achieved. On subsequent visits one or two German diviners and their rods came to England with the merchants and it is interesting to realize that the colloquial German word for the divining rod was at that time *schlag-ruthe* or striking rod; translated into Middle English this becomes the *duschan* or striking rod, and finally 'deusing or dowsing rod'. The term 'deusing rod' was perhaps first used in literature by John Locke (1632-1704), the philosopher, and his friend Robert Boyle (1627-1691), one of the original fellows of the Royal Society, reflecting the favourable position already enjoyed by the dowsing rod among English miners with a passage in Locke's scientific essays published in 1663. A century later, in 1778, a standard work on Cornish mines stated that nearly all the mines in Cornwall had been located by the dowsing rod and the instrument continued to be widely used for this purpose for at least another hundred years.

In the arid districts of southern France, during the seventeenth century, there is evidence[1] that the *baguette*

[1] Le Brun, *Histoire critique des pratiques superstitieuses* (Paris, 1702).

or forked stick was widely used, not only to discover underground and undiscovered minerals but also for a wide variety of purposes including the tracking of criminals, the tracing of deserted children's fathers, the discovery of hidden treasure and lost boundaries, and other diverse activities. When it seemed that the divining rod was beginning to take the place of the judicial powers – people were beginning to appeal to the rod instead of to the courts for solutions to their problems – the use of the divining rod became something of a scandal and, as we have seen, in the moral world was prohibited, Cardinal Camus having invoked the authority of the Inquisition. Nevertheless the rod continued to be very widely used for the discovery of underground water throughout France and many other parts of Europe. In 1659 a Jesuit priest, Gaspard Schott, stated that the divining rod was then used in every town in Germany and that he had frequent opportunity of seeing it employed in the discovery of hidden treasures.

The somewhat credulous seventeenth-century English astrologer William Lilly (1602-1681) dabbled with rhabdomancy and was, perhaps surprisingly, unsuccessful with the divining rod. He asserted that the successful operators of the rod required secrecy and intelligence in those engaged in the art and, above all, a strong faith and a competent knowledge of their work. His adventures in seeking treasure with a divining rod in Westminster Abbey are related in a later chapter.

Dr Thouvénel, a physician of Louis XVI, published, in 1781 and 1784, meritorious and lengthy reports of critical tests he had conducted with an orphan boy named Bleton who has been described as 'perhaps the most remarkable dowser known in history.'[1] A wealth of contemporary evidence is presented to show that Bleton discovered a great number of unsuspected hidden springs under the arid ground of a French province and 'converted a desert into a fruitful country'. Furthermore, it is evident that the remarkable and far-reaching results achieved by Bleton led to the most searching enquiries, examinations

[1]William Barrett, *Psychical Research* (Williams and Norgate, 1911).

and interrogations, and the severest tests produced exemplary results so that many of those who were most sceptical of the boy's abilities, were eventually convinced of his genuine capacity to discover water with the use of his rod.

Jonathan Swift (1667-1745), dean of St Patrick's, Dublin, and British satirist wrote in 1710 his 'Virtues of Sid Hamlet the Magician's Rod':

> They tell us something strange and odd,
> About a certain magic rod,
> That, bending down its top, divines
> Whene'er the soil has golden mines;
> Where there are none, it stands erect,
> Scorning to show the least respect;
> As ready was the wand of Sid,
> To bend where golden mines were hid;
> In Scottish hills found precious ore,
> Where none e'er look'd for it before;
> And by a gentle bow divined
> How well a cully's purse was lin'd
> To a forlorn and broken rake,
> Stood without motion, like a stake.

Another British author, Thomas De Quincey (1785-1859) wrote of the wonderful success of 'jowsers' (as dowsers were vulgarly called at that time) in parts of Somerset where the location of underground water is extremely difficult and where 'scientific skill' had been known to draw a blank.

In the latter part of the eighteenth century the first mention of the art of water divining in America appears, incorporated with reports of the activities of witches and the practice of witchcraft, and it seems likely that this early association between water divining and witchcraft accounts for the American term 'water witching', which remains to this day the popular term for the use of the divining rod; the only other possible origin of the term lies in the fact that early American dowsers usually preferred the wood of the witch hazel for their divining rods. At all events in no other English-speaking country is the term 'water witching' used, although the practice of using a twig to find water spread and grew, and there are many reputable accounts of the success of the divining rod throughout the nineteenth century and right up to the present time both in the United States and throughout Europe.

Perhaps a couple of examples from the nineteenth century will suffice at this point. Near Horsham in Sussex, according to Sir William Barrett, Sir Henry Harben built a mansion on his fine estate and he had a 90 foot deep well sunk, in the hope of finding water, but he was unsuccessful. He took advice and sank another well, this time 55 feet deep, at the spot pointed out by the experts, but still he found no water. He tried a third time, again led by the specialists in the matter, and this time he sank a 100 foot well deep into the Sussex clay. From the bottom of this well he was advised to run horizontal tunnels or adits which he did at considerable cost, but still he found no water.

Finally, against his better judgement, he contacted a notable dowser, John Mullins of Wiltshire, who surveyed the estate armed with his forked twig and after searching for a long time found that his divining rod reacted violently at a certain spot and he declared that an abundant supply of water was available there at a depth of no more than twenty feet; while another spot, close by, would also yield water.

The positions Mullins had indicated were situated on a slight elevation, and two wells were dug at the places suggested, through sandstone rock, and a perennial supply of excellent water was discovered at a depth of 15 feet.

A second case involving John Mullins was even more remarkable for it concerned a large bacon factory whose proprietors were considering moving their premises elsewhere, until they sought the help of the dowser.

In 1887 the firm of Richardson and Company of Waterford found that they needed a larger supply of water than they possessed so they arranged for a 62 foot well to be sunk at what appeared to be a promising place, but no water was found. They then went to a professional firm who, after themselves taking geological surveys and soundings, suggested another place as that most likely to yield results. Here a bore-hole 292 foot deep was sunk, but still no water was found; the bore-hole was widened and, although a little water was then found, it was such an insignificant amount that the bore-hole was abandoned.

The following year the Irish firm tried again. This time, acting on skilled advice, they sank a bore-hole, 7 inches in diameter at the bottom of the original 62 foot well. This work was undertaken by the Diamonddrill Rockboring Company and, not without some difficulty, they bored through ancient and incredibly hard silurian rock no less than 612 feet and still they found no water. They continued boring for a further 333 feet – a sum of 945 feet – and a total well-depth of more than 1000 feet, and still they found no water.

After this complicated and expensive failure to locate water yet another spot was selected for boring, and again acting on the finest geological advice obtainable, a bore-hole 52 foot deep was made. The layers of rock were found to be identical to those previously encountered and the geologists advised the firm that the search was hopeless. So Messrs Richardson were considering the advisability of the enormous inconvenience and expense of moving their factory when someone suggested they try John Mullins, the English dowser.

Mullins travelled to Ireland. He was told nothing about the previous abortive efforts to find water. He walked around and over the factory premises, about 700 feet by 300 feet in area, asking no questions but silently concentrating on the ground, holding his divining rod in his hands.

Suddenly, at a spot only a few yards from the deep bore-hole, the twig twisted so violently in his hands that it broke in two pieces. Here, said Mullins, there was plenty of water, at a depth of about 90 feet. He also pointed out two or three other places nearby where his rod twisted as he walked, showing that there was water below ground. Although, in view of past experience in that area, everyone felt that it would be a complete waste of time, boring at the place indicated by Mullins resulted in a wealth of water being found at a depth of just under 90 feet.

Sir William Barrett mentions that a local geologist was asked to report progress to an official of the Irish Geological Survey and that he had personally consulted these letters. There can be no doubt that John Mullins found water where the scientific authorities of the day were baffled – a well that from that time (1889) until Barrett's report (1911) yielded an unfailing supply of excellent water at a rate varying from 3000 to 5000 gallons an hour. One official from H. M. Geological Survey investigated this whole matter for Sir William Barrett and in his report stated that Mullins must have struck a line of fault or narrow fissure in the hard, primitive rock, as the water-bearing points the dowser indicated all fixed on a straight line. Though this fissure probably streamed from the adjacent high ground, there was no surface indication of this fissure as the rock was buried by 40 feet of boulder clay.

One other example of the dowser's ability recounted by Barrett in his book[1] and in person at a meeting of The Ghost Club concerned an amateur dowser, Mr J. H. Jones of Waterford. At the time he researched and wrote *Psychical Research*, Sir William Barrett lived at Kingstown, County Dublin. His friend Sir John Franks, C.B., former Secretary to the Irish Land Commission, required water on some property in West Kilkenny and, being sceptical of dowsing and divining, he arranged to subject Mr Jones to a series of tests.

It so happened that there were some long-forgotten wells on the property; they had not been in use for many years and there was nothing above ground level to show their whereabouts, or any sign on the surface of the ground – not even old paths leading to them. Mr Jones, a complete stranger to the locality, set to work in the area in the presence of Sir John Franks.

First he quartered the ground backwards and forwards, 'like a dog looking for game'. Apparently finding the direction of the flow of water, he carefully followed it

[1]*Psychical Research* (Williams and Norgate, 1911)

until he reached exactly the place where the hidden wells existed. For the next test Sir John took the dowser a good half mile away to a spot where it was impossible to have any idea where the well might be, a place that was in fact out of sight until one reached a position within 2 yards of the place, yet the dowser did not hesitate and indicated the position of the unused well with absolute accuracy.

Mr Jones then selected a precise spot to sink a new well, about half a mile from any of the old wells. It was necessary to cut and blast through solid rock but 38 feet down they hit a spring of water and the new well resulted in a plentiful supply of good water.

Sir William Barrett decided to test the theory of dowsing himself by comparing the findings of two independent dowsers. He wanted to see whether both men would indicate the same places for water and also the same places where water would *not* be found. He selected a site on a mountain slope in County Wicklow which had, to his knowledge, never been visited by a water diviner and where there did not appear to be any indications whatever either that there was any underground water or that there were no hidden springs. Indeed, the selected spot was a grass-covered field with a bed-rock believed to be only a few feet below the surface of the ground.

First Sir William employed the services of an English dowser of repute, Mr W. Stone from Lincolnshire, who went over specially for the purpose. After walking back and forth across the field Mr Stone said plenty of water would be found 20 feet below the surface at two definite places and he indicated another adjacent spot where he said no water would be found. Sir William then took him to another field on the other side of the mountain where the dowser's forked twig showed no indication of moving and Mr Stone declared that no water would be found anywhere in the field.

Sir William then obtained the services of a successful amateur dowser and tried the same experiments at the same places a few weeks later. The results were precisely those obtained by Mr Stone. A series of bore-holes were made; first in one field and then in the other. The bed-rock proved to be deeper than had been anticipated but, after boring through 16 feet of hard and dry boulder clay, at the spot where the dowsers had said water would be found, a splendid spring of water was encountered.

A short distance away, where the diviners had said no water would be found, a week was spent boring into solid rock and no water was located. A third boring, again at a spot indicated by both dowsers as a place to find water, water was found at a depth of 18 feet. In the other field, where both dowsers had said no water would be found, although in fact it appeard if anything to be the more likely place, several more bore-holes were made in likely places but, although nearly a month was spent on the site, no water was found.

Sir William Barrett was so struck by the unexpected and plentiful supply of water discovered in the first field that he eventually bought the plot of land, built a cottage there and sank a well in place of the bore-hole and, even in times of great drought when many springs ran dry, that well at Carrigoona never failed to produce a plentiful supply of good water.

The work and borings carried out at the field showed that a bed of sand and gravel lay above the bed-rock and below the surface of boulder clay; through this the underground water flowed. But how had the dowsers hit upon this permeable water-line, Sir William asked himself, when there was nothing whatever to indicate its presence? These and subsequent tests, in all over a hundred, convinced Sir William Barrett that water divining worked. Some of his conclusions as to the possible explanation for this 'peculiar gift', as he called it, will be explored in a later chapter.

And so we reach the present century when water divining is used throughout the world without anyone really knowing how it works. In Spain the ministry of agriculture issued a technical manual in 1953 on the methods of finding underground water and one chapter is devoted to the use of the divining rod. Societies and organizations have been formed to further the aims of dowsing and the day may not be far distant when the art is accepted as a scientific fact. To this end there exist such associations as the Society of Dowsers in Britain, L'Association des Amis de la Radiesthésie in France, Gesellschaft für Wissenschaftliche Pendelferschung in Germany, Centre International d'Étude de la Radiesthésie in Belgium, as well as several in the United States of America; and an International Congress of Radiesthesia meets periodically. There are several businesses catering for the dowser's needs and supplying manufactured apparatus and a few firms, such as one named 'Wright Rain', even specialize in finding water for industrial contractors by dowsing and divining methods. It is a far cry from Moses and his rod and even from the itinerant prospectors in the mining districts of Germany in the fifteenth century.

2. The Authenticity of Dowsing

To establish the authenticity or otherwise of dowsing or divining by a rod or indeed the whole realm of rhabdomancy which includes radiesthesia, which is just as rational as dowsing, it is necessary to explore every possible avenue that might lead to the discovery of the cause and reason for the undoubted successes that are achieved by many users of the divining rod.

Radiesthesia is a 'fringe medicine' technique that has been described as an attempt to apply to medicine the style and mechanics used in dowsing. Most radiesthetists use a 'black box' – an object of much antagonism and ridicule – and, by inserting into the box a specimen of the blood of a patient, they claim to be able to diagnose the disease or illness from which the person seeking treatment or advice is suffering. It is emphasized that the spot of blood itself has no intrinsic value; it is merely used as a means of 'tuning in' to the patient and creating a rapport with him.

Investigation of radiesthesia suggests that some extra sense may be involved – as may be the case in the use of the divining rod – and that certain people are indeed able to create a bridge between the spot of blood and the person concerned. Unfortunately the employment of the 'box' has brought the whole subject into disrepute, for there seems to be no logical reason or sense in the apparently purposeless electrical layout and circuit contained within the box, and this fact (emphasized by a court judgement a few years ago) has caused radiesthesia to be scorned by doctors and scientists.

Yet the two basic concepts of radiesthesia may equally apply to the *modus operandi* of divining for minerals or of any other related activity of the diviner. One is that all matter radiates on its own wave-lengths – an idea that most rational people will accept as at any rate within the bounds of possibility; and the other concept is that all living organisms emit electromagnetic wave radiations that vary in intensity and frequency with the general vitality, health and metabolism of the subject – an idea that an increasing number of people regard as likely.

Alternatively, the radiesthesic faculty, as far as man is concerned, may be something similar to the strange ability utilized by homing pigeons and by dogs and cats, as a way of finding their way back home from great distances and over strange terrain. A similar sense may be employed by moths and other creatures as a way of locating a mate. It has been suggested that the antennae of insects are used for vibratory wave selection within that insect's environment and that one antenna is negative and the other positive.[1]

If this is so it opens up ideas of vibratory resonance and interaction between frequencies of the human organism and 'tuning' to the frequencies of incoming wavelengths pertaining to the substance being sought. But perhaps this takes us out of the realm of authenticating the divining rod and might be looked at within the various theories that can be put forward to account for the phenomenon of the divining rod.

Yet we must not leave the animal world before noticing in passing that ant-hills are almost invariably built over an underground stream and that storks never nest above one; do the ants' antennae (highly developed in the case of the male, incidentally) act in a similar way to the diviner's rod? And can the long, conical bill of the stork, with that bird's love of wading, act in a comparable way and tell the bird where to nest without danger from water beneath them? Perhaps it is a point in favour of the authenticity of dowsing that the same thing seems to happen in the animal kingdom where some of the intrinsic characteristics of certain members of the animal

[1]Christopher Hills, *Supersensonics* (University of the Trees Press, California, 1975).

world (and particularly birds) represents a possible parallel with the motivation of the divining rod.

We have no real knowledge of the mystery of migration or navigation of birds, although there is some evidence that birds use the sun as a compass, and experiments have shown that, if migrating birds cannot observe the sun, their movements are quite random; indeed if mirrors are so arranged that the sun, as viewed by the bird, is made to appear in a different part of the sky, the birds' orientation is altered through an equivalent angle. But this is by no means the whole story of navigation by birds for they also learn landmarks. But what of the birds that, without the benefit of known landmarks, return to their homes hundreds – and in some cases thousands – of miles away? A marked Manx shearwater, sent across the Atlantic to Boston, returned to its nest on Stokholm Bird Observatory in Wales in twelve and a half days having covered more than 3000 miles of territory previously unknown!

One explanation is a sensitivity to the earth's magnetism, with the bird measuring directly the three components of the earth's field: intensity, declination and melination. Since these cover the surface of the earth very regularly and independently, their gradients will cross, forming a navigational grid, with any one point characterized by unique values of the components, and measurements of these at the release point would give its position relative to that of the bird's home. But there is no known organ capable of acting as a magnetometer, so this theory, first suggested by a Frenchman named Viguier at the end of the nineteenth century, is not generally accepted, although direct sensitivity, if it exists, could provide a clue to the activity of divining for minerals.

Another idea to account for the remarkable navigation of birds is indirect sensitivity to electrical effects produced by flying through the lines of force and varying the intensity of the field, and here too may lie a clue to the authenticity of dowsing. Theoretically any electrical effect, whether static or dynamic, can be shown to be exceedingly small and impossible to detect against the vastly stronger electrostatic fields of the earth and clouds, or against much greater currents of physiological origin in the body. Here, experiments that involved attaching small magnets to the birds' wings to set up a pulsating electro-motive force and swamp any effects due to the earth have resulted in no disturbance either of orientation or of the homing instinct. It rather looks as though the navigation of birds is based on some kind of observation of the sun; possibly certain species possess some kind of internal chronometer but, whatever the explanation, there does seem to be some form of automatic mechanism at work and it may yet prove to be akin to an unknown ability possessed by the practitioners of water divining.

In a completely different direction, it is possible to look at the authenticity of the divining rod from a historical viewpoint. More than twenty years ago I remember hearing L. J. Latham, a dowser with considerable practical experience, remark that the story of Moses standing before the rock and smiting it so that his people might have water, held more than a suggestion of the divining rod at work. It is an example that is often used but to the non-dowser it may seem rather far-fetched.

However, from earliest times the sceptre has been regarded as an emblem of power and one is reminded of the sceptre of many of the gods of aborigines (the inhabitants found in a country at its first discovery) and especially of those deities who presided over metallurgy.[1] Such are Indra, the giver of riches, whose paternity is ascribed to Dyaus, the sky; the mythological Vedic Hindu god with his 'spear' and 'thunderbolt'; Hephaestus, the fire god of Greece, skilled in metallurgy and (according to one theory) purifier of the land, with his hammer and 'pincers'; and the enormously powerful but benevolent Scandinavian Thor, the god of thunder, one of the oldest of the gods since he had the earth for his mother, and his father Odin had the power to change himself into a serpent. As we have seen, serpents were from earliest times regarded as guardians of mines and the repeated

[1]William Jones, *Credulities Past and Present* (Chatto and Windus, 1880).

discovery of stone hammers, associated with the first metallurgic gods, in such widely separated locations as the copper mines of Anglesea and those of Peru, cannot be insignificant, and the numerous legends concerning serpents, or even god serpents, who interfere with the working of metals serve to reinforce the argument of a very long association between a rod (or 'sceptre' or 'hammer') and an entwined serpent; a symbol that is with us to this day in the staff and serpent symbol of the Royal Army Medical Corps.

An officer at Aldershot, with whom I discussed this matter in January 1979, said straight away that he had always understood the symbol had its origin in the story of Moses smiting the rock and producing water. ... At all events there can be no doubt that the use of rods for divining is very ancient indeed and it may be thought that a history of more than 2000 years is in itself a testimony of authenticity.

Biblical scholars point to Exodus 17:5, where we read:

And the Lord said unto Moses, Go on before the people, and take with thee of the elders of Israel; and thy rod, wherewith thou smotest the river, take in thine hand, and go.

Behold, I will stand before thee there upon the rock in Horeb; and thou shalt smite the rock, and there shall come water out of it, that the people may drink. And Moses did so in the sight of the elders of Israel.

Numbers 17 speaks of Aaron's rod being the only one to flourish. Aaron and Moses were of course brothers:

And the Lord spake unto Moses, saying: Speak unto the children of Israel, and take of every one of them a rod according to the house of their fathers, of all their princes according to the house of their fathers twelve rods: write thou every man's name upon his rod . . . .

And it shall come to pass that the man's rod, when I shall choose, shall blossom: and I will make to cease from me the murmurings of the children of Israel, whereby they murmur against you ... and the rod of Aaron ... was budded, and brought forth buds, and bloomed blossoms, and yielded almonds.

From time immemorial the desert bedouin has carried

a staff, usually the undressed branch of a tree, as a support and as a weapon; and also as a symbol of authority. For centuries the eastern shepherd slept with his staff at his side, often thrust inside his tunic, ready for instant use in defending his flock; likewise, the desert sheikh carried his staff as a hereditary rod of office and mark of his chieftainship. In Genesis we find Jacob, after praying to be delivered from the vengeance of Esau, saying, 'With my staff I passed over this Jordan; and now I am two bands' (i.e. camps). In the hereditary sense the staff should have belonged, after their father's death, to Esau, the elder brother, who had sold his birthright to Jacob for a mess of pottage. It has been claimed that such staffs or rods were greatly valued because of their divining qualities which are touched on from time to time in the scriptures.

According to the Talmud, when Moses was living with Renel the Midianite, he noticed a staff in the garden and he took it to be his walking stick. This staff was Joseph's, and Renel carried it away when he fled from Egypt. This same staff Adam carried with him out of Eden. Noah inherited it and gave it to Shem. It passed into the hands of Abraham, and Abraham left it to Isaac; and when Jacob fled his brother's anger into Mesopotamia, he carried it in his hand and gave it at his death to his son Joseph. Such are the reputed antecedents of Moses' Rod, a name by which the divining rod is sometimes called to this day, after the rod with which Moses worked wonders before Pharoah and with which he 'drew water and filled the troughs . . . .'

Incidentally the place where Moses smote the rock and produced water is, according to ancient Arab tradition, known today as the Spring of Moses or the Waters of Meribah, a stream that has worn a way through a low ridge of white sandstone. This is pointed out as evidence of being the place where water 'came out abundantly'. It is near Kadesh and flows through the Wady Musa; in the main valley at Petra the same tradition is to be found.

Historical scholars have pointed out that the Chaldaean astronomers and astrologers, wise men from Babylonia and later Assyria, were famed for divination with the use of the rods; Herodotus mentions the same method as a custom of the Scythians; Ammianus Marcellinus recalls its use by the wandering Mongol-type Alani nation; and Tacitus refers to the same practice by the old Germans. To kiss the rod was long regarded as a signal of willingness to submit to punishment meekly. All these examples stress the *power* of the rod – could it have been the power to divine water and other minerals?

In an issue of the *Gentleman's Magazine*, dated November 1751, it is stated:

... so early as Agricola the divining rod was in much request, and has obtained great credit for its discovering where to dig for metals and springs of water; for some years past its reputation has been on the decline, but lately it has been revived with great success by an ingenious gentleman who from numerous experiments hath good reason to believe its effects to be more than imagination. He says that hazel and willow rods, he has by experience found, will actually answer with all persons in a good state of health, if they are used with moderation and at some distance of time, and after meals, when the operator is in good spirits. The hazel, willow and elm are all attracted by springs of water: some persons have the virtue intermittently; the rod in their hands will attract one half hour, and repel the next. The rod is attracted by all metals, coals, amber and lime stone, but with different degrees of strength. The best rods are those from the hazel or nut-tree, as they are pliant and tough, and cut in the winter months ...

The great eighteenth-century zoologist and traveller, Thomas Pennant (1726-1798), of whom Dr Johnson said, 'he observes more things than anyone else does', writes that the divining rod was still employed and credited within living memory and was supposed, by having a sympathy with the hidden ore, to supersede the necessity for ordinary methods of searching. The instrument used by a foreign adventurer in the writer's neighbourhood is described by him as being no more than a rod forked at one end which had been cut in a planetary hour – on Saturn's day and hour – because Saturn was the significator of lead. Jupiter, Venus, Sol and Mercury also participated in the operation according to their reputed several attributes and powers.[1]

Whatever the final explanation for dowsing and divining, and I am sure, as with many other currently unexplained mysteries, we shall eventually discover the cause and reason for the simple fact that dowsing works – usually; present knowledge seems to suggest that there may be a sixth sense which we all possess but have to learn to develop. If dowsing is authentic it transcends normal limits of both time and space; and, as it did for T. C. Lethbridge[2] and others, the practice can widen the possibilities and potentialities of the art to unimagined horizons.

If we do in fact possess a sixth sense it could account for many 'paranormal' phenomena at present unexplained – without the necessity to call in discarnate spirits. There could be natural laws of which we have little or no knowledge and indeed the scientific work of Professor J. B. Rhine at Duke University, North Carolina, has clearly demonstrated the existence of previously unknown forces. Rhine has himself told me that there can be no doubt that the mind has an extra and muscular power to do things and affect things in a manner that we cannot control and have no real knowledge of. Dowsing is almost as much a mystery today as it was in the fourteenth and fifteenth centuries in Hungary and Germany but the evidence that it works is overwhelming.

A sixth sense? Perhaps. A sense that is more developed in some people than in others? A sense that we have to learn to develop, just as we have to learn to develop the other five senses: the delicacy of touch, the fastidiousness of smell, the exactness of sight, the delectation of taste and the refinement of hearing? And once developed it may be that this sixth sense can be used both for good and for evil. The art of using a divining rod has always been predominantly for good, and the authentication of the practice will ultimately lead to greater happiness for mankind.

There are hundreds of practising water diviners in

[1]See Thomas Pennant, *Tours in Wales* (1778-1781)
[2]See Selected Bibliography

Britain and thousands of people active in 'water witch-ing' in the United States of America. In an issue of the *Christian Science Monitor* dated 25 August 1972, some readers detailed their experiences; individually perhaps they are insignificant, but collectively, and in association with hundreds of thousands of similar experiences throughout the world, such a wealth of evidence cannot but be significant.

America seems to have been very 'dowsing conscious' at that particular period and the *Los Angeles Times* of 10 December 1972, carried the news that a town relied on a 'water smeller' to find its water!

The report stated that in an age when men walk on the moon and computers are used for just about every-thing the little town of Mountville, 5 miles west of Lancaster, Pennsylvania, continued to rely on the unex-plained reactions of stocky, seventy-three-year-old George Keck who went to the United States from Germany in 1926.

Apparently, it had long been a common sight in the town to see Keck walking steadily at the head of workers for the Lancaster Area Sewer Authority, checking the course the workmen were taking and advising them, for example, when the sewer line they were excavating was about to approach any water. He achieved his remarkably accurate prognoses time after time by using only a pair of chromium-plated pliers. Whenever he passed over a water pipe or underground stream, the pliers would react so violently that they were almost jerked from his hands.

John Hess, Mountville's Public Works Director at the time, stated that he often called on Keck's services. 'It really does help us,' he is reported as saying. 'Our water lines were installed in 1908 and we don't have any records showing their location, but George Keck invari-ably finds them.'

It seems that Keck discovered that he had the power to locate water in this way when he was twelve years old and while he was still in Germany. During a drought at his home town, he happened to have with him a pair of pliers and he discovered that with them he could find water, and he has been finding water ever since!

In a later chapter we will look at the possibilities of tests of various kinds that can be carried out in an effort to authenticate water divining but for the moment we will leave this aspect of the subject with the thought that Evelyn Penrose, who at one time acted in an official capacity for the British government as a diviner for water, used to say that the emanations given off by water underground were sometimes so powerful that they could pass through twenty storeys of a building and affect a sleeping person . . . .

3. Theories of Dowsing and Divining

Astrology is a good example of an empirical science since it relies on trial and experience and on human observation over a long period of time, thereby making it difficult to check by modern scientific methods. Attempts have been made to use computers to obtain statistically convincing results in astrology but, as with any empirical science, accuracy and really significant effects are only as good as the practitioner. The same is true of radiesthesia and divining, and indeed clairvoyance and other forms of extra-sensory perception. All are subject to the same limitations and the results obtained are often only as good as the experimenters concerned. This is a point that must always be kept in mind when considering any theory that might explain the why and the wherefore of the diviner and his craft.

Those diviners with a scientific outlook will seek a scientific explanation for the faculty of dowsing and they will suggest, for example, that electromagnetic disturbances affect the muscles of the diviner or the person attempting to find water, or they may tend to be sympathetic to the theories of Louis Turenne, whose experiments and experience and research led him to look for the explanation in terms of vibration. Writing in the second decade of the present century, Turenne – and indeed many people who followed him in practising various forms of radiesthesia – became convinced that everything in the universe vibrates with an individual rhythm and that these vibratory rhythms or influences are transmitted to the atmosphere where they have a subtle effect.

It is suggested, and it is a theory that is possible – indeed probable – but very difficult to prove, that these vibratory patterns of any given substance or object or living thing indicate its inherent qualities. Furthermore, it is claimed by the adherents of this theory that these rhythmic vibrations can be located, picked up and shown to exist by affecting delicately balanced apparatus held in the human hand.

Involuntary movements of a forked twig or a pendulum indicate, it is maintained, the vibratory emissions of the substance sought by the dowser or diviner.

A theory on the same lines is accepted by a considerable number of diviners, namely that the answer lies in attraction of some unexplained kind. This is an idea that makes sense of incorporating a sample, or witness, of the substance that is sought in the divining instrument used – if a kind of sympathy or attraction exists between like substances. Yet it is rather difficult for an unbiased observer to visualize an active attraction or sympathy between, say, water and a twig – be it hazel, willow or any other type of wood – and still less so when the divining instrument is made of metal or even plastic.

On balance it seems more likely that the answer to the mystery of the divining rod and the undoubtedly high proportion of dowsing success lies with the dowser rather than with the implement he uses. Some dowsers have suggested that the twigs are 'thirsty for water', others talk of 'electrical forces', 'magnetism' and 'chemical reasons', but what is interesting is that most diviners assert that it is necessary for the operator to 'have faith' in what he is doing; he must be confident that he *will* find water before he can succeed.

I recall a conversation with the late Robert Leftwich, who had many remarkable successes in dowsing for water and oil both in England and America, sometimes under test conditions. When he visited my home in Hampshire, he admired a collection of blue and white plates that my wife had collected from various parts of the world, and he suddenly asked me, 'Do you think, if you concentrated *hard* enough, that you could make one of those plates jump off the shelf?'

When I had to admit that I very much doubted whether I could achieve such a demonstration of the power of thought, Robert seemed a little saddened and said quietly, 'Oh, I know I could, if I really wanted to . . . .'

To Robert Leftwich, at any rate, the conviction that he *could* do dowsing played an important part in his divining work.

Another interesting aspect of the diviner's art is that many practitioners maintain that the faculty or ability is either inherent in certain individuals (the vast majority of people in fact), or inherited and passed through generation after generation, most commonly being handed down from father to son, but also from father to daughter. There are also those who believe, in common with the accepted belief for a heightened psychic faculty, that the gift is invariably to be found in the seventh son of a seventh son. Personally I have found, almost without exception that divining is an acquired talent and that diviners only begin to practise the art after they are introduced to it by seeing someone else do it. There seems little doubt that this is the general rule but it is difficult to know what deductions or conclusions are to be drawn from this fact.

The fact is that the vast majority of diviners, water and metal diviners, professional and amateurs, will freely admit that they have no idea how it works, or why it works – they simply find that 'it just works'.

A farmer who lives and farms near my Hampshire home is David Bown. The farm he manages is a modern one using up-to-date methods for milk and crop production, cattle-raising and agriculture in general, throughout its 400 acres. David himself is a very forward-looking, progressive and practical man, who uses to the full the farming technology of today; he keeps abreast of new developments and ideas and is thoroughly familiar with all aspects of modern farming. I was therefore more than a little intrigued when he told me that he had carried a divining rod in his farm car for some years.

It was about 1970 that David Bown set about establishing a drainage system on some of the pasture land he farms, and he was rather surprised when the supervisor in charge of the drainage arrangements brought out a divining rod and started to peg out the line of a water pipe that ran across tha land. Noticing David's surprise he said he had no idea why the rod indicated the whereabouts of the pipe line but it certainly did – and he was sure David could do the same thing if he tried. Accordingly David did try and sure enough the rod worked for him, and he has carried it in his car ever since.

I found this especially interesting not only because we had here a practical, hard-headed, no-nonsense farmer who owned a divining rod for the simple reason that it worked, but also because this was no twig of hazel or willow but a piece of bent wire with the ends inserted into used plastic biro pens so there was no physical contact between the dowser and his rod. And this fact and the whole incident seemed to me a fascinating sideline to the phenomenon of dowsing – so much so that I am incorporating a photograph of David Bown and his rod – and I am sure there are many other practical men, equally unaware of why the divining rod works and not particularly interested anyway, who nonetheless use it in their everyday activities. For such people, theories that may or may not account for the activity are immaterial; the point is that dowsing works.

From time to time articles appear in various periodicals that claim to have solved the problem of how the divining rod works, but they usually turn out to be one person's opinion, which can be contradicted by a dozen examples of dowsing that make it unlikely, to say the least, that the answer to this mystery has in fact been discovered.

Such an article, headed 'The Divining Rod Explained' appeared in *Fate* magazine in 1955, at a time when I was conducting a series of worldwide tests in telepathy and extra-sensory perception. The author, Hugh A. Brown, began by saying that, as long as people thought that gravitation was a pull exerted by materials of the earth, divining for water remained a miracle. He added that Sir Isaac Newton wrote that such a notion was so absurd that no competent thinker could accept the premise, yet the theory was still taught in schools . . . .

Then comes the author's explanation:

When it became known that weight was caused by radiant energy coming to the earth from celestial space, which forced the earth into the shape of a ball or sphere and caused all materials through which it freely and imperceptibly penetrated, to fall or be pushed toward the centre of the earth, the divining rod was no longer a mystery, but became a natural easily understood phenomenon of nature.

The downpouring energy rays, known as quanta and photons, penetrate all materials like radio waves; but unlike radio waves, which appear to be vibratory radiations, the quanta radiations produce the phenomenon of weight. They are an electrical phenomenon. They flow, just as lightning flows, through the paths of least resistance to the earth.

When a green sapwood branch is held in the hands and the elbows are pressed against the body, an electrical conducting path is established for a part of the flow of quanta.

The downward pull of the divining rod is caused by that portion of the quanta of radiant energy, passing through the human body, which is shunted through the parallel electric circuit of the sapwood branch to the ground. The weight of the human body will be found to be decreased to the extent that the weight of the rod is increased.

Only live, fresh greenwood can be used for divining; the reason being that such woods are conductors of electricity. It functions to establish an electrical circuit to the earth's electrical conductors, which are wet earth and metals.

Copper and other metals, which are electrical conductors, have been used successfully for divining water and minerals. Dead wood and glass rods have been tried but always without success. They are dielectric materials and insulators which do not conduct electricity and therefore they cannot divine water and metals in the ground.

If this theory held water (if the reader will pardon the pun) everyone should be able to use a greenwood divining rod, but this is not so. Furthermore, dead-wood and glass rods *have* been used successfully for divining water; and certainly we have no need to look further than to the rod with its plastic holders used by farmer David Bown, just described, to see that the point about insulatory material is invalid.

On the more involved scientific aspects of the *Fate* article I had a word with my friend and scientist, Dr Vernon Harrison, a long-standing member of The Ghost Club, and he told me:

I am afraid that this is the sort of pseudo-scientific nonsense that results when authors get hold of technical terms that they do not understand. Although attempts have been made to explain away gravitation in terms of curvature of space-time, gravitation is generally accepted by physicists as one of the four fundamental interactions between material particles, the other three being the strong, weak and electromagnetic interactions. The pull between material bodies has been demonstrated and directly measured by the experiments of Cavendish, Boys and other workers. It is therefore far more than an absurd theory.

Although it is true that radiant energy exerts a slight pressure on surfaces it meets, it cannot account for the phenomenon of weight, nor for the approximately spherical shape of the earth. Most of the radiant energy reaching the earth comes, not from celestial space, but from the sun, and the pressure of such energy is not necessarily directed towards the centre of the earth.

Quanta are not rays or a form of radiation: they are discrete quantities of energy. They are not particles that flow through paths of least resistance to the earth, and the dowsing rod does not form a closed circuit for the conduction of electric current.

What I think may be true is that the nervous system of certain individuals may be a sensitive detector of small changes in the electromagnetic field near the surface of the earth. It is known that these fields are disturbed by the presence of water, metals and certain rocks near the surface. The dowser himself appears to be the important factor in dowsing, and the stick he uses is merely an indicator. As you know a considerable variety of sticks, rods and pendulums has been used by different dowsers with satisfactory results.

While I feel that it is important to consider all possible explanations for the dowsing faculty, in respect of Hugh A. Brown's theories I thought a scientific view and assessment was necessary and I am most grateful to Dr

Harrison for his consideration of the matter and his lucid comments.

The idea that radiation of some kind could explain dowsing and divining has long been explored and discussed by such organizations as the British Society of Dowsers, the Radionic Association and the Psychosomatic Research Association and, during the course of a British Congress on Radionics and Radiesthesia, held under the auspices of these three organizations, papers were presented dealing with Reichenbach's odic force, the orgone energy of Reich, the human electromagnetic radiations, harmful rays from the earth, 'fundamental energy' and – perhaps the most interesting of all the papers presented on that occasion – a claim that all matter radiates weakly with frequencies specific to different materials and notably determined by atomic and molecular weight, and that moving water produces an additional and stronger flow field and the human nerve-muscle system reacts to both these stimuli.

However, there were difficulties in observing and recording these reactions and many physical factors apparently interfere with observations on these alleged radiations. During the course of the congress[1] it was stated, interestingly enough, that conditions favourable for dowsing experiments favoured telepathy and clairvoyance experiments to such an extent that an almost entirely correct score could sometimes be obtained with good subjects over short time periods. The originator of these claims, J. C. Maby, also maintained that an imaginative person could project a psycho-radiant energy and influence suitable physical instruments, and it seemed that such radiations from bystanders sometimes interfered with dowsers at work. In summing up the whole congress it was stated that at that time (1950) radiesthesia and radionics occupied an intermediate position between science and psychical research.

The experimental and theoretical basis for these supposed forces is as slender today as it was then but that does not necessarily rule out all such forces for it is not

[1]See *The Proceedings of the Scientific and Technical Congress of Radionics and Radiesthesia* (London, 1951).

beyond the bounds of possibility that 'orthodox science can be influenced by an internal ferment arising from the minds of scientists who have been presented with clear and repeatable evidence', as Dr A. J. B. Robertson put it in his review of the published report of the congress.[1]

A completely different theory for the action of a divining rod in the hands of a dowser was propounded about the same time by Dr C. M. Cooper of the American Society for Psychical Research in a paper entitled 'Self-Experimentation in Water Divining'.[2] Both Dr Cooper and his brother discovered that they obtained a reaction with a divining rod and Dr Cooper then began to fiddle with the twig, trying to 'make it behave as it seemingly behaved of itself . . . keeping the wrists and elbows slack'. He goes on:

I separated the ends of the prongs sufficiently to produce a decided tension where they join. I then with the fingers and forearms rotated the prongs downwards and inward. At once the stem began to dip. As I continued to rotate the prongs, the twig dipped more and more, and then quite suddenly the rod itself took command and jerked my hands downwards, stretching the wrists.

On the basis of this self-experimentation Cooper propounded the interesting theory that the reaction of the divining rod is a function of the anatomy and gait of the dowser. He explained the theory in this practical way:

I am sway-backed, and as I walk I project my body forward and brace back my shoulders. This carries my elbows backward, upward, and outward. As this occurs my forearms pronate. The result of these movements is that I produce a decided tension where the prongs join, and also rotate them. This causes the stem of the rod to begin to dip. I grip tighter to stop the movement, but in so doing I automatically further pronate and hence without realising it, increase the force that is causing the movement.

[1]See *Journal* of the American Society for Psychical Research, volume 36, no.666.
[2]See *Journal* of the American Society for Psychical Research, volume 45, no 3.

During the course of further experimentation Cooper discovered that when he approached a pail of water holding the prongs very slackly, he reached a certain distance from the pail when he subconsciously tightened his grip, thus alerting his muscles, and he obtained the usual dowser's reaction. He deduced that, in his own case at any rate, the ability to obtain a dowsing reaction in the vicinity of water depended upon his ability to read terrain and from that he not unreasonably deduced that professional dowsers who possessed a 'marked flair' in that direction 'would achieve a correspondingly high percentage of dowsing success'. Obviously much more experimentation would be necessary before any general conclusions could be reached but it is an aspect of the subject that could well repay patient and repeated experiments with many different dowsers.

Sir William Barrett, in the chapter on the divining rod in his *Psychical Research*[1] introduces the intriguing suggestion that the miners of Saxony and the Hartz mountains (seemingly the first documented users of the forked rod for locating minerals) were possibly led to use the rod from the belief mentioned earlier, which was 'once universal, that metallic ores attracted certain trees which thereupon drooped over the place where those ores were to be found', but in the end Barrett tries his best to find an explanation for the 'peculiar gift or instinct' that is possessed by a good dowser or diviner. He asserts that the dowser himself usually thinks it is electricity[2] but suggests that this explanation is only a convenient word (and to the ignorant a meaningless one) used to account for any mysterious occurrence. Interestingly enough Barrett says that when a dowser knows that he himself or his forked twig is insulated from the ground, the rod does not work; but if the dowser is insulated and does not know it, the rod works as well as ever!

Thus suggestion or auto-suggestion must play a part in the operation of divining, says Barrett; for, if the dowser

[1]William and Norgate, 1911.
[2]Barrett was writing, of course, long before a national electricity system was in operation in Britain and when electricity was far less well understood than it is today.

is working with radioactive substances and believes that such substances affect his rod, or if he believes the rod will move upwards when he approaches water and downwards on receding from water, or that it turns for minerals when he holds a sample of the sought-for one in his hand, it will assuredly do so, and all this must emphasize the fact that, as Barrett puts it, 'the dowser is a very suggestible subject'.

Although in some instances the sudden twisting of the rod, even the snapping of the twig as attempts are made to restrain its gyration, are involuntary and almost certainly an example of unconscious muscular action, it is equally true that some intelligent observers and practitioners utterly deny this explanation and maintain that an unknown force is in operation or is manifesting itself. If this is so, says Barrett, 'it must be an external force of which we have not the remotest conception'. But the important question is: what is the nature of the faculty which leads a good dowser to discover a hidden spring of water or a lode of metallic ore when other means have failed? And here Barrett discloses that he believes the explanation not to be physical at all, but psychical, and he points out that 'all evidence points to the fact that the good dowser subconsciously possesses the faculty of clairvoyance' and this gives rise to an instinctive, but not conscious, detection of the hidden substance which he is seeking.

Barrett believed that this 'obscure and hitherto unrecognized human faculty reveals itself by creating an automatic or involuntary muscular spasm that twists the forked rod'. It is a theory that is difficult to prove and perhaps its weakness lies in the fact that most people can dowse successfully; does this mean that most people are clairvoyant, albeit unconsciously so?

Barrett even concluded that this activity sometimes produced 'a curious *malaise* or transient discomfort, which furnished some dowsers with a sufficient indication to enable them to dispense with the use of a forked twig'. He put this hypothesis to the test with 'a good amateur dowser' and discovered that the man really possessed this kind of second sight! This being so, reasoned Barrett, dowsers should be able to use the faculty for finding other things besides water or metallic ore and he was satisfied that this was the case.

During the course of numerous experiments with two amateur dowsers, Mr J. F. Young and Miss Miles, Barrett took the precaution of excluding the possibility of their having or obtaining any knowledge of the whereabouts of, say, a coin, which had been hidden in their absence. He made sure that he himself gave no unconscious indications and furthermore he took steps to ensure that the only person who knew where the coin was hidden was excluded from the room – in an attempt, says Barrett, to get rid of possible telepathy – although, of course, putting a person out of sight does nothing of the kind.

However, all his precautions made no difference to the results which were, he tells us, 'far beyond any success that could be achieved by mere chance'.

Barrett seems to have totally comitted hmself at this time to the idea of the good dowser possessing a 'supernormal perceptive power – seeing as it were without eyes'. He suggests that 'like other supernormal faculties', this ability 'usually reveals itself through some involuntary muscular action ...' and he goes on to compare the capacity for 'discernment beyond the power of vision' to that which exists in the homing and migratory instincts of certain animals and birds. He draws the following conclusions: those dowsers who really possess this curious faculty are rare, and many pretenders exist; a good dowser is born rather than trained; 'involuntary motion of the forked twig which occurs with certain persons, is due to a muscular spasm that may be excited in diferent ways'; the explanation for dowsing is a matter of further physiological and psycho-logical research, 'though provisionally we may entertain the working hypothesis' of unconscious clairvoyance or perception at a distance.

Unlikely as it may seem, colour has been advanced as a theory to account for the strange power of the water diviner. There are those, mostly mystics and followers of meditation, yoga, spiritual discovery, self-knowledge and increased awareness, who believe that the essential ingredient among successful dowsers is colour and emanations of consciousness.

It has been postulated that everyone has a coloured aura which absorbs and reflects cosmic radiations. In some people, those with a predominantly red aura, reaction is highly developed and they are extremely sensitive to the entire electromagnetic spectrum and their consciousness is such that it blends with this sensitivity and the two, consciousness and colour, become one awareness. In dowsing, the radiations of water and metallic ore are easily and unconsciously picked up by the dowser and he is invariably successful.

In other people, those with a prevailing violet or blue aura, this particular sensitivity is not so highly developed and the colour of their aura has the opposite effect to those who possess a red aura. The violet or blue reflects the rays emanating from the unseen minerals and these have to be absorbed and transmitted to the more sensitive red inside of the aura before these people respond to dowsing. According to this theory everyone is able to dowse but some are better dowsers than others and some people take longer to achieve results. Few researchers or investigators or even dowsers would disagree with the latter observation but, until we can satisfactorily establish that auras do in fact exist, prove that they are sensitive to cosmic radiations, and indeed substantiate that radiations are emitted from minerals, then we really are not in any position to draw conclusions from the hypothetical assumption that colour has any connection with divining.

In 1962 one of the more distinguished physicists in France, a professor of physics at the Sorbonne, Yves Rocard, claimed to have discovered and established that a substantial quantity of water in the ground is accompanied by very weak changes in terrestrial magnetism and that many people seem to be capable of biologically distinguishing the slightest magnetic gradient. He became convinced that magnetic currents cause a dowser's muscles to relax with a consequent movement of the divining rod when underground water is present and he published the results of his discoveries and conclusions in a book entitled *La signal de Sourcier* (1963).[1]

It is a theory that leaves many aspects of dowsing and divining completely unanswered. If it is the gradient that causes magnetic currents, which in turn affect the dowser, how is it that dowsers can also locate static water where, presumably, no gradient is evident? And it is a theory that entirely disregards the faculty for so-called map dowsing or divining from a distance, which many dowsers are able to do with considerable success.

It is to the late Guy Underwood (no relation to the present writer) that we are indebted for the suggestion that dowsing is connected with ley lines. Those 'old straight tracks' of ancient mounds, standing stones, hilltops, dew ponds and old churches that seem to criss-cross the countryside forming a network of straight lines may be lines of force which were known to our pagan forebears and along which flow a subtle energy. Certainly some ancient stones, circles and megalithic remains do seem to contain centres of energy and at certain times seem to be charged with a power akin to electromagnetism.[2]

A few years before the outbreak of the Second World War a leading ley hunter of the period, Major F. C. Tyler, discovererd that leys often consisted of two parallel tracks. The original idea had been that leys were simply primitive roads – trade routes – and it was purely the fact that they linked up so many old pagan sites and ancient landmarks that aroused interest; but what possible reason could there be for two ancient trackways running parallel?

Guy Underwood, a Wiltshire solicitor, Justice of the Peace and local councillor, had noticed that two prominent dowsers, Captain Robert Boothby and Reginald Smith had independently commented upon the existence of underground streams in the vicinity of prehistoric tumuli and other ancient relics. Boothby had noted that Stone Age burial mounds and other prehistoric remains

[1] See Jean Jurion's *La Radiesthésie, Techniques et Applications* (Presses Select Ltee, Montreal, 1976).
[2] See the present writer's *Dictionary of the Supernatural* (Harrap, 1978).

were situated across underground streams, while long barrows were invariably built over a subterranean stream with the water flowing longwise in relation to the barrows.

Smith was intrigued by the fact that at the centre of every prehistoric site he discovered what he called a 'blind spring' from which a number of underground streams radiated. After his retirement Guy Underwood spent his days exploring prehistoric sites with a divining rod and he soon discovered that his rod showed water at the various sites, exactly as Boothby and Smith had said.

But he also found something else. The main pull at these sites seemed to be on the left or negative side; and then he found that there was a quite separate pull on the right or positive side and this pull he thought was not the result of underground water but seemed to be more magnetic in origin. He eventually came to the conclusion that there were two tracks of magnetic force, one much wider – possibly twice as wide – as the other. He named the narrow parallel trails 'track lines', and the more powerful set of *two* parallel lines he called 'aquastats'. Sometimes he found that the positive aquastats and the negative track lines ran side by side along the same course and, when he began to realize that the presence of these double lines could provide an explanation for certain of the sites being chosen and known, since time immemorial, as holy places, he called these double tracks 'holy lines'.

Linking practical fieldwork with historical study he found that the track lines – the narrow, parallel lines of magnetic force – were often used and had been for centuries, by animals for their regular walks and wanderings, and furthermore practically all old roads followed the contours of these strange tracks of force. This suggested to Guy Underwood that early man had either recognized the trackways instinctively or had followed them for some specific reason.

The problem was that these winding and curving lines could hardly be compared with the old straight tracks – the grassy paths discovered and lovingly plotted and photographed by Alfred Watkins in the 1920s for his

monumental work *The Old Straight Track*.[1] In fact, both
the types of leys or lines discovered by Guy Underwood
meandered here and there, traced a zigzag pattern, an S-
bend, and even formed loops before wandering away
again. Underwood was intrigued to notice that sometimes, when the lines went round and round in a spiral,
this curious formation seemed to mark a particularly
'holy' place. Furthermore these singular lines seemed to
cross at more or less regular intervals so that a tracing of
a track line or aquastat resembled nothing as much as a
string of sausages!

Alfred Watkins, the re-discoverer of leys and old
straight tracks, had no idea that there was anything
occult or mystical about the ley lines; he believed that
they were ancient pathways used by our primitive
forebears as trade routes. Possibly a few – those that led
to old churches built on pagan sites – might have
religious connotations, and a few more seemed to be
associated with astronomy and in particular with the
rising and setting of the sun; but by and large Watkins
considered the ley lines to be a purely practical means of
communication. Guy Underwood, on the other hand,
became convinced that he had discovered a principle of
nature unidentified by science, and in his book[2] he states
that 'its main characteristics are that it appears to be
generated within the earth's surface; that it has great
penetrative power; that it affects the nerve cells of
animals; that it forms spiral patterns; and is controlled
by mathematical laws involving principally the numbers
3 and 7'.

This 'earth force', as Guy Underwood called it, formed,
he believed, a network on the surface of the earth,
manifesting itself in lines of discontinuity, which he
called 'geodetic lines'. He points out in his book (published posthumously) that the philosophers and priests
of the old religions seem to have associated this 'earth
force' with the generative powers of nature – and
particularly so when the force manifested in spiral forms.
They believed it was an essential part of the mechanism

[1]Originally published in 1925, reprinted by Garnstone Press, 1970.
[2]*The Pattern of the Past*, originally published in 1969.

by which life comes into being and, in fact, to be the 'Great Arranger': the balancing principle which keeps all nature in equilibrium 'and for which biologists still seek . . . .'

Guy Underwood's investigations, especially at Stonehenge, a place that fascinated him, showed that such mysterious, exciting and enticing places are a centre of geodetic lines and he found that the great outer ditch at Stonehenge, the earliest part of that mighty monument of the past (*c.* 1800 BC) is defined by the enormous loop of an aquastat which forms an almost complete circle, one end curling in a double loop around the enigmatic heelstone with its encircling ditch. To Guy Underwood, Stonehenge represented a veritable whirlpool of geodetic lines, a unique centre of earth force, and it cannot but be of interest that this sacred and profane place should have been used by Neolithic followers of the moon cult.

So we have many theories for the positive results obtained by the divining rod: electromagnetic disturbances; unexplained attraction or sympathy or magnetism; faith and the power of conviction; radiant energy; a function of the anatomy and gait of the dowser; an unrecognized psychic faculty; colour and emanations of consciousness; earth force; or perhaps a combination of any or all of these.

Study and examination of the subject and the literature and of diviners themselves suggest that there is no single, simple explanation for the fact that for many people the divining rod works. No universal reason for the success of divining has yet been established. There is a lot of evidence pointing in one direction, a lot of evidence pointing in the opposite direction, and not a little that points in neither. Theories may be thick upon the ground but the indisputable fact is that, for a great many people, perhaps for most of mankind, divining does work to a greater or lesser degree.

4. Aspects of Dowsing and Divining

So far we have, in the main, concerned ourselves with the commonest form of dowsing – doing so with a divining rod and seeking to locate water or metal. But there are other deeply interesting aspects of the diviner's art: indirect or map dowsing; the use of the pendulum; sexing eggs and unborn children; radiesthesia and the possibility of diagnosing and curing illness; locating and detecting criminals and missing people.... The list appears to be endless, and as fascinating as it is puzzling. Is it possible to find a common link in all these diverse aspects of the subject?

It is not beyond the bounds of possibility that there is indeed a common factor or bond; certainly the authors of *Water Witching, U.S.A.*[1] thought so and in a chapter entitled 'From Talking Horses to Talking Twigs' they trace a plausible relationship between so-called 'talking horses' the ouija board and the divining rod.

Of a number of 'talking horses' the most famous were the Elberfeld Horses[2] but there were others: in Berlin, the Russian trotting horse, Clever Hans, and in America (investigated by, among others, J. B. Rhine), Lady Wonder. All appeared to have the capacity to solve simple arithmetical problems and to answer questions aptly and intelligently. In fact they were almost certainly specially trained, or had somehow developed the knack of noticing involuntary movements that indicated when to begin and when to cease tapping with their hoofs, shaking

[1] Evon Z. Vogt and Ray Hyman (University of Chicago Press, 1959).
[2] See Maurice Maeterlinck *The Unknown Guest* (Methuen, 1914).

their heads or pointing out letters or objects. There is some evidence to suggest that when the horses' view of the questioner was blocked, they were no longer able to 'answer' any questions; but the problem of the 'talking horses' was by no means as simple as that.[1]

One of the earliest references to the use of a pendulum as a dividing instument, in any detail, is contained in a work by Ammianus Marcellinus (c. 325-391 A.D.), a Roman historian – he was in fact a Greek of noble birth – who wrote in Latin a history of the Roman empire from the accession of Nerva to the death of Valens, thus producing a continuation of the work of Tacitus. During the course of this clear, comprehensive and important account, Ammianus Marcellinus tells of a gang of conspirators apprehended for planning the assassination of an emperor and one member, in his confession, describes the method they used to discover the name of the emperor's successor.

He relates that a priest suspended a ring by a fine thread over a circular platter with the letters of the alphabet arranged round the rim. The ring, seemingly held stationary by the priest, nevertheless oscillated and pointed successively to the letters T, H, E, and O, thereby telling the conspirators that the successor to the emperor would be named Theodorus.[3]

A variation of this pendulum-cum-ouija-board is to be found in another account from ancient Rome where a ball pendulum is suspended inside a glass and, when the alphabet is recited, the pendulum rings against the side of the glass to indicate the correct letter.[4]

Within the last decade, according to the authors of *Water Witching, U.S.A.*, a dowser in southern Illinois used exactly the same method – a pendulum suspended inside a tumbler – to indicate when it rings against the glass how deep the seeker will need to dig to find water.

Evon Z. Vogt and Ray Hyman explore the various uses

[1]See the present writer's *Dictionary of the Supernatural* (Harrap, 1978).
[2]See Michel Eugène Chevreul, *De la baguette divinatoire, du pendule dit explorateur et des tables tournantes* (Mallet-Bachelier, Paris, 1834).
[3]See Joseph Jastrow, *Wish and Wisdom* (Appleton-Century-Croft, New York, 1935).

The site of Borley Rectory, 'the most haunted house in England', at a time when dowsing was employed in an attempt to find the missing church plate.

Mrs Parker of Long Melford divining for the Borley church plate.

The author using a traditional hazel twig in a corner of his garden in Hampshire.

The author map dowsing; using a pendulum over a large-scale map.

The author using a dowsing stick or wand, perhaps the most primitive of all divining

to which the pendulum has been put, from spelling out
a name in ancient Rome to predicting the depth of water
below ground, and they conclude (as Chevreul had with
the divining rod in 1834)[1] that it is all due to the effect of
'expectant attention upon involuntary movements'. They
also explore variations of the pendulum, such as Rutter's
magnetometer, but the answer, it seems, is always the
same.

Rutter, aware of the possibility that the pendulum
might be influenced by involuntary movement of the
hand holding it, constructed an apparatus (which he
called a magnetometer) which suspended a ball from a
metal frame. Rutter's line of thought was that, because
the frame was sturdy and self-standing and the ball was
not suspended by the hand, any movement of the ball
could not be the result of involuntary movement on the
part of the person operating the apparatus. Rutter merely
held his finger against the frame of his magnetometer
for a moment while, with his other hand, he touched an
individual or object and the suspended ball seemingly
discriminated between various individuals and different
objects by changes in intensity and direction.

It was left to a follower of the inventor to discover the
secret of the magnetometer. Dr H. Madden, a Brighton
homoeopathic physician, began to use Rutter's apparatus
to test the value of his remedies and in 1851 the British
medical journal *Lancet* carried an account of Dr Madden's
findings, as revealed by W. B. Carpenter.[2]

Madden, as he experimented with various globules
and pills, discovered that the oscillations of Rutter's
magnometer corresponded exactly with his idea of what
they ought to be. Thus one medicine would produce, say,
lengthwise swings of the ball while a medicine of
opposite virtues would produce a crossways movement.
Dr Madden methodically went through the whole Homoeopathic Pharmaeopoeia and then he began to look at
the whole thing again with an important difference. This
time he took precautions to see that he was not aware of
the nature of the medicine being investigated: the medic-

[1]Michel Eugène Chevreul, *op.cit.*
[2]*Mental Physiology* (Kegan Paul, 1874).

66   The Complete Book of Dowsing and Divining

aments were handed to him by an assistant who gave no
indication of their nature to the doctor. Immediately and
completely the results ceased to present any constancy.
Oscillations at one time swung crosswise and at other
times lengthways for two samples of the same medicine,
and acknowledged and proven remedies of opposite
kinds showed no indication of any difference whatever
on Rutter's magnetometer. Dr Madden promptly
acknowledged that the whole system which he had built
up had no foundation other than his own anticipation of
what the results should be. Human nature being what it
is we should not be surprised to learn from recent
publications that versions of Rutter's magnetometer are
still sold, under such names as Psionic Machine and
Hieronymus Machine.[1]

On the subject of table turning the two authors of
Water Witching U.S.A. quote what is described as a typical
spiritualist session with a number of individuals seated
around a table with their hands placed, palms downwards, on the table top. It is generally arranged before-
hand in which direction the table will rotate, and the
party sits and waits, sometimes for a considerable time,
with the idea impressed on their minds that the table
will move in a certain direction. After one or two slight
movements (which tend to excite the eager participants)
the actual turning begins. Should those present remain
seated, the table will only revolve as far as they can
reach but often, it is stated, the 'sitters' feel obliged to
'follow' the table and, first standing, then walking, then
running, they eventually find themselves no longer able
to keep pace with the spinning table. And this is all done
'not only without the least consciousness on the part of
the performers that they are exercising any force of their
own, but for the most part under the full conviction that
they are not.[2]

The researches of Michael Faraday (1791-1867), the
distinguished natural philosopher and physicist, pointed
in the same direction, and in particular he revealed by

[1]See Martin Gardner, *Fads and Fancies in the Name of Science* (Dover, New York, 1957).
[2]W.B. Carpenter, *Mental Physiology* (Kegan Paul, 1874).

experimentation that once he was able to show immediately to the sitters that they were pressing with their hands – downwards or obliquely – then all effects of table turning ceased, even though those present, earnestly desiring motion, persevered hour after hour. Once a visual indicator was introduced and everyone present was made conscious of what they were doing, the 'power' disappeared immediately, for the sitters could no longer unwittingly deceive themselves.[1]

Later table turning sessions (the table tilting and rapping in answer to a pre-arranged code), an alphabet board and pointer used in conjunction with a tilting table, the ouija table and the modern ouija boards: all, it seems, are likely to produce 'messages' that are in fact in practically all cases, the result of unconscious muscular action or expectant attention. And, if this is so, might not the explanation for the movement of the divining rod rest with the diviner and with him alone? Certainly experiments carried out in this area suggest that it could be in this direction that we should seek for at least part of the solution to the mystery of the moving rod.

And what about the pendulum? Research over many years and in several countries suggests that, irrespective of the instrument used – hazel twig, pendulum or metal divining rod – the mechanics of movement remain the same. Movement takes place when forces and stresses on the twig or rod become greater than the force by which the diviner holds the instrument. In the case of the pendulum, as with the rod, the tighter the grip the more easily the balance is upset. In fact there is little doubt that in any act of delicate balance the slightest relaxation or strengthening of the grip visibly affects the article being held.

The American University of the Trees at Boulder Creek, California, tells its students that 'radiational paraphysics' can enable them to use supersensonic methods not only to discover the weather in a certain area by studying a map of the locality, but also to find lost objects and missing people or solve crimes by 'getting a reaction'

[1] See 'Experimental Investigation of Table Turning', *Athenaeum*, July 1853.

from a map or territory thousands of miles away; they can do this by using one of the various 'amplifiers such as a magnetic compass or radium block as a stimulator of the "thought fields" '.[1]

Some fifty years ago the celebrated Abbé Mermet used a pendulum in hitherto unexplored regions. His profession and calling probably protected him from much of the derision that most other people would have attracted for he gradually built up a considerable reputation as a valuable and reliable aid to police investigators and he repeatedly helped them when they sought missing people and they began to appreciate the apparent powers that either he or his pendulum possessed for time after time he was able to indicate the whereabouts of a corpse.

The Abbé claimed that he possessed clairvoyant powers which, with the help of the pendulum, enabled him to 'see' the actual location or whereabouts of a missing person or indeed a lost object.

The Abbé's chief interest was in healing but he was always willing to try to find missing persons and, according to the records, he appears to have been successful on many occasions. Once a girl came to him for help because her brother was missing and the police could find no trace of him. Abbé Mermet asked for something that had belonged to the missing boy and the girl gave him a photograph. Once he was alone the priest sat at his desk with the photograph in one hand, a map of the area in front of him and a table of figures at his side. He took his pendulum and held it over the map, asking direct questions as he did so, questions that required only an answer of 'yes' or 'no'. When heights and distances and measurements were required, the Abbé held the pendulum over the table of figures.

Next day, when the girl returned to see what he could tell her, the priest said he was sorry but he had bad news for her: her brother was dead. He pointed to the map still spread out on his desk and to one particular position. 'I followed your brother to that spot', he said. 'There he stopped and I believe that there he was murdered. Then

[1] Christopher Hills, *Supersensonics* (University of the Trees Press, California, 1975).

the body was moved by a man 1¾ metres in height. Your brother was stabbed to the heart.'

After a moment Abbé Mermet continued with more detailed information. He said the body of the girl's brother had been thrown into the River Hongrin, not far from a place which he indicated on the map, and he said the body would in fact be found in 4 metres of water; he surmised that robbery had been the motive since there was neither gold nor silver on the body.

In the event, Abbé Mermet was proved right in every particular. The boy's body was discovered very near to the place he had indicated and an empty purse, which his sister recognized, was recovered from the River Sarine, not very far away.

Since the days when Abbé Mermet became one of the best known practitioners and theorists on the subject of dowsing in rationalist France, other dowsers in many countries have claimed to possess the same ability. Robert Graves and Alan Hodge, in their social history of Great Britain from 1918 to 1939,[1] referred to one dowser who found four drowned bodies within a few months; but in general the results, although spectacular in some instances – in common with those of other 'psychics' who help the police from time to time – are undependable and costly when many false trails are followed. So, understandably, the police – while welcoming help from any quarter – do not go out of their way to seek the assistance of the dowsing fraternity when they are at a loss in knowing where to look for a missing person.

And yet there have been undoubted successes with a pendulum used over a map, and here any physical explanation such as may be advanced for the act of divining for water with a hazel twig or rod, seems to be under a severe strain. I remember a well-known expert on the subject, L. J. Latham, saying to me at a Ghost Club meeting that the pendulum was not as accurate as the divining rod for finding water and he did not support the theory that extra-sensory perception came into dowsing, but with map dowsing and the use of a pendulum

[1]The Long Week-end (Faber and Faber, 1941).

he was not so sure.

The same evening that I talked to Mr Latham I heard, first hand, a very strange story about pendulum map dowsing. Mr and Mrs King became fascinated by the subject following a remarkable exhibition of the apparent success of the procedure. They told me that their seventeen-year-old daughter Jane had taken the family dog, a pedigree pug, for a walk one evening and it had been stolen. The dog had been let off its leash on a common near their home, and Jane had been chatting to a boyfriend when she had been vaguely aware of a car slowly driving along the road nearby. Engrossed in conversation, she had hardly noticed that it had gradually come to a stop, then moved on, picking up speed, soon to disappear out of sight. At the same time she became aware that the pug was nowhere to be seen. With growing desperation, despair and suspicion, she and her boyfriend spent almost an hour looking for the dog, calling it by name and asking people whether they had seen a pug – but the dog seemed to have vanished from the face of the earth.

At length Jane returned home, hoping against hope that somehow the dog had made its own way back, but it seemed to have disappeared completely. And then Jane remembered the car, and with mounting apprehension the family telephoned the police with their suspicions, but the authorities had very little to go on. Neither Jane nor her friend had noted the number-plate of the car and in fact they could not completely agree on the description or even the colour of the mysterious car. But the police agreed that the dog had probably been stolen and they promised to make all possible enquiries.

The days passed without any news of the pet and then, four days after the dog had been lost, Jane remembered reading about some people being able to locate missing persons by using a pendulum over a map. They thought it was worth a try and Jane removed the clip fastening from the dog's lead and threaded it on to a piece of twine so that it formed a pendulum. They had no idea where the dog might be so they took a road atlas and slowly worked through it page by page without obtaining any reaction from the pendulum, apart from a slight reaction when the atlas was open at a map of north Yorkshire, but so slight was the movement of the pendulum that they ignored it. However, when they reached the last page of the atlas without any further reaction, Jane turned back to the north Yorkshire page and tried again.

Carefully holding the thread so that the clip fastening was completely stationary, she laboriously went over the whole map a little at a time and this time she received a definite reaction at a certain spot. Her father suggested that to test that there really was a reaction, she should cover her eyes so that she could not see anything and when this was done he moved the map under the pendulum and again traversed the whole page – and again there was a movement of the pendulum at the same spot.

Convinced that they were now on to something, the family obtained a large-scale map of the area concerned and tried again. This time the pendulum seemed to react strongly in the vicinity of a group of isolated buildings, which Jean and her family thought might be a farm.

The upshot of the affair was that Jane and her parents travelled to Yorkshire, located the farm and obtained an interview with the occupant who was most friendly and helpful. He listened to all they had to say and then said he thought he might have some good news for them, but would they first provide him with a detailed description of the dog, its collar and anything else that would establish its identity. When they had done so the man gave them tea and asked them to excuse him for a short while.

After about twenty minutes he returned with the lost dog, and he asked them to be good enough to let him explain as well as he could what had happened. It transpired that his teenage daughter and her older brother had long wanted a pug dog of their own, ever since they had stayed with relations who owned one. They had, a few weeks earlier, spent a holiday in the south of England and on their way home, as they had driven over a common, they had seen what they thought was a stray dog – a pug. After convincing themselves that there was no one about and that the dog must indeed be a stray for it had no name and address on its collar, they took the dog away and brought it home.

Jane and her family were so delighted to have their pet back, and the farmer was so charming and so upset at the distress his children had caused that the Kings decided to take no further action. In fact the two families later became friendly and the young girl who took the dog has since been to stay with the Kings where she and Jane equally enjoyed the company and companionship of the pug, who was none the worse for his adventure. Needless to say, there is no way in which it is possible to convince Jane and her parents that the pendulum does not work!

There are scores of similar stories of map dowsing but unfortunately, as with a lot of tests for finding water by means of a divining rod, whenever tests are controlled, they practically always fail. It may be that this has something to do with the person in charge of the test or it may be that the fact that it is a test and not the real thing prohibits the faculty from working. Whatever the reason there really is very little scientific evidence for establishing the veracity of map dowsing with a pendulum. I may say that, after hearing the story of Jane and the family dog, I arranged a series of tests with Jane, all of which failed completely – yet the one time the method was used when it was really needed it worked.

As long ago as 1933 tests of dowsing from plans were carried out at Avignon under the auspices of the Congrés de Souriers in an attempt to decide once and for all whether there was anything in the claims that were being made by map dowsers and pendulum users. The tests were entirely negative and it was found to be impossible to produce positive results under test conditions.

In 1947 the dowsing fraternity made much of the fact that an award of 50,000 francs had been given to François Gramenis of Anrecy, France, for his part in the discovery of the body of a young man who had fallen to his death in the Alps. Gramenis had pinpointed the spot by map dowsing with a pendulum over a large-scale map of the area. Referring to the case in his book, *The Psychology of the Occult*,[1] D. H. Rawcliffe reminds us that the area in which the young Frenchman was climbing must have been known and could not have been very extensive, so such a success may well be attributed to chance, if not due to prior knowledge. 'Against thousands of map dowsing failures, we must expect an occasional chance success. It will be surprising if the dowser of Anrecy is fortunate enough to hit the jackpot again.' To the best of my knowledge, that success of forty years ago was not repeated by François Gramenis.

How and why map dowsing works is difficult to understand without attributing success to some form of extra-sensory perception on the part of the person using the pendulum and, although, as with so many aspects of divining, scientific and controlled tests have proved indecisive, there is no doubt that on occasions – not under test conditions – it has worked.

The author of a fascinating account of personal experience of many aspects of dowsing, Major General Scott Elliot[2] says that map dowsing or distant dowsing really involves a combination of simple questions and answers with a horizontal map or plan, or vertical sections of them; indeed he maintains that 'virtually all dowsing is a matter of question and answer'.

After rightly drawing attention to the fact that one must always be alert to the possibility of 'brain intrusion in the form of preconceived ideas or wishful thinking', Elliot asserts that map dowsing enables the qualified dowser to study ground, or the seas, in any part of the world while in the comfort of his home, for locating such things as: oil, gas, minerals, precious stones, water; ships on or under the sea; previously unknown archaeological sites – not to mention such mundane items as field drains, council drains, pipes and cables and faults in them.

Elliot says much of the success of map dowsing depends on the existence and accuracy of maps, plans, diagrams and charts, and here perhaps it is possible to

[1] Derricke Ridgway, 1952.
[2] *Dowsing One Man's Way* (Neville Spearman, 1977).

obtain an inkling of this strange faculty, for he goes on to say that it may be necesary to improvise when good maps or plans are not available, using a sketch map of sufficient accuracy or to define the area by the use of latitude and longtitude, or draw an improvised grid between known objects or locations for 'everything in the world lies in relation to other things, even moving things move in relation to other things'.

Having obtained a large-scale map of the area, or produced a grid, Elliot concentrates on the area and is able to attune his mind to it and to the relationship between all the things inside the various rectangles, which in turn have a relationship with each other and to other things in the world. In this way he selects a certain rectangle for search and holds the pendulum over the appropriate part. He can often use his mind to do the work but at other times a series of questions and answers helps to produce a reaction in the pendulum and to achieve the required results.

In his contribution to *Practical Dowsing: A Symposium*[1] Major General Scott Elliot reveals that he started out as a complete sceptic about the validity of dowsing and divining, then he discovered that he could detect underground water whenever he stood over it but, when he heard about the ability of some dowsers to find water by working over a map, he couldn't accept that it was possible. He decided to give the idea a try with a young nephew who had just learnt to dowse and they made a plan of the tennis court outside and obtained definite reactions. Outside they discovered that there was indeed water in the exact places they had marked; they had no idea how it had happened but the fact was it had worked.

Curiously enough, for Major General Scott Elliot map dowsing became the first method of dowsing that he would always try, and he developed a number of individual features of map dowsing that work for him. He accepts that it is an involuntary contraction of the muscles of the hands, arms and shoulders that cause a dowser's rod to lift or dip; the actual holding of the rod

[1] Bell, 1965.

slightly contracts the muscles so that, with influence of underground water, the muscles tighten a little more, causing the rod to move.

In map dowsing Elliot holds a pencil in the usual way that he would hold one for writing but with slight pressure and, as he passes the poised pencil over the map or plan or diagram or sketchmap where there is underground water, he finds that his fingers tighten on the pencil, he feels a definite 'pull' and at that point he lets the hand move wherever it wants to go and before long he has traced the course of any underground water.

For estimating the volume, depth and quality of the hidden water, he has worked out a system of using different coloured chalks and by gradually using larger and larger scale maps or plans he has found that he can often be accurate in his measurements to within inches.

In the same book *(Practical Dowsing: A Symposium)* the editor, Colonel A. H. Bell, states, as he told me personally at a Ghost Club meeting some years ago, that a pendulum is usually used for map dowsing and, while some dowsers find it necessary to orientate the map or plan, most do not do so; the map is minutely examined, exactly as if it were an area of ground, and the dowsing reactions apparently occur in a corresponding manner. In this way a stream might be picked up at some point on the map and its course traced with the pointer following the pendulum; but a necessary requirement is that a state of mental detachment is maintained throughout when dowsing at a distance.

Major General Scott Elliot has often remarked on the fact that, while the subject of ordinary dowsing with a divining rod is a subject that interests many people and is accepted without great hostility, map dowsing is something that no one really understands and it may incite scepticism for there is an aura of mystery about it and, while science and scientists and dowsers themselves can make guesses as to how and why it works, so far we do not know the final explanation.

As we have seen map dowsing usually involves the use of a pendulum and this brings us to another aspect of the subject for here, it seems, we enter a mysterious realm where not only the sexing of eggs and unborn children and the diagnosis of illness is claimed but also the location of missing objects and people and even healing.

Pendulums of sorts have a very long history in the story of divination and the occult arts. There are ancient Chinese documents describing an object, usually a ring, suspended from the hand by a silk thread, being used to foretell the future and warn of misfortune. The Romans were not averse to resorting to the pendulum for divination purposes and indeed there are records of people being condemned to death for such practices before the year 400 A.D. It is possible to find variations on the pendulum theme in many obscure races and communities all over the world as indeed it is possible to find variations of a forked twig or rod used by the Greeks and Romans and Persians, but the use of the pendulum as a guide to health is of more recent date and became a branch of fringe medicine under the name of radiesthesia.

In the same way that almost anyone can get a reaction from a divining rod, so it is claimed, most people can obtain guidance as to the health of himself or someone else, armed with a pendulum; the various types of pendulums are discussed in a later chapter. Usually a pendulum swings in a clockwise gyration to indicate health and in an anti-clockwise gyration to indicate ill-health, but there are always exceptions. The late Captain W. H. Trinder used to obtain the opposite indications while the venerable Abbé Mermet worked on the basis of a gyration for healthy tissue and an oscillation for unhealthy tissue.

Captain Trinder once demonstrated his abilities as a dowser and pendulist at a meeting of The Ghost Club, and a psychic former chairman of that organization, researcher Harry Price, in the company of Dr C. E. M. Joad, conducted several experiments with Trinder and came to the conclusion that the captain's dowsing and pendulum faculties were clairvoyant in origin, although Trinder himself repudiated this. Some very interesting and carefully planned experiments included Captain

Trinder successfully locating a submerged lake merely by working with a wooden bobbin suspended over an estate map on which the lake and other water courses, situated 50 miles away, were not marked. They were reported in some detail in a letter to *The Times*.[1]

A common method that pendulum users recommend for beginners to 'prove' for themselves that there is something in radiesthesia or medical diagnosis by pendulum is for the amateur to hold a pendulum over his thigh when he should obtain a reaction for a healthy tissue. If he then slaps his thigh smartly with his other hand, he will find that the pendulum will give a different reaction – that for damaged tissue. A short time afterwards the reaction will be seen to change and after a moment or two will revert to the original indication for healthy tissue; the temporary injury having by then disappeared!

The prescribed method for making a complete pendulum examination of a person or an animal is to arrange for the subject to lie flat on his back and then on his front, so that every part of his body can be covered by the pendulum. It will often be found that unhealthy reactions are obtained from parts of the back and shoulders but these are often due to strains or injury in the past or the presence of fibrositis or rheumatism.

Many medical pendulists or radiesthesiasts practise homoeopathy and have favourite herbal remedies such as arnica tincture and ruta liniment. Once the injured or unhealthy part of the body has been discovered, the experienced practitioner will prescribe a remedy and holding a specimen of the tincture or liniment in the pendulum hand he will explore the area again with the pendulum asking himself mentally, 'Is this the right remedy?' and if the treatment is the correct one, the pendulum will indicate this with a positive movement.

The procedure for diagnosing a particular infection or disease is for the pendulum to be held over the hand of the patient and to touch with the free hand a 'sample' or 'witness' of a number of common diseases in turn.

[1] 6 September, 1938.

Several 'witnesses' may give different reactions from those obtained with the rest and these are thought to be those of the diseases affecting the subject. Sometimes more positive reactions can be obtained if each 'witness' is held against the thread of the pendulum as it is suspended over the hand of the patient. Other pendulists diagnose by means of a printed list or pictorial representation of ailments.

One expert in direct pendulum work, the late Dr Ernest Martin, quoted in the contribution by V. D. Wethered, B.Sc., in *Practical Dowsing*[1] was in the habit of testing patients for a particular medicine or item of diet by getting the patient to place his or her hand over a sample of the object in question and then Dr Martin would hold his pendulum over the patient's hand. The pendulum would then oscillate or gyrate with a positive or negative reaction indicating whether or not the medicine or food agreed with the patient.

Dr Martin was one of the many pendulists who maintained that it was possible to detect the outer edge or 'skin' of the etheric body, usually about ½ inch from the skin surface. He also claimed that the human body, and indeed the separate limbs, were polarized: one side of the body or a limb (usually) gave a positive or clockwise gyration while the opposite side usually gave an anti-clockwise gyration when tested inside the etheric body. Accordingly, a pendulum held to the right of the navel, about ½ inch from the body surface, will give a different reaction to a pendulum held on the left side; and, directly above the navel, along the median line, the pendulum is likely to oscillate inside the etheric skin. The polarity of a limb can be ascertained, it was claimed by Dr Martin, by holding a pendulum first on one side of a patient's leg and then on the other side, about ½ inch away and with a fairly short thread.

Dr Martin also used the fingers and hands for testing the principal organs; different parts of the hand representing radiesthetically, it was believed, certain organs of the body and 'hand charts' have been produced by

[1]Bell, 1965.

various people indicating the parts of the hand and the organs they represent. Unfortunately these charts frequently contradict one another but the one reproduced in *A Radiesthetic Approach to Health and Homoeopathy*,[1] based largely on the chart produced by a prominent researcher in this aspect of the subject, A. Bovis, is probably the most generally accepted.

Dr Martin and his fellow pendulist, Dr E. T. Jensen, believed that the 'general polarity' or general health of the subject was represented at the tip of the thumb. Both doctors used to include in their treatment the injection of a herbal hormone at points on the skin surface indicated as favourable by the pendulum and it was claimed that by this means a bad pendulum reaction could be changed into a good one almost instantaneously.

Some pendulum healers used to use lengths of insulated wire wound around the damaged or injured limb; the ends of the wire had to cross each other at the median line and the wire had to be correctly applied but the object was to correct the etheric field around the imperfect limb and so improve it. One notes with interest that when commenting on this 'wire treatment' one author warns newcomers to radiesthesia to be careful in using this technique as 'highly sensitive people may soon have had enough of one particular treatment and may be unpleasantly overstimulated by it if it is prolonged'.[2]

There is a story of an ideal but sadly not typical co-operation between a pendulist and a physician. The Belgian radiesthetist M. Autrigue was consulted about a young lady who had complained of severe headaches for a period of several weeks but refused to see a doctor. Using a pendulum over a photograph of the girl M. Autrique could find nothing wrong in the area of the girl's eyes where he had expected to find the seat of the trouble but eventually he discovered what he believed to be a tumour near the pineal gland.

He said nothing of his discovery but insisted that the

[1]V. D. Wethered, British Society of Dowsers, 1961.
[2]V. D. Wethered in *Practical Dowsing* (Bell, 1965).

girl must see an eye specialist without delay. The specialist confirmed the presence of a tumour and following his recommendation an immediate operation saved the girl's sight. In the event a tumour the size of a pigeon's egg was removed from near the pineal gland. Many people would regard this example as a lesson in how the faculty of dowsing with a pendulum to diagnose illness can be used to the best advantage in concurrence with established medical practice.

The location and discovery of criminals and missing persons by means of a pendulum has been claimed to be one of the most useful purposes to which dowsing can be applied. We have already looked at the remarkable case of Jacques Aymar and the famous story of his discovery of the murderers of a Lyons wine merchant and his wife in 1692. Aymar was already established in the vicinity of his home as a water diviner when he was in his twenties and it was while he was engaged in this work that he discovered his ability to locate missing persons. A violent reaction of the divining rod led him to think he had discovered an excellent water supply and he suggested that a well should be sunk at the spot. Instead of water the diggers unearthed the head of a murdered woman.

When she had been identified Aymar was taken to her house and there he directed his rod at each of the people present, obtaining a strong reaction when the rod was pointed at the husband of the murdered woman. The husband promptly fled, thereby admitting his guilt to the satisfaction of the authorities, and thereafter Aymar found himself much in demand for using his dowsing talents to trace other murderers and criminals.

Since then, right up to the present time, dowsers and pendulists have helped the police to locate missing persons and dead bodies; significantly perhaps they seem to be especially successful in finding the bodies of drowned people.

John Clarke, the Leicestershire dowser, built up a considerable reputation for his ability to locate drowned bodies and, between March and May 1933, he successfully indicated the positions of the bodies of five people who had met their deaths by drowning.

Several examples of assisting the police in this type of enquiry are recounted by a Torcross dowser, W. H. Burgoyne, in his contribution to the symposium *Practical Dowsing*.[1] In each case the dowser used a 'sample' – an object associated with the missing person – to assist his mental concentration.

The first incident took place early one morning in March 1945 when Mr Burgoyne heard sounds of a disturbance outside his home in Devon and on making enquiries he learned that two boys were missing from the nearby village of Slapton. The boys' father had a shop in Torcross and in his van Burgoyne found a pair of braces belonging to one of the boys. Using this article as a 'sample' he soon picked up reactions that led him to a bridge and then he followed the trail to the edge of the lake where he thought the boys had taken to the water in a small rowing boat.

Here the dowser and the boys' father engaged the services of a fisherman who took them on to the water and by laboriously criss-crossing a line from the spot where the boys had left the land, the dowser eventually felt a strong pull on his 'sample' and having marked the spot the police soon discovered the bodies that were found to be entangled among the branches of a tree in deep water.

Nine years later Mr Burgoyne read in a newspaper that a certain Mr Card of Callington in Devon was missing. He immediately offered his services to the police and in the company of a friend of the missing man and with a pair of the absent man's spectacles as a 'sample', the dowser began his search for a trail by visiting the place where the man had last been seen. There he picked up the trail and made his way across three fields until he arrived at the edge of an expanse of swampy land where Mr Burgoyne said he experienced a strong feeling that the body of the man they sought was very close by. When the marsh was searched by the police they quickly found the body of Mr Card.

[1] Bell, 1965.

Finally, one morning in September, 1959, a police sergeant came to Burgoyne's home and asked him whether he would help in looking for a man who was missing from his home at Cornworthy near Totnes. The man, an antiques dealer, had not been well and had been staying with his daughter at Dartmouth. The dowser obtained a handkerchief that had belonged to the missing man and at Dartmouth he picked up the trail that led across several fields to an old farm where the man had worked as a young man. From there the trail turned back towards the daughter's home but, just past an old mill in the middle of a copse, they found the man's body, hanging from a tree.

An example of the pitfalls that a pendulist and indeed any dowser must guard against is what happened to M. Henri Meier, a dowser from Luxembourg who had helped the police to find the bodies of missing persons on several occasions.

M. Meier was interned during the Nazi ocupation of his country and, when the water supply ran short, he found a new well for the internment camp. Shortly afterwards the German commandant sent for Meier and asked him to locate a spring of water beneath the floor of his office. In vain Meier explained that in his search for a new water supply for the camp he had already been over the area covered by the commandant's office and there was no underground water there. The commandant would brook no argument and he insisted that there was water and Meier was to find it – and he could start over the commandant's desk.

Resigned to the inevitable Meier produced his pendulum and chart and sat down at the desk and began to look for reactions as he had been instructed to do. To his utter amazement the pendulum quickly began to rotate, indicating a spring of water and Meier began to concentrate and to ask questions as to the depth of the spring and the capacity of the water. With puzzled surprise he worked out that there was a spring 3 metres beneath the desk with a water capacity of 10 metres a minute. When he handed over his results to the commandant, he laughed in his face and told Meier he knew a little about dowsing himself and he had played a trick on the unsuspecting dowser.

Lifting the blotter pad from his desk the commandant revealed a drawing of a spring of water and underneath the information that the depth of the spring was 3 metres and the water capacity 10 metres a minute!

These are but a few of the many fascinating aspects of the faculty we call dowsing or divining. Reading between the lines it seems indisputable that there is a psychic element in dowsing; it can hardly be simply a physical reaction, unless there is anything in the idea of some sort of system of ultra-short waves of a very high frequency that dowsers unconsciously tune into.

In recent years it has been suggested, by Madeleine Barnothey of the University of Illinois among others, that some biological systems may have evolved a remarkable sensitivity to very small changes in ambient magnetic and electromagnetic fields. Yet even this theory would not account for all the aspects of dowsing that we have considered in this chapter and perhaps it would be wise to look a little deeper into the various types of dowsing instruments, some of the historical and recent case histories of dowsing, and also at some of the dowsers themselves and their work in the world today, before we attempt to explore some dowsing tests and perhaps reach some sort of conclusion as to the explanation for this curious faculty.

5. Dowsing Instruments and their Uses

It has been said that almost anything can be used for dowsing and certainly it is possible to find a wide variety of objects in common use, both as pendulums and as divining rods. This fact seems to emphasize the point that the *modus operandi* of dowsing and divining has little if anything to do with the actual instrument or object being used; these articles serve merely as a convenient focus on which to centralize and concentrate the force or reaction that tells the dowser that he has discovered the substance he seeks.

Sometimes the instrument selected is consciously chosen by the dowser but more often, in the case of everyday articles, adapted to the dowser's use. It is a case of the object being readily to hand and, having once been used and found successful, the same instrument is used again and again.

In the case of instruments consciously chosen by the dowser, these are in the main accepted and marketed products produced for the special purpose for which they are required. Before we look at such useful articles and where they can be obtained, let us consider some of the common and less common objects that have been pressed into the service of dowsing and divining.

The article most frequently used for dowsing is, predictably, a forked twig or stick, 'preferably newly picked to ensure pliability and maximum sensitivity'.[1] At one time, as we have seen, there were special conditions

[1] Robert H. Leftwich, *Dowsing: the Ancient Art of Rhabdomancy* (Aquarian Press, 1976).

attached to the selection of the twig and the operation of the rod. One had to face east when cutting the forked twig (so that the rod caught the first rays of the morning sun) or, according to other sources, the eastern and western sun had to shine through the fork, otherwise it was useless. The selection and cutting should be at a time of the new moon, the twig should grow towards the east or the north or straight upwards, and so on . . . .

Well over 100 years ago a chap-book, *The Shepherd's Calendar and Countryman's Companion*, contained explicit instructions for selecting and using a divining rod or as they put it a 'Mosaic Wand to find hidden treasure':

Cut a hazel wand forked at the upper end like a Y. Peel off the rind and dry it in a moderate heat. Steep it in the juice of wake-robin or nightshade and cut the single lower end sharp, and where you suppose any rich mines or treasure is near, place a piece of the same metal you conceive to be hid in the earth near to the top of one of the forks by a hair or very fine silk or thread and do the like to the other end. Pitch the sharp single end lightly to the ground at the going down of the sun, the moon being at the increase, and in the morning at sunrise, by a natural sympathy, you will find the metal inclining, as it were, pointing to the place where the other is hid.

In similar vein Theodore Besterman revealed in a lecture at the Folklore Society[1] that, according to a twelfth-century manuscript, you should find a mountain ash (*Eberesche*) which has grown from a seed dropped out of a bird's beak. Go at twilight between the third day and night after Lady Day and break off a twig. This twig must not come into contact with iron or steel, nor must it be allowed to fall to the ground. The manuscript then proceeds to describe various pseudo-magical directions for the use of the rod.

The hazel, known as the 'Tree of Knowledge' in Ireland, has long been regarded as possessing magical qualities, in common with the rowan or mountain ash, another favourite wood used for divining rods but many modern advocates of the art of divining maintain that a

[1]Theodore Besterman, *Water Divining* (Methuen, 1938).

forked twig from any tree will serve equally well the same purpose.

Nor is it only a forked twig that can, apparently, be used as a divining rod. Metal rods, a pair of pliers, a coat hanger, barbed wire, whalebone, copper wire, clock springs, surgical scissors, plastic rods – just about anything in fact that is forked can, it seems, be employed; there are even cases of a dowser using nothing but his hands to indicate the presence of underground water or some other hidden mineral. A South African, Pieter Van Jaarsveld, achieved a kind of fame with his repeatedly successful demonstrations in locating diamonds as well as water and other underground substances with his hands. It is interesting to note that dowsers who do not use any kind of rod or focus maintain that they are able to sense and see, with an inner perception, the underground matter. Unfortunately, they are unable to explain exactly how they know what they know.

Furthermore it does not necessarily have to be a forked stick, which may be held with the fore-fingers placed against the diverging arms of the rod and the elbows held back against the sides of the body, simply balanced between the fingers, or, more commonly, by gripping the branched arms with the palms uppermost. Other variations include balancing a straight stick or wand between the thumbs and fore-fingers and simply resting the rod on the palm or back of the hand. Some dowsers use a straight rod cut in half; one end of one half is hollowed out and one end of the other half sharpened to a point and inserted into the hollow of the corresponding half and held lightly between the fore-fingers. Then, it is said, the pointed stick revolves in the presence of underground water.

Even in the early days of dowsing and divining there were these variations in the use of twigs and, in the seventeenth century, a straight, springy rod was often held in front of the dowser, in the form of an arc; usually the ends would be held one in each hand and sufficient pressure applied to cause the stick to bend and reach a rigid arc. Occasionally such a twig would merely be balanced on the forefingers of the two hands. Even such articles as a stalk of dry grass and a German sausage (!) are said to have been successfully employed by competent dowsers.

But it is the flexible wood divining rod that is still the commonest and the easiest and the cheapest to find, make and use. More than 200 years ago the Abbé de Vallemant recommended 'a forked branch of hazel, a foot and a half long, as thick as the finger and if possible not more than a year old'.

The forked divining twig is generally accepted as consisting of two branches of equal size and of the same length taken from shoots at the top of the tree, cut below the knot so as to form a fork, and stripped of any minor branches and leaves. The two branches should form an angle of between 25 and 50 degrees and the whole rod should be sufficiently pliable to enable the ends of the branches to be bent almost at right angles and strong enough to resist twisting. The main stem should be cut clean and at right angles, avoiding any slant in the cut; the two branches should be cut clean and both in the same direction. All the leaves and excess twigs should be removed and any little scars levelled off flush with the bark.

Some dowsers say that all kinds of wood can be used for dowsing although the more porous and lighter the wood the better. Other dowsers assert that it does not matter whether the wood is green or dry, pithy or not. But in practice the smoother and less rough woods are easier to handle and seem to give the best results.

Apart from hazel and rowan, other woods have been preferred for dowsing. The laurel has, it is said, special virtues as do the almond tree, the alder, beech, apple, privet, hornbeam, ash, maple, whitethorn, laburnum, oak, chestnut, elm, pear, bramble, plum and birch. Among the woods *not* recommended – as long ago as 1826 by Count de Tristan – are lime, Spanish broom and horse chestnut. Lime rods do not apparently give movements as well as other woods, possibly due to active properties inherent in the tree; Spanish broom has a thin bark and its branches are largely pith, while the horse chestnut is not very flexible and breaks easily – although horse chestnut rods are said to produce very powerful reactions.[1] In America a popular divining rod is made from two 12-inch lengths of whalebone bound together at one end with two strands of thick, black thread. A more recent innovation is the aluminium or wire divining rod with plastic handpieces.

During the course of a television programme, 'Now You See It, Now You Don't', broadcast by the BBC in December 1977, instructions for making such a rod resulted in a flood of reports of successful first attempts at dowsing by amateurs. Viewers were advised to take a plain wire coat-hanger, snip off the handle or hook, cut the remaining wire in half, straighten the two pieces, bend them at right angles about 6 inches from the ends and insert the short ends into the barrels of old ball-point pens. These plastic ends were the handles of the rods and, by holding the rods with the longer struts straight forwards, it was found that they turned inwards, met and crossed in the presence of underground water.

More recently still, low density polyethylene rods have been used for commercially manufactured 'pointing rods' with cylinders to accommodate samples of the substance being sought. These rods are sprung outwards in a flaring arc and remind one of the antennae of insects, especially butterflies. Can it be that the dowsing faculty of detection has a parallel in nature and that this phenomenon is a natural attribute in some creatures, giving them the powers of location and perception at a distance?

Pendulums as divining instruments are even more varied than divining rods: they may be hollow metal, plastic, perspex or wood containers; torpedo shaped, square or ball shaped; there is the spectrum pendulum with its phial of radioactive salts in a solution of tritium or radium and the rings, beads, coins, keys and solid pendulums of everyday usage. It is quite obvious that, for whatever reason pendulums work, they do so irrespective of the apparatus used.

In fact there are reports from Europe and America of

[1]Bruce Copen, *Dowsing for You* (Academic Publications, 1975).

all kinds of things being used as a pendulum: a garden
spade, a pitchfork, a bottle of minerals, a bunch of keys
suspended from a Bible, a metal nail file, an amulet, a
walking stick, a stone with a hole in it – just about
anything that can be suspended or held in such a way
that it swings free can, it would appear, become a
diviner's pendulum.

Such a weight, usually suspended on the end of a
piece of string, that swings or gyrates to indicate the
presence of unseen water or some other substance also
has a very ancient origin; perhaps it is even a relic of
primitive magic.

There are reasons for acknowledging the assertion that
the ancient Egyptian ankh is the oldest divining rod of
all. In this ansate cross, which may represent a human
being, the eye of the loop portrays the head or the
vaginal orifice being penetrated by a phallus – represented by a straight line – or a dam holding back the
life-giving waters of the Nile. Whatever its origin, the
ancient sign of life has long been a favourite amulet and
could well represent a divining rod or pendulum.

There are stories of several 'experiments' reputedly
showing that certain rods are 'sympathetic' to certain
metals. In 1659 (as we have seen) a Jesuit priest, Gaspard
Schott, maintained that a 'rod' was then in use in every
town in Germany and that he had frequently observed
the discovery of hidden treasure by its means. He says:

I searched with the greatest care into the question of
whether the hazel-rod had any sympathy with gold and silver,
and whether any natural property set it in motion. In like
manner, I tried whether a ring of metal, suspended by a thread
in the midst of a tumbler, and which strikes the hours, is
moved by any similar force. I ascertained that these effects
could only have arisen from the deception of those holding
the rod or the pendulum, or, maybe, from some diabolic
impulsion, or more likely still, because imagination sets the
hand in motion.

Many dowsers find a pendulum far more sensitive
than a forked divining rod but, while it has the disadvan-
tage of only being usable while the dowser is stationary,

it is so sensitive, it is claimed, that it will register to a far greater degree the whereabouts of whatever the user may be seeking. It does this by moving in various ways, swinging to and fro, from side to side, in a circular, oval, clockwise or anti-clockwise motion and each movement and the extent of the activity has a specific meaning for the pendulist.

Some pendulists, including Robert Leftwich, as he told me himself, condition their minds to associate clockwise gyrations with positive responses and the reverse with negative ones, while plain oscillations represent indifference or neutral attraction. Once he had 'tuned himself in' to the particular object or substance he was looking for, Leftwich would set the pendulum oscillating and on reaching the object of his search the swinging movements would alter to clockwise gyrations. However, he admitted that this concentration idea was a personal choice and some pendulists preferred to begin their approach to the problem in hand with the pendulum motionless.

Not infrequently a combination of dowsing methods will be used with the divining rod employed to locate the whereabouts of whatever is sought and then the pendulum will be used to obtain additional and more exact information. The pendulum alone is used for map dowsing or divining at a distance and usually for indoor work.

A fairly modern innovation is the idea of an aluminium rod which incorporates a bottle or container suspended from between the forks of the rod or inside the pendulum which is hollow. Into this container the dowser will insert a specimen of the liquid or mineral or substance he is seeking. It is a practice that inevitably leads us back to the idea of sympathetic magic so beloved of witch cults. The dowsing fraternity look on the matter rather differently and suggest that a specimen of the subject he is seeking may help the dowser to think of the substance more accurately or to 'reinforce his tuning ability'.

To such people pendulums or suspended weights, 'give a visible effect to the human powers of perception;

[and] the releasable internal energy manifesting as vibratory waves or ultrasonics of an object can be detected and well recorded by various methods of perception using amplifying instruments such as rods, dials, rules, grids and the biometer'.[1] To the more critical observer the sensitive pendulum will 'register the tiniest involuntary movements of the hand, and as is well known, any simple idea in the mind can be reflected to some extent in the movements of the pendulum'.[2]

The type of divining instrument described on BBC television and made from wire – in this particular instance, from a wire coat-hanger – is more properly an 'L' or angle rod. It is an instrument that turns inwards or outwards rather than dipping or rising as happens with the more conventional divining rod. 'L' rods are often recommended for beginners and newcomers to the art since they almost invariably function for everyone and they are probably the simplest and easiest instrument for locating straightforward underground water, pipes and streams. The rods are held loosely, one in each hand at body width apart and almost waist high, parallel with the ground, while the dowser walks slowly forwards. It is a good idea to keep the smallest finger on the inside of the rod as this helps to keep the instrument parallel with the ground and rigid without a firm grip.

Manufactured angle rods can be purchased and these usually comprise metal rods with sealed tips and the short ends of the rod inserted into wooden handles. These type of rods, so readily available and easily 'manufactured' have been used in many cases of emergency. Many years ago Sir William Barrett at a meeting of the The Ghost Club revealed that Sapper Kelly used copper angle rods to locate water.

During the First World War Sapper Kelly served with the British Expeditionary Forces in the Dardanelles and the soldiers were in great difficulties because of severe shortage of drinking water. Sapper Kelly, an Australian soldier who had long practised the art of dowsing in his

---

[1]Christopher Hills, *Supersensonics* (University of the Trees Press, California, 1975).

[2]D. H. Rawcliffe, *The Psychology of the Occult* (Derricke Ridgway, 1952).

native land, informed his commanding officer that he had found scores of springs with the aid of divining rods, and he was permitted to try his hand.

Not only did Sapper Kelly succeed in quickly locating a spring that resulted in an abundant supply of excellent fresh water, thereby saving the British forces from 'much privation and suffering', as Sir William Barrett put it, but he is credited on one occasion with finding no less than thirty-two wells in the period of one week!

There are one or two curious variations on the more usual angle rods and pendulums and divining rods. At one time a lot of work was expended on an aerial dowsing rod invented by an experienced dowser who made a rod comprising a length of uninsulated wire with a double loop, one at each end, and handles on each of the wires between the loops. It was claimed by the inventor, a man named Clarke, that his metal detecting rod could locate aeroplanes in the sky that were out of sight, a person moving inside a building, and other objects out of the line of view, but the rod never reached any degree of popularity with the dowsing fraternity.

Major Pogson, a member of The Ghost Club whom we shall meet in a later chapter, invented another wire device that he called a 'motorscope'. A single piece of stout wire was bent in two places at right angles so that a shape reminiscent of the old-fashioned car starting-handle was obtained. This was held in an upright position and a pointer, soldered to the central part and positioned so that it pointed away from the dowser, acted as an indicator to the location of water or metals.

At first, with a hand holding each end of the crank, the indicator would show the direction of the substance being sought; then the instrument would be turned on its side and, when the dowser walked in the direction indicated, the pointer would dip when it was over water or metal. This was another instrument that never really caught on.

A dowsing tool that has enjoyed a degree of popularity is the amplifying pendulum which is really a cross between a single type rod and a pendulum. The instrument consists of a non-metal handle from which emerges a single, strong wire. About 1 inch from the handle the wire forms several circles, making it into a sort of spring, and then the wire continues straight for about 12 inches and ends in a weighted knob. It is so balanced that the rod is highly flexible and so delicate that most people desirous of performing the act of dowsing will find that it works for them, and it is claimed that it is not affected by wind or weather.

A smaller but simpler amplifying instrument is made of spring silver and is still more sensitive; it can be used at unusual angles and in difficult positions. Amplifying pendulums react as other pendulums with clockwise, anti-clockwise and oscillating movements. They can be held in either hand and can be used vertically as well as horizontally, or indeed in any other position. They are also very light and easily transported.

Signor Elio Pasquini of Rome designed the Pasquini amplifying rod/pendulum which is claimed to be able to plot the entire three-dimensional radiesthetic field for the evaluation of the investigator. The Pasquini amplifying pendulum incorporates either a single cavity or a double cavity in the handle and this permits the dowser to use 'witnesses' or samples while the second space acts as a resonator chamber.

An even more sophisticated model is known as the aurameter, considered by many people who should know to be 'one of the world's most sensitive radiesthetic detectors'. Essentially, it is a pointing wand and similar to other amplifying pendulums except that it has a plated pointing weight which is fixed to a balanced spring system, which in turn is fixed to a polished handle. The makers point to its special variable sensitivity control incorporated in the handle for the purpose of controlling the amount of sensitivity.

And so we find ourselves in the realm of fringe medicine: radiesthesia, which is basically rational enough, is nothing more than an attempt to apply to medicine the techniques of dowsing and divining that we have discussed. But it is the nature of the equipment used by some of the practitioners of radiesthesia that has caused so much ridicule to be poured on the subject: the notorious 'black box'.

To understand the principle of radiesthesia it is necessary to recall that the dowser himself does not really understand the act of dowsing. Most dowsers will readily admit that the twig or rod or pendulum reacts to an unconscious mental signal, triggered in some unknown way by the presence of underground water or whatever substance is being sought.

Whereas many people unacquainted with the principles and practice of dowsing might consider clairvoyance, telepathy and other forms of extra-sensory perception to be some form or expression of an unexplained mental process which will one day be understood by science, the majority of dowsers believe that the process is a result of radiation.

Everything, they say, radiates on its own wavelength, and the human mind which, under certain conditions and when correctly tuned, is able to act as a receiving set, generates a force or 'neuro-muscular energy' resulting in the movement of the dowser's rod or twig or pendulum.

It is a faculty – whatever the explanation – that seems to result in thought projection and many parallels are to be found in nature, in particular in the flight of birds in formation. Here anyone can marvel at the uniform movements, far too minutely exact to be accounted for by some form of call signal, and it seems indisputable that a process is taking place about which we know nothing. Perhaps the answer lies in the region of resonance, or possibly radiation is the solution and the dowsers are right.

Other examples in nature of an undiscovered faculty that may be related to dowsing is to be found in the homing instinct of pigeons and the occasional stories of remarkable achievements of animals in finding their ways home.

In October 1978 a cat in Australia walked over 1000 miles in twelve months to reach its home. It happened when Kirsten Hicks, about to leave Adelaide with his parents on a long sea journey, arranged for his grandparents, 1000 miles away on Queensland's Gold Coast, to look after his white Persian cat while he was away.

When the family returned home the grandparents had to tell Kirsten that his cat had disappeared and all their efforts to find it had failed. Kirsten and his parents made numerous enquiries themselves but, after several weeks with no word or sign of the cat, Kirsten gave up all hope of seeing his pet again. A year after the cat had been taken to the grandparents, it turned up on the doorstep of its old home.

Kirsten Hicks said at the time that, although the cat's white coat was matted and filthy and its paws sore and bleeding, the cat was purring when he found it. Kirsten's father pointed out that to reach its home the cat had travelled more than 1000 miles, crossing rivers, deserts and vast wildernesses in the process. 'Not surprisingly,' he adds, 'it is still a little nervous. No wonder it does not stray more than a few yards into the garden.'

There are many other examples of an 'unknown power' inherent in animals that may well be related to the dowsing power that is to be found in many practitioners of rhabdomancy. Not very long ago a cat, seemingly mourning his owner's death, leapt from a car window and disappeared. It was found 5 miles away in the cemetery where its owner had been buried. The cemetery is 10 miles from the house where the cat had lived with its dead owner and the animal had never been to the cemetery before.

There are odd reports of wild geese flying to a town and circling round the hospital, 'honking' their last respects, it would appear, when a wild geese sanctuary's founder died in the hospital ... and there were scores of reports of the strange, unprecedented and inexplicable behaviour of animals and birds before the earthquake that affected Friuli in Northern Italy in May 1876. Deer wandered down from the hills and seemed to be moved by some inner compulsion to leave the safety of their natural habitat and stray out into the open. All the pet cats of the village, some carrying their kittens, left home and did not return for two days. Dogs barked, fowls became terrified and broke out of their pens, rats and mice scurried about in daylight above ground. And then, that cloudless spring day, without any sign or warning, the earth suddenly shook, buildings fell and people ran for their lives . . . .

The scientific journal *Nature* suggested that the animals were affected by a build-up of atmospheric electricity just before the earthquake and biochemist Dr Helmut Tributsch of Berlin's Max Planck Institute, collected seventy-eight reports with supporting evidence of the strange behaviour of animals just before the calamity. An interesting clue to what may have been happening can be found in the report from a watchmaker who, just before the earthquake and at the same time that the animals were behaving so strangely, tried repeatedly to assemble the tiny components of a watch and found that they repeatedly jumped out of place, for no apparent reason.

If these parts had become charged with electricity, possibly liberated by rock movement underground which preceded the earthquake, it might account for what happened. The build-up of electricity just before a thunderstorm has long been known to affect animals and some people. Can it be that some similar invisible but powerful force affects the dowser and enables him to produce verifiable results with his rod or pendulum?

Radiesthesia – sensitivity to radiations – may not be such a far cry from the dowser and his hazel twig, for so-called radiesthesia – the technique of using a pendulum to acquire information about an object or a person and even to diagnose illness – uses exactly the same principles. And pendulists point to the fact that many animals have been using radiesthesic techniques for centuries. Such creatures as antelopes and wild pigs possess horns and tusks very similar in shape to the traditional forked twig of the dowser and both these families of animals are known to be resourceful and successful in locating sources of hidden water.

Dr Lyall Watson considers these facts and poses an interesting question in his book, *Supernature*.[1] He refers to the fact that 'the best' human dowsers can work with

¹Hodder and Stoughton, 1973.

Farmer David Brown with his angle rods.

The interior of Borley Church, Essex, where dowsers and other sensitives (including Michael Bentine) have encountered a strange force. The Waldegrave tomb is on the left.

Opposite: A chapel in the catacombs of Rome. It has been suggested that the 'staffs' may be early divining

A typical Biblical illustration of what may be a divining wand: Ruth and Naomi, after a painting by A. Hopfgarten.

their bare hands and suggests that it is possible that even animals without antennae can navigate in this way. 'If the willow twig works in man's hands, how does it function when attached to the tree? The roots of trees are positively geotropic – they grow directly toward the source of gravity – but they also seek out sources of water. Perhaps they do this by dowsing?'

The sexing of eggs is just one of the practical aspects of radiesthesia, an activity that has been described as the detection by refined human sensitivity of ultra-fine radiations which are given off by matter, alive or dead. The Japanese, in particular, are adept at this practice and with no more apparatus than a bead on the end of a silken thread they have long claimed to be able to establish the sex of day-old chicks.

They even improved on this by determining the sex of the chicks before they were hatched by arranging for the eggs to pass along a conveyer belt after they had been arranged in a north-south direction. The bead, it is claimed, swings along the same axis if the egg is sterile but circles in a clockwise direction if the egg contains a cock and in the opposite direction for a hen. The pendulist and the egg factory maintain that they get 99 per cent accuracy.

If this is so, and there are pendulists in Britain who do the same thing, then it is not very surprising to learn that there are practitioners of the pendulum who say they can differentiate between the blood of a male and that of a female. A single drop of blood – or saliva – will, it is claimed, suffice for this to be ascertained. The method involves questions being asked and the subsequent movement of the pendulum provides the answer.[1]

It is even claimed that this form of pendulum activity can cure illness or indisposition. I recall the late Percival Seward, sometime president of the Association of Psychical Research and chairman of The Ghost Club, relating to me an instance which he knew about from first-hand knowledge.

A man Seward knew suffered from obscure symptoms

[1]Major J. F. F. Blyth-Praeger in *Practical Dowsing – a Symposium*, edited by Colonel A. H. Bell (Bell, 1965).

and his general health and physical condition began to degenerate. He consulted one doctor after another and several specialists, for his health became worse and his work and happiness at home began to suffer. He obtained little or no benefit from any member of the established medical profession and then he heard about radiesthesia.

He became interested in the subject and in particular studied, with a pendulum, the various foods and their suitability to his body. He found, having tested every article of food that figured in his menu, that most of the items of food to which he was most partial registered an unfavourable reaction when subjected to the scrutiny of the pendulum. Much of his food was cooked with aluminium utensils and here again the pendulum indicated that aluminium was harmful to him.

Having decided to see whether his health improved if he took notice of the pendulum, he discarded his aluminium pots and pans, eliminated those items of diet upon which the pendulum had pronounced unfavourably, and substituted for them articles of food which had obtained a favourable response from the pendulum. Within a very short time his adverse symptoms disappeared and his general health showed a marked improvement.

It is interesting to recall that M. E. Chevreul, a director of the Natural History Museum in Paris in 1830, became interested in the subject of clairvoyance and the pendulum and came to the conclusion, after exhaustive investigation of both subjects, that movement of the pendulum was not consciously imparted, but that some force of which the person using the pendulum was not conscious must be responsible, and he always maintained that a pendulum would follow its holder's thoughts and not his will.

The original idea of applying radiesthesia to medical diagnosis, according to a former member of The Ghost Club, the late Dr Tertius T. B. Watson, belonged to Mlle Chantereine who had the idea after observing that the character of polluted water could 'be identified by holding samples of bacterial cultures'. As we have seen there is evidence for accepting that some dowsers do obtain an increased reaction from their rods or pendulums when they also hold a sample or specimen or 'witness' of the substance they are seeking and, when it was found that it was possible to discover what was causing pollution in an underground stream by holding different samples of polluted water; it was not long before someone thought of trying the same theory on a sick person. If it was possible to diagnose the 'sickness' of an underground stream, should it not be equally possible to identify the sickness of a human being by studying the different reactions obtained?

It is interesting to consider the possibility that human beings are sensitive to the earth's magnetic field. Professor John Taylor points out in his *Superminds*[1] that admissions to hospitals rose during large fluctuations in the magnetic field and there is experimental support for the claim that dowsers are especially sensitive in this way. Exhaustive experiments by Professor Rocard show that a good dowser can accurately detect a variation of about 3/10,000t gauss per second. If dowsers can detect such minute variations that could well be caused by underground water filtering through porous clay, for example, electric currents could be produced which would generate a small but sufficient magnetic field at the soil's surface that might cause nuclei molecules in the blood to rotate at different frequencies and produce a muscle twitch in the dowser.

Once the idea of radiesthesia was born various practitioners used various methods – as with dowsing. Some used a pendulum, some nothing, and not a few invented strange and wonderful devices, but before we look at some of them a brief word on the methods of using the pendulum for radiesthesia.

Some radiesthetists diagnose from watching the swing or some other movement of the pendulum while mentally asking questions, others use charts and lists in unison with a pendulum: cards and charts are marked out to form a 90 degree arc and are used as a guide to the severity of the complaint. Once the illness has been diagnosed, treatment may be prescribed in the same way,

[1]Macmillan, 1975.

the pendulum deciding the best treatment or drug or medicine or diet.

A practice of radiesthetists that led to the construction of the much criticized 'radionic box' was the claim that diagnosis could be made from a spot of the patient's blood. (One is reminded of the line by Mephistopheles in Goethe's *Faust*: 'Blood is a very special kind of juice.') Yet the idea was a logical one and an attempt to remove or reduce the human element. To be fair to the radiesthetist who used blood for this purpose, he maintained that the drop of blood meant nothing in itself; it was likened to a dial on a radio set, a useful piece of equipment for adjusting the wavelength to obtain the correct tuning but then of no further value or use. The radiesthetist believed that the blood sample helped him to tune in to his patient's mind, to get on his wavelength; but if the radiesthetist was sufficiently sensitive, even this aid was not required.

It is to a San Francisco man, Albert Abrams, that we owe the first medical or radionic or black box. A neurologist of standing both in America and in Europe, Dr Abrams came to believe in radiation as a universal property of matter at a time when such a view was far from widespread and he argued that if matter and energy were so blended, it could be that the basis of disease might be electronic and in that case health and disease should be reflected in different radiations emanating from the body. So, decided Dr Abrams, the thing to do was to construct an apparatus that might be likened to the clinical equivalent of a radio set – an instrument that would indicate the radiations of a patient which could then be studied for diagnosing purposes, and doubtless something could also be developed for treatment and remedy.

So far so good, and up to this point the ideas and reasoning of Dr Abrams might well have found favour with many of his fellow physicians but then he made a fatal, if understandable, mistake. He decided, after experimenting with an apparatus that he called a dynamixer, to manufacture and market a machine he called an oscilloclast for diagnosing and treating illness and disease, and he began to lease the 'boxes' to anybody for a sum of about $300 with an additional tuition charge. The medical profession could hardly accept the commercial attitude plus the apparent willingness to encourage unqualified persons to treat themselves and others. Furthermore, examination of the machine seemed to indicate that it was fraudulent to claim that it could do what it was supposed to do, for it consisted of meaningless electrical gadgets wired together in a haphazard fashion.

The boxes, with their weird circuits, bird's nest of wires and several dials and knobs, looked scientific enough from the outside but, as Dr Christopher Evans tells us, some of these dials 'which were twiddled and set with great solemnity by the operator, may even be found not to be connected to anything at all inside!'[1] Nevertheless Dr Adams died a millionaire.

The box came to England and a committee appointed by the British Medical Association conducted an investigation, fully expecting to discredit the contraption but, after the results of a series of suitably supervised tests had been carefully analysed, the committee decided that the claims for its diagnostic value had been proved. However they were unable to come to any conclusion concerning the physical basis for the results they had obtained and consequently they could not recommend doctors to use the mysterious box. Some members of the association were anxious to explore the whys and the wherefores of the box but no funds were forthcoming for this purpose and before long the findings of the BMA's report were forgotten amid the public outcry against the black box diagnosis and therapy. Variations of Abram's box continued to be marketed, however, in a variety of designs, one of the best known in America being developed by Dr Ruth Drown and by far the best known in Britain by George de la Warr.

Dr T. T. B. Watson described in detail the theory and principle of these radiesthesiac boxes at a meeting of The Ghost Club. He said that for the purposes of discussion they consisted of nine variable rheostats scaled from 1 to

[1] *Cults of Unreason* (Harrap, 1973).

10 connected in series with a detector unit consisting of a thin sheet of rubber over a metal plate. The contraption was not electrically powered. The patient could be personally linked to the instrument, or a blood spot might be used. In the latter case, the patient could be any distance away and it was believed that the information obtained referred to the state of the patient's health at the time of the examination. A vibration rate (which bore no relation to any known physical vibration rate) was allotted to each organ and tissue in health and disease, as well as to parasites, bacteria, viruses, chemicals, hormones, vitamins, and so on.

To make a diagnosis, organ rates were set up in turn on the dials and, to determine the energy output of any organ, the rubber pad would be stroked with a finger while the ninth dial was rotated from 10 to 1. At the number representing the energy of the organ, the rubber was said to become sticky and adhere to the finger. To discover the nature of the pathological condition of the organ, disease rates were set up on the dials. In this way it was claimed that a complete picture of the state of the mind and the body of the patient could be ascertained. In addition anatomical diagrams were sometimes used. A pointer connected to the instrument was then moved over the diagram while the detector pad was being operated, and the precise site of the injury detected. Dr Watson emphasized that the mind of the operator played a dominant part in the diagnosis and treatment and at each item under investigation the operator would ask himself: 'Is this patient suffering from so-and-so?' Efforts to make the instrument entirely automatic were never successful.

George de la Warr (1904-1969) was originally an engineer. It is probably pertinent that his mother was greatly interested in homoeopathy and de la Warr, while regarding the theory (that minute doses of drugs which would produce symptoms in a healthy person of the disease being treated, will cure that illness) as rubbish, he was impressed by the fact that it seemed to work and he came to the conclusion that there existed some kind of fundamental energy or force in all living things, and that the presence of this energy could be detected and measured by scientific means.

It was during the course of another Ghost Club meeting that members were told of the early experiments and the construction of the black box that was to cause the inventor so much trouble. De la Warr's box consisted of a number of control knobs, a rubber detector pad and containers for samples of blood or hair. There were no valves inside the box, no condensers – in fact nothing. The diagnosis was carried out by rubbing a finger on the rubber pad at each figure on each of the dials and, when the finger stuck, that figure was noted. By this means a series of numbers was obtained and with the aid of the *Guide to Clinical Conditions* (supplied with the black box) it was possible to match up the 'rate' number with an ailment, disease or affliction. By using different combinations it was claimed that psychological conditions could also be detected.

De la Warr then produced a special 'treatment' box. This consisted of another box with dials on the outside and without any orthodox power source or transmitter inside. Having obtained a diagnosis it was only necessary to look up in the catalogue supplied the 'bloodcast treatment rate' for the malady, adjust the dials accordingly and the treatment box did the rest. This box was followed by the appearance of the latest marvel from the Delawarr laboratories: a 'camera' capable of photographing human thoughts.

But it was the diagnostic black box that found its way into a sensational legal case when, in 1960, De la Warr was sued by a black box operator, Miss Catherine Phillips. The main complaint was that George de la Warr 'fraudulently represented that there were associated substances, distinctive waves, vibrations or radiations capable of affecting a device of the defendant called a Delawarr diagnostic instrument'; Miss Phillips also complained, among other things, that some of her subjects, according to the results she obtained from the machine, appeared to change sex from day to day . . . .

The case lasted a full thirteen working days and represents a turning point in the public history of radionics. Miss Phillips's counsel presented a string of reliable witnesses: surgeons, pathologists, physicists, photographers and electrical experts to say that the equipment was ridiculous and completely unworkable. Counsel for De le Warr was Mr Christmas Humphreys and he called as witnesses Air Marshall Sir Victor Goddard, former head of technical services in the RAF; the Rev. Dr Leslie Wetherhead, Minister of the Inner Temple, and Dr Kenneth Walker with his impressive medical and scientific background, who all said that De la Warr's work was important, that it involved scientific investigation, and that it could not possibly be called fraudulent.

In his summing up of the case in the Queen's Bench Division Mr Justice Arthurian Davies suggested that the nonsensical interior of the box was irrelevant to the case in question as no one had claimed that they knew how it worked, but merely that, on occasions, it did work. He emphasized that he was not saying that the box did work and indeed he considered that to be 'a very open question'. On the matter of the camera and the photographers which had been brought into the case, the judge went so far as to say that it all seemed 'completely bogus'; but he was satisfied that De la Warr honestly believed in his devices and his methods and consequently he could not be guilty of fraudulence. He therefore awarded judgement for the defendant.

The triumph of George de la Warr and his friends (including a Mr Corte who addressed The Ghost Club on the subject) was shortlived, however; they had won the case but not only had the judge made it quite clear that he had the gravest reservations about the various De la Warr boxes but, owing to a technical anomaly, De la Warr was unable to get costs, and these amounted to some £10,000. Following this court case the black box and other radionic devices fell into disfavour, although similar radionic appliances, including 'mnemonic charts' and 'vertical magnetic tuners', as well as the original black box, are still available.

In much the same way as the black box was an attempt to eliminate the human element, we now consider the

'Revealer' which might be regarded as a similar and logical extension of the divining rod.

This instrument first came to my notice in conversation with my friend the late Dr George Medhurst, then Chairman of the ESP Committee of the Society for Psychical Research. That committee became interested in the device then being marketed by J. C. Oliver (Leeds) Ltd and the publicity leaflet issued claimed that 'the Revealer detection instrument was invented by Mr L. J. Veale, a building contractor, in 1956'. The brochure further stated that the instrument:

... is largely used for building and civil engineering work and, by using it, the operator can easily determine the position of underground services. It is possible to locate both metallic and non-metallic objects, determine their composition and approximate depth and in the case of pipes, the approximate diameter. The instrument has been used to detect a buried service at a dept of 205 ft, thus an operator can easily locate sewers, pipes and cables and other materials usually found much nearer to the surface of the ground.

The Society for Psychical Research, in publishing the results of its investigation,[1] pointed out that these were impressive claims to make for a device that was in essence a divining rod, 'for despite its more elegant format the Revealer is a quasi-hazel twig rather than a piece of scientific apparatus'.

In fact the Revealer is a sophisticated pair of angle rods, two L-shaped metal rods with the short limbs set into cylindrical handles which allow the rods to rotate freely. The long arm, referred to as the 'indicator' is composed of two parts for convenient storage and when screwed together form a rod of 21 inches in length. The rods are marked with calibration figures. The handle containing the short limb is chromium-plated copper, 9 inches in length and ¾ inch in diameter, a cylinder closed top and bottom by metal caps. These cylinders are divided into compartments by floating copper discs. Within the cylinder are needle compartments, each

[1] *Investigation of a Divining Instrument Called the 'Revealer'*, S P R Journal, volume 47, no.757 (September, 1973).

containing eight copper needles with the eyes set into dimples in the surface of the discs; the needles are arranged in a circle around a central sleeve extending along the length of the cylinder in which the rod rotates.

There are also dust compartments filled with metal filings, and spring compartments, each containing a light coil spring to hold the needles in position. The short limb of the rod may be provided with a wire that twists in and out through the apertures in the rod 'for greater sensitivity'. When the rods are held with the cylindrical mounting vertical, the slightest tilting movement will cause the rod to rotate on a vertical axis. There is also a 'mineral bracket' which can be attached to one of the cylinders for the purpose of determining the composition of the located object or substance. Specimens of various materials can be threaded on an elastic cord mounted on a curved frame that clips on to the cylinder and, when seeking a material or substance not included in the bracket, the user is advised to hold a specimen to confirm a finding, for example a tube of water or oil.

Since the distributors of the Revealer supplied with their literature a 'selected list of users' the investigating committee of the Society for Psychical Research sent a questionnaire to most of the hundred or so local authorities, statutory undertakings, public utilities, engineering companies and other commercial enterprises to enquire about their satisfaction and the actual results that they had obtained with the £72.10 instrument.

In the event ninety-three organizations were sent questionnaires and sixty replied. Very few gave the Revealer a positively unfavourable report – although three denied all knowledge of the instrument – two said they considered it useless and four found it to be of little use. The other replies were favourable, although no more than nine claimed consistently successful results. Since the replies were on the whole favourable the Society decided to hold some field tests to attempt to see the instrument at work. It might be appropriate to mention here that the members of the investigating committee were well aware of the difficulties in obtaining unbiased reports: some of the people who completed the questionnaires were the same people who had authorized the purchase of the Revealer, so it might be thought that they would hardly give an adverse report.

For the purpose of the field tests (for precise details of the tests the Society for Psychical Research report should be consulted) five operators concerned with organizations who had returned questionnaires were examined, the first one in the garden of Dr Medhurst's home at Wembley and then in Bushey Park, and the rest in Bushey Park only.

The first volunteer, a civil engineer, had no success in Dr Medhurst's garden and very little in Bushey Park; the second operator did no better; the third achieved marginally better than chance expectation; the fourth somewhat complicated things by suggesting several locations and refusing to prefer one, but he did seem to be the most promising of the subjects tested, although unfortunately a later test ran into difficulties because of the weather and this subject was not able to repeat his promising performance; the fifth participant achieved results worse than chance expectation.

The general consensus had to be that the claims made for the Revealer were not altogether justified, although the instrument may be an inspirer of confidence; certainly the instrument does not seem to endow its practitioners with the elusive gift of consistent performance under test conditions and in this respect, it may be thought, the Revealer is no better and no worse than any other divining instrument.

During the course of his recent book, *Divining, the Primary Sense*,[1] Herbert Weaver explores the possibility of ray-paths that can be used to find missing persons and objects, and can locate, for example, ships at sea, even if they are thousands of miles distant; such ray-paths can be detected by the late Lawrence Veale's Revealer Field Detector, obtainable from Mrs Lawrence Veale, price about £75, at St Lawrence, 5 Fluder Hill, Kingkerswell, Newton Abbot, Devon.

Herbert Weaver, a rationalist who takes a physiological

[1]Routledge and Kegan Paul, 1978.

view of divining, conducted a number of experiments with the sophisticated Revealer and in his book he describes in detail the investigations that led him to conclude that the divining faculty is due to unconscious sensitivity to electromagnetic fields. He wrote to me in June 1979, explaining that the photograph he has kindly allowed me to reproduce relates to a successful experiment quoted in the Board of Trade journal *The Coastguard* in January 1968. Lawrence Veale and he successfully located the hidden Trinity House ship *Stella* from some miles away through the uniquely individual signal of her captain. The measuring scale, in front of the operator, was the first primitive attempt to resolve the centre of the ray-path, then to be read on a 360 degree protractor (not shown in the photograph). Another device found in 1971 reduces the error to .25 degree. The bracket on the right handle is to identify the detected metal underground or 'voids' or underground 'fissures' which can then be marked in outline on the ground surface.

Understandably, Herbert Weaver is reluctant to divulge the special techniques and extra apparatus necessary to extend the Revealer to distant use and discrimination for, as he pointed out to me, if this information fell into the wrong hands it could perhaps be used for such unfriendly purposes as hunting down dissidents – a use that the early mineral and water diviners could hardly have dreamt that dowsing might one day be used for.

6. Dowsers of the Past

One of the earliest stories of dowsing in the past concerns William Lilly (1602-1681) the English astrologer who was also interested in the subject of dowsing. Lilly had long been intrigued by stories of buried treasure in the cloister of Westminster Abbey and he obtained permission from the Dean to search for the missing treasure at dead of night, armed only with divining rods.

The Chapel of the Pyx, a vaulted chamber built between 1040 and 1100 is undoubtedly part of Edward the Confessor's original building. The only stone altar *in situ* at Westminster shows that it must have been used as a chapel sometime before the fourteenth century when it was the monastic treasury and here was housed the 'pyx' or box containing the standard pieces of gold and silver and here, once a year, took place the trial of the pyx, the testing of the current gold and silver coinage which later took place at the Mint. The king's treasure house was once the crypt under the nearby Chapter House and it is part of this treasure that has never been found.

In 1303, when Edward I was occupied with his Scottish wars, money and jewels were stolen by thieves who entered with the asistance of confederates in the monastery. It is said that several millions of pounds worth of treasure was carried away. Access is supposed to have been obtained through a tunnel that began in the Great Cloister.

The peaceful, grassy plot in the middle of the Great Cloister was a vital factor in the daring theft of the treasure for, preparatory to the robbery, the monks who were in league with the robbers arranged for a crop of flax to be sown in the plot of ground. When the flax had grown tall a tunnel is said to have been dug from here to the Chapel of the Pyx and by this means entry was effected and the treasure removed and buried in the growing flax until it could safely be removed from the holy precincts.

However Edward I acted promptly; the abbot and forty-eight monks were taken to the Tower and tried. The abbot and the rest of the fraternity were released but the charge was found proven against the sub-prior and the sacrist and while much, but not all, of the treasure was recovered, the thieves were executed, skinned, and their skins tanned and used to cover both sides of the door opening into the passage from the Cloisters to the Chapter House.

It was through this doorway, at that time, that the monks had to pass to their dormitory on the floor above, so presumably the idea was that they would be continually reminded of the theft and what had happened to those who had committed it. The original door still exists and leads to the old dormitory, a part of which is greatly changed, while another part is used as the Abbey library.

On the inside and outside of the door were found, under iron clamps, fragments of human skin and attendants at the entrance to the Chapter House will show visitors a small piece of the skin of one of the thieves, Richard le Podlicote, carefully framed for preservation, after having been nailed to the door for centuries.

The astrologer Lilly was convinced that the successful operation of the dowsing rod demanded secrecy and intelligence in the agents, and above all a strong faith and a competent knowledge of the work. He learnt all he could about the robbery of the Abbey treasure and, satisfied that he could recover the missing treasure with the help of his divining rod, he impressed the Dean of Westminster with his competence and obtained the necessary permission.

Accordingly, at dead of night, watched by the Dean and others, Lilly searched for the missing treasure in the Great Cloister where the thieves had arranged for the crop of tall flax to be grown to hide the digging of the tunnel. It was here that some of the treasure had been recovered and Lilly found a definite reaction on the western side of the cloister where his rods 'turned over each other with inconceivable rapidity'.[1] Yet, on digging, no treasure was found – only a coffin. Tired from his efforts Lilly retired to the Abbey and then a storm arose, so violent that all the candles were extinguished save one which burned dimly, and for a time the elements threatened to destroy the west part of the church.

Lilly, it was suggested, must have released a demon intent on destroying the ecclesiastical edifice where it had been imprisoned and, although Lilly 'succeeded at length in charming away the demon', his divining rods became immovable and no persuasion could induce him to make another experiment of that kind.

In his *Memoirs*, published posthumously, Lilly states his personal opinion regarding the incident. He says 'the true miscarriage of the business was by reason of so many people being present at the operation, for there were about thirty, some laughing, others deriding us; so that if we had not dismissed the demons, I believe most part of the Abbey church would have been blown away; secrecy, and intelligent operators, with a strong confidence and knowledge of what they are doing, are best for this work'. Towards the end of his life Lilly amassed a tolerable fortune and he bought a small estate at Hersham in Surrey where he diverted his talents to the practice of medicine.

Carl von Linné Linnaeus (1707-1778) the Swedish botanist, during the course of his visit to Denmark, heard his secretary highly extol the virtues of his divining rod.[2] When questioned on the subject the secretary intimated that he was perfectly willing to convince Linnaeus of the power of the rod. Thinking to convince the secretary of the insufficiency of the power of his divining rod, Linnaeus concealed a purse containing 100 ducats under a ranunculus (a plant of the buttercup or crowfoot family) which he came across, growing in a meadow; he removed all traces of his having disturbed

---

[1] William Jones, *Credulities Past and Present* (Chatto and Windus, 1880).

[2] See the *Gentleman's Magazine* (established in 1731 and discontinued in 1914) for February, 1752.

the ground, made a mark that he would recognize, and then bid his secretary find the purse if he could.

After repeated efforts the man had to acknowledge himself beaten; the wand or rod showed no reaction anywhere but the mark that Linnaeus had made to indicate the whereabouts of the purse of money was soon trampled down by the company who turned out to witness the experiment, so that, when Count von Linné Linnaeus went to recover the gold himself and so bring the trial to an end, he was utterly at a loss to know where to seek the purse!

Then the secretary offered to be of any assistance that he could and, in the relaxed atmosphere after the test, he quickly announced that the purse of money they were seeking could not be in the direction that he and Linnaeus were following but quite the opposite in fact, and he followed the direction of his divining rod and quickly reached the place where the purse had been hidden and he found the gold. Carl von Linnaeus freely admitted afterwards that just one more experience like that would be sufficient to make a convert of him!

200 years after the convincing proceedings witnessed by Carl von Linnaeus, I had long discussions at The Ghost Club with the late Major Charles Aubrey Pogson, who has been generally considered to be one of the great dowsers of all time. Theodore Besterman, a psychical researcher of considerable standing and experience, maintained that he had considered more evidence pertaining to dowsing than any man alive and that Major Pogson was second to none in his divining abilities.

By the time I knew him Major Pogson had a wealth of successful dowsing work behind him, work he had undertaken during his Army service (from 1905 to 1925), during his time in India, where he was official Water Diviner to the government of Bombay from 1926 to 1930, and during the latter part of his life he continued divining in a private capacity, when he lived on the south coast of England. During the course of his war service Major Pogson was mentioned in despatches and awarded the Military Cross.

I found it interesting to learn that Major Pogson's wife,

whom he married in 1914, was the daughter of W. N. Pogson (a very distant relative) of Madras, who was himself well-known as a water diviner, and furthermore Major Pogson's mother remembered watching her grandfather use a hazel divining rod. Major Pogson's wife also possessed the ability to dowse, the only one of three daughters who could do so. These facts suggest that in some cases the ability may be inherited; certainly Mrs Pogson thought so. Incidentally, both Mr and Mrs W. N. Pogson, after being introduced to the subject through the chance reading of a pamphlet and afterwards themselves successfully locating water, oil and metals in many different locations over a long period, came to the conclusion that the reaction of the rod to any substance they sought had nothing to do with the actual rod moving as a result of the subtle activity of the dowser's hands; the rod merely acted as an instrument registering such minute movements. Having reached this conclusion, they gave up using a forked twig and took to using wire rods which they found gave a finer expression to their hand movements. They also came to the conclusion that different substances produced distinctive and characteristic reactions which they were able to recognize, that affected their hand movements, and that some matter affected the right hand to a greater degree and other matter the left hand.

In 1916 Major Pogson (as he was to become) first became interested in the subject of dowsing when he assisted his father-in-law with some experiments, and he soon discovered that there was a slight but definite movement in the rod when he held it over some metal, although he had no belief whatever in the ability to dowse at that time. This reaction awakened his interest in the subject and he practised whenever he was able to do so, trying to find underground streams on hillsides, which he found he was able to do, and to trace them to where they emerged as springs. Later, when he obtained a strong reaction, he would arrange for wells to be dug and invariably he was successful in finding a good supply of water.

By 1922 he was carrying out water divining projects

for Indian rulers and others, having obtained special sanctions from the authorities to do so. Early in 1925 his many successes in divining for water in a land where water was in short supply, caused his work to come to the attention of the Bombay Government, who applied for him to be loaned to them so that they might test his dowsing abilities.

The scenes for the resulting tests were carefully selected by the Agricultural and Boring Department of the government as being areas where normal methods of finding water had failed and the areas were therefore thought to be dry. Pogson found water in several places and the Bombay Government made application through the government of India to the Secretary of State for India for the extended loan of his services for an initial period of three years. And so Major Pogson became official Water Diviner to the Indian government, a post created specially for him.

Not that the appointment passed unnoticed, indeed *The Times* commented in their issue of 30 April 1926 that there was 'much criticism' of the appointment but went on to say, '... The facts now published show how successful Major Pogson has been and how fully he has justified his appointment at a high salary.'

Even the staid *Indian Journal of Engineering* had to admit Major Pogson's achievements: 'Major Pogson can find water, it appears, when the machines specially designed for the purpose have failed,' the *Journal* commented in its issue of 1 May 1926. 'It is an interesting situation. Out of forty-nine wells which have been sunk upon spots indicated by Major Pogson, only two have failed to produce water. It is a notable achievement.'

During his years as official Water Diviner Pogson proved again and again the efficiency of dowsing and divining for water, especially during periods of famine when he was held responsible by the Indian government for the provision of water for villages and agriculturists in rural areas badly affected by shortage of water and where scores of wells dug by ordinary engineering methods proved to be failures. Pogson told me, in all modesty that, when he was perfectly sure that he had found water, he was never wrong and he had never failed; his appointment was twice extended and only ceased when he was retired as a measure of enforced economy in 1930. During the course of an official white paper, GRN 9182 RD dated 18 July 1929 it is plainly stated that, 'the services of Major Pogson are being dispensed with, not for any reason of dissatisfaction with his work, in which indeed he has achieved a considerable measure of success, but solely on the ground that this Goverment can no longer afford them'.

During his unique official appointment Major Pogson visited all districts of Bombay, locating sites for wells and bores for municipal and village supplies, for government departments and agriculturists, and all reports and enquiries on the subject of underground water were submitted to him for scrutiny and advice. He covered many thousands of miles during the course of this work and his services were requisitioned by the Bihar, Orissa, Central Provinces and North-West Frontier Province for town waterworks, village water supplies, and by government railways, industrial enterprises, schools, clubs and private individuals.

During the course of one official report on his work it was stated that he surveyed 577 fields for possible well sites and pronounced the presence of water in 220 of them; water was duly located in every one of those he had selected. Another report contains the following sentence: 'The percentage of success obtained in the wells fully excavated during 1928 is a very high standard and is remarkable in view of the fact that, with one exception, all of these wells have been sunk in localities where the shortage of water is a most acute problem.'

Following his return to England and making his home in Sussex, Major Pogson caried out thousands of projects for District and Urban Councils, factories, farms and private individuals and again, he told me, he never failed to locate water where there was water. He found water at depths varying between a few feet and 500 feet and continued successfully to find water for the rest of his life.

In one instance he stated that water would be found at

a certain spot at a depth of 32 feet which would yield a sufficient supply indefinitely. Water was indeed found at a depth of exactly 32 feet and the well produced an adequate supply of water throughout nine months of drought, but then the water yield fell considerably and the well became useless. Pogson was sent for again and he discovered that a new well had been dug in a neighbouring field some 300 yards away and this was feeding on the same spring that fed the original well. He recommended that the well be deepended to 60 feet and then bored, if necessary, to 120 feet in order to tap a source of water at a lower depth. The well was deepened to 60 feet and a bore-hole sunk to 81 feet, where a supply of water was struck which rose to within 19 feet of the surface and remained at that level. The well easily supplied a withdrawal of 500 gallons a day and there was no shortage thereafter.

A small laundry in Worthing required about 2000 gallons of water a day to enable it to operate and here Pogson was somewhat restricted as the available area was small, but he eventually located a fissure current in an open garage where, he estimated, a 6 inch bore-hole would produce more than sufficient water for the laundry's requirements at a depth of about 96 feet. Such a bore-hole was sunk and water was found at 92 feet. Pumping tests gave 1500 gallons of water per hour.

Major Pogson had no illusions about dowsing, and he believed that it could be done both on a physical and on a psychical basis and that the majority of dowsers employ, often unknowingly, a psychical sense that they attribute to a physical basis. A few, he thought, operate purely on physical lines and a greater number used a combination of the two factors.

His long residence in India and considerable experience of dowsing and dowsing practice there led him to conclude that in the East much, if not all, of the dowsing is actuated on a psychical basis (a point he dealt with at some length in his paper on 'Water Diviners of India' which he presented at the British Society of Dowsers); in the West, on the other hand, where psychical and occult matters are not held in such high esteem, dowsers sought to ascribe a physical basis to the faculty, even to the extent, in Pogson's opinion, where the factors involved make such a claim ridiculous.

When I pressed him on this aspect of the subject Pogson argued that if, as dowsers favouring the physical explanation claimed, water or some effect of water exerts a physical impression upon a person, it surely follows that that person must be within such distance from the water that the effect is felt without the interference of any other water nearer to the person. Yet there are many dowsers who appear to be able to locate water several miles away, while others employ a rod or pendulum over a map or plan to locate water successfully, although the actual ground where the water exists may be hundreds of miles away.

Pogson went on to instance a dowser locating water for a client a mile away from where he stands on the chalky Sussex downs, yet it is known that the quantity of water in the chalk must mean that there is water between the dowser and where he has located it: how can he possibly ascribe a physical basis to the fact that he feels the water at his chosen spot to the complete exclusion of the quantities of water that must exist between him and the place he selects, not to mention the other vast supplies all around him in every direction?

Such a dowser may say that he is locating the strongest source of water but Pogson argued that, if the water was energizing some force that the dowser could locate, then all the water around him must be energizing similar forces, and how could he be affected by one without being affected by the total sum of all the other water nearer to him; and furthermore, why was he not affected by even larger and stronger sources of water at greater distances from him. Where is the limit, asked Pogson. And how can he find his particular spot, for when he walks towards it he may come within range of an even larger and stronger supply of water – presumably this would blot out his original site . . . .

Pogson always maintained that without any limit of operation practical dowsing, on a physical basis, was impossible, for there must always be a stronger supply beyond his 'strongest supply'. Pogson believed that such dowsers worked within a boundary without realizing it. Before attempting to find water the dowser is usually given particulars of his sphere of operation and unconsciously sets his mind to work to see whether he gets any impression of the presence of water. When he does receive such an impression, it is transmitted to his consciousness, which immediately relays the effect to his nerves and muscles which register the actions he associates with the presence of water.

This type of dowsing, Pogson told me, seemed to be very similar to the dowsing that he often encountered in India, where the dowser, on being taken to a field or area and asked to locate water, would lapse into a state of meditation and then pronounce that water would be found at a certain spot and at a certain depth. On those occasions when such attempts at finding water were successful some psychical basis was evident for, if the result was obtained purely on a physical basis with an unlimited range, then all the forces and attractions that were present would intermingle and the result would be a hopeless muddle.

On the specific subject of map dowsing Major Pogson was always sceptical. He told me frankly that he remained to be convinced that such divining had ever been accomplished – without the dowser obtaining some knowledge other than from the map or plan. All the tests in map and distance dowsing that he had been associated with, and indeed every one that he had first-hand knowledge of, had proved to be utter failures. He believed that those who thought they had accomplished map dowsing had been 'led away by their enthusiasm' and had in fact obtained their results by other means, usually by visiting the site personally.

Major Pogson has been described as 'perhaps the most successful of all water diviners'.[1] It is a claim that is difficult to dispute. During those few years in India he located water in no less than 465 sites, in 199 cases the water was suitable for drinking and in 266 cases accept-

[1]D. W. Rawcliffe, *The Psychology of the Occult* (Derricke Ridgway, 1952).

able for irrigation purposes: he achieved a success rate
calculated at 97 per cent. It is equally difficult to argue
with the view that he 'helped considerably' to change
'the climate of opinion towards dowsing'.[1]

Yet there was one occasion on which Pogson drew a
blank, not that this reflects on his dowsing ability; rather,
in view of his undisputed success rate, it strongly
suggests that there was nothing present to affect his rods,
but it was an interesting experiment and exercise for it
was a search for treasure at the Tower of London.

There is considerable historical evidence that treasure
has been buried at the Tower at various times, the best
known being the Barkstead Treasure. I have talked to my
friend Yeoman Warder Geoffrey Abbot (who has produced a book on the Tower ghosts) and he tells me that
this treasure was buried by Colonel Sir John Barkstead,
one of Cromwell's men and Lieutenant of the Tower. An
unscrupulous man, he extorted loot from the prisoners
in his charge and, when King Charles II was restored to
the throne, Barkstead buried his ill-gotten gains somewhere within the precincts of the Tower and fled. It was
reportedly worth between £7000 and £20,000 when it
was buried in wooden butter firkins so it would be worth
a fortune today, – if it is still there.

John Barkstead was a wealthy jeweller in the City of
London. He became a Member of Parliament and a
favourite of the Lord Protector who appointed him to
the Lieutenancy of the Tower. While it was the usual
custom for men in such authority to enrich themselves at
the expense of the prisoners in their care, there is no
doubt that Barkstead carried his nefarious activities to
shameful lengths and he kept his spoils at his official
residence in the Tower. He was one of the signatories to
the execution warrant of Charles I and, with the return
of Charles II and his Royalist adherents, Barkstead had
little time to make his escape to Holland.

In fact he was sought and found by two Royalists who
seized him and smuggled him back to England where he
was hanged, drawn and quartered at Tyburn; his execu-

[1]Francis Hitching, *Pendulum: the Psi Connection* (Fontana/Collins, 1977).

tion was carried out in such haste that no enquiries were made, it seems, regarding the whereabouts of his undisputed and missing wealth.

Three months after his execution in July 1662, the diarist Samuel Pepys (1633-1703) heard about the treasure from his cousin Lord Sandwich and having obtained the necessary permission Pepys and his party descended to the cellars beneath Barkstead's residence, looking for the marks which they had been told would guide them to the treasure. This must have struck a chord in Pepys's memory for on two occasions he had buried his own wealth and later, when he wanted to recover it, had the greatest difficulty in recognizing the signs he had left to indicate where he had buried it!

It was arranged that the king was to have a good share of any treasure found and Pepys himself takes up the story:

> So our guide demands a candle, and down into the cellars he goes, enquiring whether they were the same that Barkstead always had. He went into several little cellars, and then went out a-doors to view, and to the Cole Harbour;[1] but none did answer so well to the marks which was given him to find it by, as one arched vault, where, after a great deal of council whether to set upon it now, or delay for better and more full advice, to digging we went till almost eight o'clock at night, but could find nothing. But, however, our guides did not at all seem discouraged; for that they being confident that the money is there they look for, but having never been in the cellars, they could not be positive to the place, and therefore will inform themselves more fully, now they have been there, of the party that do advise them. So, locking the door after us, we left here tonight, and up to the Deputy-Governor, my Lord Mayor and Sir H. Bennet, with the rest of the company, being gone an hour before; and he do undertake to keep the key of the cellars, that none shall go down without his privity.[2]

It has been speculated that the arched and vaulted cellars described by Pepys are likely to have been the lower of two vaulted chambers contained within the Bell Tower. These cellars are in fact the ground floor of the Bell Tower which is on the same level and adjacent to

[1]The meaning of this expression has never been satisfactorily explained.
[2]*The Diary of Samuel Pepys* for 30 October 1662.

the Tower Lieutenant's official residence and indeed these chambers can only be entered from the 'Lieutenant's Lodgings' and there is no other direct entry. It would appear that the search, when it was resumed by Pepys and his friends, was again confined to this area.

This time, says Pepys,

> ... we staid two or three hours, and dug a great deal all under the arches, as it was now most confidently directed, and so seriously, and upon pretended good grounds, that I myself did truly expect to speed; but we missed of all: and so we went away the second time like fools.

That same day however, at the Dolphin Tavern, Pepys met Mr Wade, the original informant, and Captain Evett, their guide,

> ... who now do tell me plainly, that he that do put him upon this is one that had it from Barkstead's own mouth, and was advised with by him, just before the King's coming in, how to get it out, and had all the signs told him how and where it lay, and had always been the great confident of Barkstead, even to the trusting him with his life and all he had. So he did much convince me that there is good ground for what he goes about. But I fear it may be that Barkstead did find some conveyance of it away, without the help of this man before he died; but he is resolved to go to the party once more, and then to determine what we shall do further.

Next evening at his office where he was working Wade and Evett went to see Pepys. The diarist says they had,

> ... been again with their prime intelligencer, a woman, I perceive. And though we have missed twice, yet they bring such an account of the probability of the truth of the thing, though we are not certain of the place, that we shall set upon it once more; and I am willing and hopeful in it. So we resolved to set upon it again on Wednesday morning; and the woman herself will be there in a disguise, and confirm us in the place.

Charles Quarrell, with whom I discussed the question of the Tower treasure at a meeting of The Ghost Club, was highly suspicious of this woman and her motives.[1]

[1] See Charles Quarrell's *Buried Treasure* (Macdonald and Evans, 1955).

He regarded the promised co-operation of the person who had been the confidante and probably the mistress of Barkstead as simply too good to be true. Having been the friend of Cromwell's favourite, she was unlikely to have much in common with the Royalists who had murdered her friend and so left her alone and without support. Why should she help Pepys and the other treasure-seekers? There was the possibility that she hoped to obtain some reward and she would hardly have the opportunity of herself retrieving the treasure – if she really did possess clues as to its whereabouts. But on balance it seems unlikely that she would be well-disposed, or even appear to be well-disposed, towards these or any other Royalists. Quarrell also looked askance at the original £7000 of treasure 'growing to a much more impressive £50,000' – but my edition of Pepys's Diary retains the original figure of £7000:

Being by appointment called upon by Mr Lee, he and I to the Tower, to make our third attempt upon the cellar. And now privately the woman, Barkstead's great confident, is brought, who do positively say that this is the place where he did say the money was hid in, and where he and she did put up the £7000 in butter firkins; and the very day that he went out of England did say that neither he nor his would be the better for that money, and therefore wishing that she and hers might. And so left us, and we full of hope did resolve to dig all over the cellar, which by seven o'clock at night we performed. At noon we sent for a dinner, and upon the head of a barrel dined very merrily, and to work again. But at last we saw we were mistaken; and, after digging the cellar quite through, and removing the barrels from one side to the other, we were forced to pay our porters, and give over our expectations, though I do believe there must be money hid somewhere by him, or else he did delude this woman in hopes to oblige her to further serving him, which I am apt to believe . . . .[1]

It would appear likely that at this stage Pepys would have given up all efforts to recover the elusive treasure but King Charles II was short of money and Pepys was

[1]*Diary of Samuel Pepys*, deciphered by the Rev. J. Smith, MA from the original shorthand MS in the Pepysian Library, Cambridge; with notes by Richard Lord Braybrooke. Two volumes (Dent, 1924).

encouraged to continue his endeavours to locate the money. So a few days later we read:

To the Dolphin Tavern, near home, by appointment, and there met with Wade and Evett, and have resolved to make a new attempt upon another discovery, in which God give us better fortune than in the other; but I have great confidence that there is no cheat in these people, but that they go upon good grounds, though they have been mistaken in the place from the first.

Being satisfied by their own efforts that the treasure did not lie buried in the 'vaulted cellars' as they had thought, they turned their attention to another place entirely; a part of the garden which seemed a likely place. The planned attempt was postponed because of bad weather but eventually took place. Pepys seems to have quite lost interest in the matter and all hope of finding the treasure:

Up and by appointment with Mr Lee, Wade, Evett and workmen, to the Tower, and with the Lieutenant's leave set them to work in the garden, in the corner against the mayne-gate, a most unlikely place. It being cold, Mr Lee and I did sit all the day till three o'clock by the fire in the Governor's house; I reading a play of Fletcher's, being "A Wife for a Month" wherein no great wit or language. We went to them at work, and having wrought below the bottom of the foundation of the wall, I bid them give over, and so all our hopes ended.

Although Pepys's attempts to find the Barkstead treasure came to nothing, there is no reason to suppose that it has ever been recovered; indeed it would appear likely that it is one of several hoards of treasure that lie deeply hidden in the Tower where the ground level, in some places, has risen 20 feet or more over the years, due to the accumulated deposits of centuries.

Charles Quarrell refers in his book on *Buried Treasure* to an observation made early in the present century by an architect during the course of some repair work being carried out near the Governor's Residence. The architect noticed an unusual resemblance between the methods of construction adopted in erecting the walls of two separ-

ate towers within the general fortress and Charles Quarrell suggests that this peculiarity might have misled
Pepys and his fellow seekers and the woman friend and
confidante of Barkstead and it could well be that the
treasure lies buried beneath a stone building, formerly a
dairy, on the north side of the Bell Tower – it is certainly
a likely and convenient place to hide treasure. Not only
would the ground be soft and covered with straw which
would show little sign of disturbance, but a dairy would
be the place where 'butter firkins' would normally be
found, and it was these articles that the woman said had
been used to contain the gold. Furthermore, Barkstead
would have needed to bury the gold as quickly and
easily as possible since it would be heavy and he would
not want to move it very far, so the dairy seems a distinct
possibility.

Charles Quarrell was at one time the honorary secretary of the Speleological Society and about thirty years
ago permission was obtained for three members of that
society to explore the possibility of locating the Barkstead
treasure. The party included a scientist 'engaged in
research into the field of radio', and also a man who
'possessed strange gifts'. The secret nature of the latter's
work prevented Charles Quarrell revealing any details
about him but it seems obvious that the instrument he
used was a divining rod of some kind – perhaps the first
occasion that dowsing had been used in an attempt to
obtain confirmation of the whereabouts of the treasure.

The dairy and its vicinity were thoroughly explored
by the scientist, armed with his 'detector' and, in accordance with his instructions, various parts of the floor were
marked. At these places, he maintained, there were
reactions consistent with deposits or accumulation of
non-ferrous metallic objects, buried at a depth of not
more than 5 feet below the surface.

The Speleological Society's findings have not been
proved or disproved since digging and excavation would
involve disturbance and inconvenience, although nothing of historical interest or antiquarian value would need
to be destroyed or even moved.

But to return to Major Pogson. He always had misgivings about his ability to dowse for hidden treasure in the Tower and he told me that he was never as confident about finding metals by divination as he was about finding water. He had carried out many tests and experiments but he was never totally successful and it was certainly refreshing to hear him admit the distinct possibility of failure and his practical and sensible observations on the whole subject of dowsing and divining. So many dowsers claim to be infallible and interestingly enough entertain the notion that, unless a dowser is completely confident, he will fail.

Major Pogson believed that there were four distinct things that had to be born in mind when dowsing for treasure and he always said that each one had to be thought about very seriously. There was the possibility that the story of the treasure had no foundation in fact; there was the possibility that its reputed location was completely erroneous; there was the possibility, even if the story was true, that the treasure had already been discovered and removed; and finally he was well aware that he was by no means infallible in dowsing for metal and could easily fail to find any indication of the treasure. One could not wish for a more honest and straightforward consideration of the difficulties and possibilities before beginning a treasure hunt.

At the Tower Major Pogson made a series of protracted searches in several areas, including the former dairy and the 'cellar' of the Bell Tower, but he experienced no reactions whatever that he associated with buried treasure or metals, except for in one place, which he never exactly pinpointed for me; he said that at one spot he gained the distinct impression, from a pull on his rods and a kind of psychic intuition coupled with his vast experience, that there might be a mass or collection of precious metals or coins buried there and he sensed some kind of ruined temple and the disturbance of human bones.

It is, of course, within the bounds of possibility that a temple of some kind once stood where Major Pogson obtained that reaction. The early history of the Tower is lost in antiquity but it is likely that the Romans had a fortress there (Roman remains have been unearthed and part of a Roman wall is still visible near the ditch) and the Saxon *Chronicle* leads us to the belief of there having been a Saxon fortress on the site so it is by no means unlikely that some sort of temple and the burial of ancient human remains prompted the reactions and impressions that Major Pogson received. He suggested digging at that particular spot to establish whether or not he was right.

Digging was duly carried out and at no great depth a fair-sized cavity was revealed, filled with surface debris. It seemed highly likely that some receptacle or receptacles had once been buried there and had later been removed and the resulting cavity filled up. If this had happened, it had all taken place 'long ages past' as Major Pogson put it. He regarded the venture as interesting and not a complete failure, but certainly not conclusive evidence of the location of the site of the long-lost Barkstead treasure.

My friend and former vice-president of The Ghost Club, the late Dr Paul Tabori, talked to me on several occasions about the researches of his father, Cornelius Tabori, a Hungarian journalist and writer who was interested in psychical research for more than forty years until he was murdered by the Nazis in July 1944. In 1938 Cornelius Tabori talked at length to Dr Camillo Reuter, Director of the Clinic for Nervous and Mental Diseases at Pécs, an old town in south-western Hungary, famous for its unique historical Turkish monuments.

Shortly before Tabori went to see Dr Reuter, a very well-known water diviner and head of the Austrian Franciscans, Father Anthony Csucsek, had been at Pécs at the invitation of the local Franciscan friars who were finding great difficulty in locating sufficient fresh water to supply their new chapels and guest houses at Maria-gyuid. It is an area where there is little surface water, but being a place of pilgrimage owing to the existence of a famous sanctuary, thousands of pilgrims made their way to the region and the shortage of water became an embarrassment to the religious population.

Csucsek had the reputation of obtaining a 90 per cent

success rate with his hazel twig divining rod and within a comparatively short period he had successfully located water in more than 300 places where water had not been thought to exist! With such a reputation it is not surprising that while he was in the vicinity the city authorities took the opportunity of consulting Father Csucsek about the borings they were in the process of making in an effort to provide more and better water for the city. The famous water diviner was able to tell them that some of their efforts would prove fruitful while others, which he indicated, were not worth proceeding with; he also pointed out several places that they had not considered before his visit where they would find water.

Dr Camillo Reuter told Cornelius Tabori that he had studied the phenomenon of water divining for many years. He maintained that those who had explored the subject had found the first trace of the divining rod in the world of fairy tales and that it also figured in mythology. He outlined the known history of the divining rod and the magical power that early users ascribed to it, saying that it was extremely important that the twig should be cut with a single stroke and with an appropriate spell being intoned, and that such twigs were reputed to be especially efficacious if they were 'obtained under the dominating influence of the planet Mercury, on St John's Day or Christmas Night'.

Reuter spoke of Athanasis Kirchner (1601-80) who thought that divining rods might be affected by the 'exhalation' of metals, and Roessler in his *Speculum metallurgiae*, published in 1700, mentioned for the first time divining rods made of metal. He thought that, to find any particular metal, rods made of the same substance had to be employed. Reuter talked of the days when the Catholic church considered dowsing to be the 'work of the devil' and of the attempt to ascribe the undoubted success of some dowsers to magic, and later to explain the movement of the rod on the grounds of sensitivity to the nervous system of the human body. He also said that Volta and Galvani had conducted experiments on these lines and deduced that the rod was moved as the result of the discharge of electricity in the human body when it was above or in close proximity to water and metals.

Reuter told Cornelius Tabori about a man named Ziedler who had had some success in locating lost objects with a divining rod and, when his son strayed into a forest and could not be found, he employed the assistance of the rod, concentrating his thoughts on the boy, and the rod led him to the frightened child hiding in the wood.

Among all the fascinating facts and incidents that Dr Reuter told Cornelius Tabori, many of which were reproduced by his son Paul Tabori,[1] I was particularly interested in the idea that the first traces of the divining rod had been found in the world of fairy tales. I made some exploration of the subject but came up with nothing and then I remembered that Iona and Peter Opie were the acknowledged authorities in the realm of nursery rhymes and fairy tales, authors of many celebrated books on these subjects, and I asked them whether they had ever come across anything that might have given rise to the idea of a divining rod in any version of a nursery rhyme or in any fairy tale. They said they had thought about the question – which they had not considered before – and did not really think they could help; however, they added: 'The equation of fairy wands with divining rods is a nice thought' – which it certainly is.

But perhaps it is time to turn from speculation to users of the divining rod themselves and see what manner of people they are.

[1]Cornelius Tabori, *My Occult Diary,* translated and edited by Paul Tabori, (Living Books, New York, 1966).

7. Meet the Dowsers

During the course of his fascinating talk with Dr Camillo Reuter, touched on in the last chapter, Cornelius Tabori finally asked Reuter for his conclusions on the subject of dowsers and the divining rod. Reuter replied that it was indisputable that in the hands of certain people the divining rod moves, apparently of its own volition. Dowsers, he had found, were usually men of great nervous sensibility and the expected results caused them to be excited in advance of the act of dowsing, when, it seemed, they fell into 'a peculiar nervous tension', a state of expectancy that might be similar to that experienced by someone waiting for an expected friend at a railway station, or a hunter waiting for the firing of his gun. 'The dowser arrives at the spot where he expects water with all his muscles tensed and this idea and hope is sufficient for the tension of nerves and muscles to relax or become heightened, whereupon the rod rises or jumps.' So Dr Reuter decided that the cause of successful dowsing must be sought within the dowser himself and he added: 'Most dowsers betray their nervous tension.'[1]

It is an interesting observation and, while it may be true of some highly competent and professional dowsers, even some amateurs, it does not seem to be true of all dowsers.

I knew Major Pogson fairly well and I don't think anyone could describe him as the type of person ever likely to betray nervous tension, but then I never saw him actually use a divining rod and it may be that when

[1]Cornelius Tabori, *My Occult Diary* (Living Books, New York, 1966).

he was working he did indeed betray nervous tension. It is a point that is not easily proved.

During the course of my correspondence with Legory H. O'Loughlin, president of the South California Chapter of the American Society of Dowsers for over fifteen years, he never mentioned any feeling of nervous tension, but he did tell me about the great success of his organization and the considerable interest in the subject in America. And I am grateful for his co-operation for he not only runs the South California Chapter, the oldest continuing branch in the USA where he used to get an attendance of eight or ten people when it began and he now gets an average of between 200 and 300, but he also teaches dowsing at Los Angeles City College and was busy organizing special meetings and a convention early in 1979 – all concerned with dowsing.

'Gory' O'Loughlin has been known to refer to an early dowser 'pictured' in an 8000-year-old cave drawing in the Atlas Mountains of North Africa and to cap that by saying that dowsing has probably 'been around even longer.' He says American farmers have always known certain individuals in their communities who can find water and, like musical ability perhaps, it is regarded as a gift that runs in families. He freely admits that most dowsers' earliest recollections of the subject go back to some relative or friend who had the gift of finding water, and it was from them that they learnt how it could be done; and he also freely admits that he has no idea how it works. He does have an idea that the pituitary gland may be connected with the mysterious ability; he believes so anyway, in the same way that he believes that everyone has a guardian angel.

O'Loughlin vividly remembers his grandfather hiring a dowser to find water on his land but as a boy he took little interest in the subject and it was only years later, when a friend showed him how he used a divining rod, that O'Loughlin tried his hand, found that it worked for him, and became hooked on it to such an extent that he gave up public relations work and compression foot massage to devote himself full-time to the subject. He has had such success that he now spends a lot of time giving talks and lectures and appearing on radio and television, armed with all kinds of wands and rods and visual aids to interest his audiences.

One story that 'Gory' O'Loughlin likes to relate concerns his friend Louis Matacia, a surveyor who was able to perform field dowsing and also map dowsing. While he was on military service in Vietnam he repeatedly requested the general staff in the area to allow him to show them how easy it was to dowse for enemy mines and tunnels. Eventually they agreed and set up a test area which they pointed out to him. The night before the test Matacia prepared a plan of the test area and sat up late in his tent, map dowsing over the plan. Next day he was able to locate successfully every tunnel in the area because he had discovered their whereabouts and direction the evening before as he map dowsed.

O'Loughlin is full of enthusiasm about dowsing; he tells many of his wonderful stories about the subject in the present tense, talking for all the people in the stories as though he is doing a one-man show; and he talks to his rod or pendulum (he says he can work from a map as easily as working on an open site), calling the rod, or the power that works it, 'William' – an idea that goes back to the days when a psychic person told him that his gift came from a dimly-remembered Uncle William. O'Loughlin, in common with many dowsers, is interested in psychical research and he belongs to the Southern California Psychical Research Society. A kindly, modest man, he tends to talk about other people rather than himself.

He is full of admiration for Captain Ralph W. Harris, a local man who has dealt in real estate in the area for years, but whose great interest is dowsing. When Harris was nine years old he can remember his grandfather testing every member of the family for his or her dowsing ability; he was only happy with young Ralph and he told him that he had the gift.

Within a couple of years Ralph Harris was using his dowsing ability in all manner of ways, including getting other boys to do the day-to-day jobs that he was supposed to be responsible for. Time and again he would locate a well or find water in the shape of an underground stream for a neighbouring farmer, and in return the farmer's son would gladly do some of Ralph's chores for him!

When he was grown up and involved in the real estate business, the ability to determine whether or not land or property had an adequate water supply was a considerable asset. If he knew that a piece of land had water, he bought it; if it did not he left it to others to buy!

Captain Ralph Harris served under General Patton in North Africa during the Second World War and for a time, when the enemy were on the run, there was a considerable anxiety about drinking water for the allied troops, for Rommel had blown up all the wells as the German armies retreated. Harris, then a lanky captain, sought an interview with the forthright General George Patton, who came from California as did Harris, and boldly stated that if the General would furnish him with a forked willow twig, he would find adequate water for the 600,000 men.

It was the kind of talking that Patton understood and, when Harris had related something of his wide experience and success in dowsing for water, the General promptly said Harris could have his chance, and he arranged for a complete willow tree to be flown in .... Harris cut himself a forked divining rod, tested it and, satisfied that it would serve the purpose, he walked off into the desert accompanied by a patrol and a sceptical geologist colonel.

Within a short time, Harris says, he found a vein of water 300 feet wide that yielded 2000 gallons of water per minute 400 feet below the surface, and Patton was delighted. After that Harris was repeatedly called upon to find water and locate hidden wells whenever the advancing troops were short of water, and he invariably succeeded.

Today, 'Gory' O'Loughlin tells me, Captain Harris, who also teaches dowsing at the Los Angeles City College and is a co-founder of the Southern California Chapter of the American Society of Dowsers, can map dowse and locate water at a distance. For this purpose he uses a pendulum of his own design consisting of a heavy metal spring with a handle at one end and magnets. It works in a springy fashion.

It has been suggested that this instrument may contain a secret ingredient but Captain Harris is not talking on that particular point. His unusual pendulum was made for him by an oil geologist who was also an unsuccessful dowser. Harris believes that the man failed in his dowsing and divining because he never made sure that the instrument was 'grounded' – a process that involves rubbing the instrument with the hands to impregnate it with 'vibrations'.

At one time Harris used to carry a 'witness' or sample of whatever substance he was looking for as he walked about with his divining rod and site dowsed, but these days he simply concentrates on the matter in hand and the instrument tells him when he has found it. More and more these days he map dowses from the comfort of his home.

For his map dowsing, which Harris does for water, oil, gold and many other substances, he spreads a map of the relevant area on his living room table, picks up his dowsing tool, points to a place on the map with a pencil and asks the instrument whether the mineral or object that he is looking for is to be found in that particular area. The divining rod bobs back and forth in his hand if the answer is in the affirmative; if the answer is in the negative, the pendulum remains stationary.

Another dowser in the Southern California Chapter of the American Society of Dowsers is Mrs Ellie Walker who sometimes uses her faculty for dowsing in a unique and practical way. She uses her pendulum to test fruit and vegetables to see whether they have been sprayed or not, and she has also used the pendulum to establish whether or not a particular fruit, vegetable or plant is right for her and beneficial to her health. At one time, for example, the pendulum told her not to eat spinach; but what really surprised her was when she found vegetables side by side in the same container and some (according to the pendulum) had been sprayed and some had not.

During the course of her market shopping Mrs Walker has become adroit at using her pendulum discreetly so that other shoppers and the staff of the establishments hardly ever notice her hold one hand over the produce while the other hand holds the dowsing pendulum. Mrs Walker finds that a clockwise movement of the pendulum shows that the food is good for her, or that it has not been sprayed (according to what she is seeking to discover) while an anti-clockwise movement denotes that the fruit or vegetable is not good for her or has been sprayed.

In common with many dowsers, Mrs Walker can recall seeing dowsing being carried out at a very early age. She can well remember her grandfather showing her how he dowsed when she was a small girl, but at that time she took very little notice and it was not until years later, when she was employed in public relations and advertising, that she became interested in the subject of psychic phenomena. Then, some time after her marriage, she attended a lecture on the subject of dowsing. She tried dowsing herself and found that it worked for her; then she joined the dowsing society and has been fascinated by the subject and used the faculty continually ever since.

'I don't say that it works every time,' Mrs Walker said, during the course of an interview in 1976, 'but there are dowsers who have an excellent record.' In fact most dowsers claim about 80 per cent accuracy.

Dowsers have varying explanations for success or failure but Mrs Walker believes it is the result of 'something inside you' – or it may be your own intuition, which could be the same thing. 'If you don't want to go somewhere,' she will tell you, 'and you ask your instrument what you should do and the answer is, don't go, there is usually found to be a good reason for not going.' Women, she feels, are more receptive than men and perhaps they make better dowsers, although there are as many men as women who dowse.

On the subject of map dowsing Mrs Walker, on occasions, has gone a step further than most practitioners of this aspect of dowsing: she has done it without a map.

She was once challenged to find an old garbage or rubbish dump on the property of a distant relative who doubted the ability of anyone to map dowse. Mrs Walker simply drew a rough rectangle as the shape of the property and held her pendulum over the piece of paper. She obtained an immediate reaction in one area and found that she had accurately located the rubbish dump. She had done this without ever setting foot on the property and never having seen it. She also finds the pendulum useful for locating items that are lost and she has found books, keys, and all sorts of articles that she has been unable to find by ordinary means. Her husband is a practical, efficient and objective engineer who has been astonished so many times by the results of his wife using the pendulum that he now accepts the situation and is open-minded on the subject.

Mr Harry Price, the psychic investigator and former chairman of The Ghost Club, was sceptical of the claims of many dowsers but, after a series of experiments with Captain Trinder, another member of The Ghost Club, Major Pogson, and Abbé Gabriel Lambert in Hyde Park, London, and elsewhere, Price became convinced of the reality of the faculty.[1] Indeed the water supply at his own home at Pulborough (now converted into flats) was finally discovered by a dowser from the South Downs, after the orthodox water engineers had failed to locate it.

Captain Trinder first discovered that he had the gift of dowsing – in common with the vast majority of practising dowsers – by imitating someone else. He watched an old man divining for water with a twig and, trying it himself, he found that in his young hands the twig did make a slight but definite movement when it was over water. Interestingly enough, Trinder found that the indications and movements that he obtained with a divining rod or twig became stronger the more he practised and, oddly enough, the more he found out about dowsing the better he was at it.

In later years Trinder used a whalebone rod, painted black with white binding or, if he was using a pendulum,

[1]Harry Price, *Fifty Years of Psychical Research* (Longmans, Green, 1939).

a wooden bobbin weighing about an ounce, painted black and suspended on a white string. He always found benefit from holding in his hand a sample or 'witness' of the substance he was looking for and he felt that this also helped to cut out the reactions of other substances that may be present but which he was not seeking.

During the course of a lecture at The Ghost Club, Captain Trinder recounted some of his most successful dowsing performances. He never claimed to be infallible and admitted that on occasions his diagnoses might be inaccurate; indeed he regarded it as quite wrong to be dogmatic since many of the people for whom he dowsed and indicated the best place for sinking a well never let him know whether or not his diagnosis had been correct.

The owner of a steam laundry at Lymington in Hampshire had consulted Captain Trinder after he had bored to about 60 feet at a spot where he had been told by water engineers that he would find water, but he had found none and asked Trinder whether he thought it was worth his going on with the boring at that place.

Trinder visited the laundry, taking with him his divining rod and pendulum and, after a series of tests and reactions, he told the owner that he believed there was a moderate supply of water in the form of an underground stream at a depth of 110 feet and a further moderate supply at a depth of 150 feet, but a good supply, sufficient for all his needs, would be found at about 440 feet. However, said Trinder, there was something odd about this deeper water supply: it was certainly not another stream and the reactions that he obtained were unlike those he had ever had before, so he really could not give any details about that water supply. He was more than a little puzzled and very interested when the owner told him that he intended to bore down to this deeper water supply.

In the event a stream was found at a depth of 110 feet, another was located at 152 feet and then at 398 feet they struck a good artesian flow that rose from the bore hole like a fountain and continued to supply water for the laundry for many years, in fact for as long as it was required. Captain Trinder had never previously found artesian water and so the reactions he obtained were strange to him.

A rather different exercise in dowsing was conducted by Captain Trinder at Rockingham Castle, built by William the Conqueror on the site of an earlier earthwork and formerly standing in the centre of a royal forest. There had long been stories of secret passages at Rockingham and Lady Culme-Seymour asked Captain Trinder to see whether he could find such a passage long reputed to run along the east side of the castle. Using his divining rod, Trinder marked a spot where he thought there might be a passage. Digging and excavation at the spot indicated by Trinder revealed an old archway with the passage blocked up.

Later, when he was a guest at the castle, Trinder was walking round the outside of the walls with his divining rod, idly seeing whether he obtained any reactions, when his rod lifted with characteristic distinction at a spot between the castle and the church. When he returned from his meanderings he told Lady Culme-Seymour about the reaction he had obtained and said he had marked the spot, but Lady Culme-Seymour said she thought it was most likely to be a drain in that particular place and nothing more was done about the matter.

More than two years later a new clergyman was appointed to Rockingham, a man who was interested in archaeology and, after a study of the area and existing plans and records, he said he thought there should be a passage between Anselm's Chapel, in the castle, and Rockingham church. Lady Culme-Seymour then remembered that Captain Trinder had already suggested that a passage may exist in the area now pinpointed by the new rector. She wrote to Trinder asking him whether he would like to come down to the castle again and meet the new clergyman, and perhaps do some more divining for the whereabouts of a passage between the castle and the church.

During the course of this visit to Rockingham Castle, Captain Trinder marked out with pegs where he thought the passage ran and, using his divining rod, he was able to indicate the exact route and show where the passage entered, diagonally, under the end wall of the church. Subsequently Colonel Rivers-Moore, another Ghost Club member and experienced archaeologist, dug where Trinder had indicated and established that a passage did indeed exist where the divining rod had shown it to be and furthermore it entered the church exactly where Trinder had indicated. The passage was found at the depth that Trinder had stated – eight feet – but unfortunately it could not be excavated towards the castle as this would have entailed the disturbance of a large tomb. Remembering his predilection for using a sample or witness whenever he was dowsing, Ghost Club members asked Captain Trinder whether he used anything of the kind during his search for the tunnel or passage at Rockingham Castle and were fascinated when he told them that he held a small, empty, corked bottle in his right hand.

Harry Price, during the course of experiments in map dowsing with Captain Trinder, was astonished to find that the dowser, merely using his pendulum over an estate map, indicated the whereabouts of a submerged lake 50 miles away. This lake and other water courses were *not* marked on the estate map but the information obtained by the dowser was found to be correct. Harry Price thought that this case pointed to the dowsing faculty being a clairvoyant one, but Captain Trinder did not agree. He readily admitted at The Ghost Club that many people disbelieve or refuse to accept the possiblity of dowsing from a distance, but he recounted a remarkable example of the practice that suggests that this form of dowsing is practicable, although no rational explanation is as yet forthcoming; and it does seem that, in some strange way that we do not understand, the problem of distance is eliminated.

At the time of Captain Trinder's most spectacular attempt at map dowsing a certain Colonel Rey was Commissioner for Bechuanaland and, having heard that Captain Trinder could find water by dowsing over a map, he mentioned the subject when the two men met. The Commissioner was, understandably, somewhat sceptical, and he suggested that, when he returned to

Africa (a continent that Captain Trinder had never visited except for landing for a few hours at Port Said more than thirty years earlier), he would like to send to Captain Trinder a map of the edge of the Kalahari desert and perhaps he would like to indicate on the map any underground streams that he could find with his pendulum. Captain Trinder readily agreed to make the attempt.

The 40 inches to the mile map duly reached Captain Trinder while he was on a fishing holiday at Spean Bridge, Inverness, and it was there that he went over the map with his pendulum and marked the whereabouts of underground streams that seemed to be indicated by the movement of his divining instrument. Several 'water-holes' were marked on the map and, after locating the streams, Captain Trinder went over the waterholes with the pendulum, found four of them to be dry, marked the map accordingly and sent it back to Colonel Rey having had the map in his possession for just two days.

During the course of his acknowledgement Colonel Rey told Captain Trinder that the lines of underground streams that he had marked on the map 'practically all' ran through places where water had been found: 'they do not cover quite all such places but the great majority of them'. As far as the dry waterholes were concerned, Trinder was certainly right as to the non-existence of water at some of them; as far as the others were concerned, Colonel Rey had no information but he ended his letter: 'Your results generally appear to be marvellous, not to say uncanny! You would certainly suffer severely at the hands of the other "witch doctors" if you came to Bechuanaland Protectorate, though I would do my utmost to protect you!'

Ghost Club members were particularly interested to hear Captain Trinder's theories as to how and why dowsing works, but he had no pet theories or views on the subject, although he did say that for him personally the pendulum would only work if he held the string between the first finger and the thumb of his right hand or the second finger and the thumb of his left hand. He had no idea why this should be so but in his travels he had met other dowsers who seemed to have different 'active' fingers and he assumed that the wave, or current, or whatever the power was, followed different nerves in different people. He also found that the use of spectacles prohibited or prevented the faculty of map dowsing: the pendulum remained completely motionless as long as he looked through his spectacles; however, if he pushed them up on to his forehead, the pendulum worked normally.

Finally Captain Trinder revealed that as far as he was concerned it was necessary for him to have both his heels on the ground to obtain any reaction suggesting an underground stream. Experience had taught him that, if he lifted his heels off the ground, he obtained no reaction in the divining rod, although the usual reactions would be obtained immediately he replaced his heels on the ground. He expressed the view that some sort of air-wave seemed to be involved in dowsing, since he had experimented by blowing into an empty bottle over the place where he had obtained a positive reaction of a certain metal, and he had then corked the bottle. Later he found that he had obtained exactly the same reactions from the apparently empty bottle as that which he had received over the spot where there was buried metal.

One of the first dowsers I met personally was an old Suffolk dowser who had been asked by a farmer, after a long, dry spell of weather, to see whether he could 'track down' an underground spring or stream in one of the farmer's fields. Having expressed my interest in the matter I was invited to be present. I cannot do better than reproduce the account of the incident that I published in my book, *Deeper Into the Occult*, now out of print.[1]

I met the dowser, an insignificant little man, rather serious and perhaps a little resentful that his efforts were to be under scrutiny. I did my best to put him at his ease by saying that I had read a lot about dowsing and had seen various forms of divining produce results and I much appreciated the opportunity of seeing a water diviner in action.

He produced a forked hazel stick, about two feet long, cut at

[1]Harrap, 1975.

the joint of two branches and spread at an angle of about forty-five degrees. I handled the stick, or 'wand', and it was undoubtedly an ordinary branch, but very dry and rather brittle with age. He showed me how he held it, near the ends of the two branches with the thumbs of his hands pointing outwards. Some diviners allow the wand to pass between their second and third fingers, but this man held it with the whole of both hands in a firm grip.

Having consulted a compass and turning to face North, the dowser grasped the wand in his particular way and then raised it almost shoulder-high. Then, taking a deep breath, he walked solemnly forward in a straight line and reaching the end of the field, turned and walked back. In this way he proceeded back and forth over the dry ground.

The dowser has to know what he is looking for, and in this case the farmer told him that he believed there had once been a well somewhere in the field, although long disused and filled-in; if it could be located and the dowser could say that there was flowing water there, the farmer was willing to have the place dug and explored. The dowser continued to walk up and down for nearly half-an-hour, covering most of the field, and then he paused.

The forked stick quivered. The dowser stood still, gripped the wand very firmly and slowly moved it over the immediate area. The stick seemed to be pulled in one direction and the dowser took a short step, led by the pull. He was convinced that he was then right over the water for the wand began to dip and quiver more and more violently.

The dowser still held the wand firmly and seemed to be trying to stop it from moving, but he was evidently only testing the reaction and soon his arms began to shake with the vibration of the wand and the invisible but powerful pull that seemed to come from the dry earth at his feet. Soon the wand was affected to such an extent that he could no longer control it and it dipped and pointed straight into the ground.

The forked stick turned in the dowser's hands until the butt or joined end, which had been pointing towards his chin, stood at right angles, but still he seemed to be trying to get the stick back into its original position when, with a 'crack' that made us all jump, the stick broke in his hands.

The dowser turned to the farmer in triumph and pointed to the spot where the wand had been so violently affected. 'There's water there,' he said simply. 'And plenty of it.' The farmer quickly produced a short stake and drove it into the ground to mark the spot. As he did so he asked the dowser whether he could tell him how deep the water was and the dowser produced another stick which he had evidently brought as a reserve. He repeated the careful positioning of his hands, firmly gripping the stick, and then he seriously and solemnly held it over the place now marked with the farmer's stake, concentrating hard.

Despite the strong grip of the dowser the stick dipped inexorably towards the earth, then came up again only to dip once more. It dipped ten times, its movements seeming to grow weaker with each movement. The dowser waited for the stick to remain motionless and then gave his opinion. 'The water is between nine and ten feet down,' he said. It was all over and the farmer was very happy with the result. He made plans immediately to dig for the water and I learned later that he had found an excellent supply of water, exactly where the dowser had indicated, at a depth of just under ten feet.

I talked again with the dowser. There was nothing striking or unusual about him, quite the opposite in fact. He seemed very ordinary and modest about the gift that he possessed. The faculty or whatever it was, he accepted as a matter of course. He told me he had been divining ever since he was a boy. It all began when the local squire of the village where he was born sent for a dowser to find water on his estate. It had been something of an event for the village and the boys had followed the old man as he walked over the lawns and fields with his forked twig, until he found a spring for the squire.

Afterwards the old man had invited the boys to try their hands at dowsing and, as he held the stick over the spot where the dowser had said there was water, my informant told me that he felt the stick move in his hands. He tried to hold it still but it had moved in spite of his efforts. It was a very strange feeling and at first he thought all the other boys must have felt the same movement. Then he discovered that he was the only one who felt so strong a pull on the stick. He was shy about admitting it at first, for at chapel he had been taught that diviners had sold their souls to the devil, but his initial fear was soon overcome by the fascination of being different from other people and very soon he took to practising on the quiet, away from the other boys. He soon found that he could locate water and he had been doing it ever since. He said a great many people have the power and it is far commoner than most people realize but comparatively few trouble to find

out whether or not they can discover water, minerals, oil –
even treasure.

Other dowsers have provided evidence of the variety
of purposes for which dowsing and divining can be
adopted. Robert Leftwich travelled thousands of miles to
demonstrate his dowsing talents which included locating
abandoned tunnels and other underground hazards;
Catherine Fry, a West Country dowser, possesses
hundreds of letters of gratitude from water boards, rural
district councils, surveyors and engineers – she originally
used her bare hands for dowsing. The late Major Harold
Spary used his dowsing powers to locate and track
underground cables and water mains for the Royal
Aircraft Establishment at Lasham in Hampshire before
excavation work was carried out on the site; he also used
dowsing to locate mines during his military service in
the North African campaign during the Second World
War. During the early 1970s Harold Spary was employed
by Spembley Electronics as a storeman but he turned out
to be a reliable 'cable diviner'. Instead of the traditional
wooden twig his equipment consisted of two welding
rods and his dowsing work proved so dependable that
the RAE used his skills several times in preference to
expensive machinery to locate old underground cables
when new ones had to be laid. Major Spary was yet
another dowser who maintained that anybody could
dowse – 'all they need is faith that it will work' he used
to say. For water divining Major Spary always used a
divining rod made from whalebone. One or two people
even appear to have made money out of dowsing: in
1971 William Young, then of Sheringham, was reported
to have charged £200 a day to find water for irrigation
contractors, but he often charged less to farmers and
only half his fee if no water was found. At that time he
was reported as saying that out of eighty-four wells sunk
on his advice, only once had he been wrong – and then
by just 15 feet.

Soon after I began work on this book my friend Renée
Haynes of the Society for Psychical Research asked me
whether I knew Colonel Kenneth Merrylees of Laven-

ham. She told me: 'He once took me out for a test walk and I was fascinated at an attempt in which he put one finger lightly on the back of my wrist, to find at a certain point in the path, the rod twisting like a live creature in my hands!'

I first met Colonel Merrylees, OBE, M.I. Mech.E., some twenty years ago when he addressed The Ghost Club on the subject of dowsing. When I approached him in 1979 he told me that at his advanced age (eighty-three) he is unable to be a very active dowser; in fact most of his 'best' wells had been in the Middle East or India but he had kept few records.

During the course of his many talks and lectures over the years, at The Ghost Club and elsewhere, Colonel Merrylees – who has never believed that dowsing can be taught – explored the subject from a practical point of view and suggested a possible explanation. To appreciate the logic of his argument it is necessary to begin at the end – at the time when the dowser obtains an indication which he interprets as showing that he has located that for which he is searching.

Leaving on one side the very few 'super-sensitive' dowsers who could dispense with any of the usual dowsing instruments, Colonel Merrylees would point out that all dowsers use one or more of their five senses to record the movement of some type of indicating instrument which they held in both their hands or occasionally in one hand. He had long been aware of the fact that a careful inspection of any dowser at work would reveal that any dowsing instrument (or at least any of the usual ones) merely exaggerated the minute muscular movements of the dowser himself – so it was the dowser who in fact was really responsible for the movement of the divining rod or whatever might be used, and *not* a question of the presence of water or some mineral causing the twig or rod to move.

By way of illustration Colonel Merrylees explained that the traditional forked twig is held in such a way that the join moves through a wide arc when the forearm muscles are contracted or extended, no matter how slightly. In a similar fashion the dowser who uses a pendulum builds up a swing through a succession of very small hand movements. In fact it is possible to obtain all these effects by conscious muscular effort but the true dowsing indication seems to be obtained, as far as can be established, by a completely involuntary or reflex movement. There was nothing new in this observation, Colonel Merrylees was careful to point out, but many dowsers seemed to think that it was the instrument which was moved by some outside force and this led them to look for a purely physical explanation of the art of dowsing.

Colonel Merrylees would go on to say that muscular movement of any kind only occurs when the appropriate nerve message arrives by way of the motor nerves from the brain and this in turn may have received the impulse to act from the sensory nerve system or from the mind or thoughts of the person concerned. Most reflex muscular movements appear to be intuitional or the result of past experience such as the hurried withdrawal of the hand or foot if a hot surface is touched, or the blink of the eyelid at a sudden bright light or movement near the eye. It has always seemed to Colonel Merrylees that if there is a physical explanation for dowsing then it follows that there must be some physical force or field or radiation or something, which so acts on the sensory nervous system that it triggers off the dowsing reaction.

When Colonel Merrylees talked to me about this aspect of the subject I mentioned to him that there are many reports of non-sensitive people who have held a dowsing rod or twig and, when they are touched or make physical contact with a dowser, they find that they can obtain a dowsing reaction in the twig they are holding. He agreed that this had happened and it did suggest that, sometimes at any rate, a nerve impulse could be transmitted from the dowser to the muscles of another person.

He emphasized the fact that, although the motor nerve message may be triggered off by wishful thinking or inaccurate observation on the part of the dowser, prompt investigation can usually uncover such a mistake. Unfortunately the novice or beginner in dowsing, probably in an over-anxious state to be successful, cannot recognize these thought-motivated reactions and consequently he, or she, gets lots of inaccurate indications and comes to the conclusion either that he or she cannot dowse or that there is nothing in the subject anyway.

Assuming that some form of sensitivity on the part of the experienced dowser does in fact enable him to find water or some mineral or whatever he is looking for, and the evidence that this is so seemed to Colonel Merrylees quite overwhelming, he feels that the interpretations of the indications that suggest depth and quantity and quality are a rather different matter, but he does believe there is more than sufficient evidence to show that experienced and qualified dowsers can and do locate underground water with an accuracy far beyond what might be expected by chance and frequently against the opinions and conclusions of geologists, geophysicists and hydrologists.

And were this all that was claimed by dowsers there is no doubt that a good case could be made out for a physical explanation; perhaps some form of radiation affecting the dowser and resulting in the dowsing reaction; but in fact this, Colonel Merrylees assures me, is a very incomplete picture of dowsing and its possibilities – quite apart from the fact that no such hypothetical radiation has been identified and no instrument has shown any such radiation or anything else that might account for the dowsing reaction, unless a dowser is involved.

Colonel Merrylees will tell you that it is now common for a reputable and experienced dowser to reduce the physical effort and time involved in dowsing on the actual site by a number of short cuts that are accepted as dowsing techniques. For example he may visit the area where water or some mineral is required but without actually traversing the site. Instead, he will take up a position in the vicinity of the area to be examined and decide by testing in which direction he will find the required substance; at such a distance (which may be considerable) it seems unlikely that the dowser is picking up any physical radiation or emanation from the flow of water or mineral lode.

Alternatively, the dowser may even dispense entirely with visiting the area of search and not leave his own room. By means of a fairly small-scale map of the area involved, no matter how distant the area may be, the dowser will obtain a reaction from the map. While this practice has become accepted as general procedure by some experienced dowsers, Colonel Merrylees considers that, while it can be a very useful and sound means of beginning a search, it can rarely be used as a complete substitute for pinpointing with considerable accuracy the precise spot where a well should be sunk or mineral ore will be found.

Nor is great concentration the necessary attribute to successful dowsing. At least not in the ordinary sense in which all other thoughts and considerations are eliminated from one's mind. Rather, Colonel Merrylees feels, a heightened form of receptivity or awareness is induced by the systematic and careful consideration of the problem in hand. This is usually best achieved by asking oneself the appropriate question while holding the dowsing instrument over the map or plan of the area. With experience it will be found that the receptivity generated remains constant until it is brought to an end by the movement of the dowsing instrument, signalling the conclusion of the exercise.

Colonel Merrylees has found that this receptive state of mind can be reached at any time and in any circumstances, and this means that he and other experienced dowsers can, and indeed have, selected the precise area that will be fruitful while in conversation with other people and even when travelling as a passenger in a car. At the same time, Colonel Merrylees suggests that this heightened receptivity that seems to be unique to dowsers can be switched on and off like a tap – which is fortunate as otherwise the sensitive dowser would be continually exposed to the influence and would hardly ever be free from some indications! But then again Colonel Merrylees has found that some lines of flow – the more powerful ones – create an air of discomfort after a time and he knows from experience that, for example, he would never be able to relax completely or sleep exactly over such a flow.

For the reasons he has stated, Colonel Merrylees finds it impracticable to accept the idea that a purely physical explanation of the dowser's ability covers all the facts – for he clearly feels that what dowsers are able to do cannot be explicable in terms of physical emanations or radiations on any known wavelength or system. He has, therefore, looked beyond the limitations of orthodox physics and the five known senses of man. He believes that there are two possible explanations for the dowsing reaction. Answers do seem to be given to dowsers about objects and locations that are not known to any living person, so it would appear to be reasonable to assume that the dowser is obtaining these answers from some source that is outside the known boundaries of our human existence with its five senses of sight, hearing, touch, taste and smell.

One possible explanation is that dowsers are obtaining information from discarnate entities – that they are in fact mediums in the spiritualist sense who are able to make contact with the world beyond death – but, since Colonel Merrylees and practically all the great number of dowsers he has met and known in a lifetime of dowsing do not profess to have psychic powers or to use processes similar to those employed by spiritualist mediums, he does not think this theory warrants serious consideration.

The other alternative – and one that Colonel Merrylees has come to regard as the most likely – is that there may be a direct communication between the mind of a dowser and some source of knowledge that is beyond all physical existence limits. It is a theory that conveniently fits in with the results that dowsers indisputably achieve, and it includes reasons for the limitations of some dowsers' abilities.

Colonel Merrylees envisages the unique sensitive concentration and receptivity that seems to be enjoyed by dowsers as a means of opening a channel of communication between the mind of the dowser and with either a personal or general subconscious, or super-conscious, source of knowledge. He thinks that the channel of communication for water location is probably one that everyone may have once possessed as a natural gift and that is why most people have, to some degree, the ability to dowse for water. Often of course they are completely unaware of possessing the power and it is only when they try dowsing that they find they have the capacity, the ability and the power, in some measure, to do it.

Colonel Merrylees believes, after lifelong study, application and practical investigation of the subject, that the complete availability of this channel is never complete, even with the most sensitive and successful natural dowsers, without a great deal of effort, study, practice and experience. And, while he thinks that there appear to be many other similar channels that enable dowsers to locate minerals, lost objects, missing persons and a thousand other things successfully, he does not believe that proficiency in any one type of dowsing is necessarily the prelude to equal success in any other type of dowsing.

While available evidence over many years suggests that there are few limits to what can be located and uncovered by dowsing methods, it is crystal clear that there are limitations and restrictions inherent in the human mind, and therefore in all dowsers, which may be impossible to overcome, but despite these the desired results *may*, with great effort, still be obtained.

Summing up his conclusions on a subject that he has practised in three continents, Colonel Merrylees contends that, whatever special line a dowser may try to follow – water or minerals, missing persons, disease and treatment, archaeology – none, he believes will succeed unless the dowser possesses the three essentials of his craft: sensitivity of mind, confidence and experience. Blessed with all three a dowser should be able to find the answer to any problem of search within the limits of his experience and endeavour. It is a criterion that I have yet to find inaccurate in respect of any dowser whom I have met.

8. Dowsing and Divining in the Modern World

During the course of the last chapter reference was made to a dowser named William Young who reportedly received £200 a day from a firm of irrigation contractors, named appropriately Wright Rain. A spokesman for the firm said at the time: 'William Young is always absolutely right about the place and the quantity when farmers want to sink a well. . . .'

It seems that when Young was twenty-one he met a man who had returned to this country after making a fortune dowsing in Africa. Young asked him how it was done. The man showed him and, when Young discovered that he obtained the same reactions, he began dowsing himself and for years he charged nothing for his services. Then in 1957 a house subsided when 12 acres of Norwich slums were being cleared. William Young was called in and he found eight forgotten tunnels – a discovery that probably saved the people concerned something in the region of £35,000. When Young heard that a geologist had charged £200 a day but hadn't been able to find the tunnels, Young decided to charge the same amount. Unlike some clairvoyants who find that when they charge for their services the faculty disappears, dowsers, it would seem, can cash in on their gifts.

Not that all dowsers do so, but it does seem that dowsing has a place in the modern world and, when other means of locating missing people and objects have been exhausted, sometimes the dowser is successful. A case in point occurred in the early spring of 1979 when a fishing boat capsizd off the Esso jetty in Milford Haven with the loss of three lives and no one could find the boat.

Kingfisher, a converted lifeboat, was carrying a six-man fishing party when it capsized in heavy seas. Two of the men, all of whom came from the Midlands, were thought to be trapped in the boat's wheelhouse but an extensive search of the area yielded no results and, when it seemed certain that there was no hope of finding the two men, the search in general was called off but a local diver, Kevin McCauley of Hakin, who had helped in the search that was mounted by coastguards and the Conservancy Board, decided to continue the search alone. He dived six more times but failed to find any trace of the fishing boat. Exhausted and disappointed, he still refused to give up the search, and then he remembered a Welsh water diviner he had read about who had located missing objects. At length he found William A. Lewis of Mardy, Abergavenny, and supplied him with a chart of the Haven and information about the missing boat, *Kingfisher*. 'It seemed like a million-to-one chance,' Kevin McCauley said at the time, 'but he marked the exact position of the wreck . . . and he lives a hundred miles from Milford Haven . . . .'

Soon after receiving the information from the diviner, Kevin McCauley and another diver, John Thornton, went out into the bay to search for the wreck, taking the marked map with them on board the Conservancy Board launch, *Grassholm*.

Without difficulty the coxswain, Frank Yeomans, pin-pointed the position of the wrecked *Kingfisher* with an echo-sounder. It had drifted more than 150 yards from the place where it had sunk and it was finally located at a depth between 90 and 100 feet. Now Kevin McCauley went down with the dangerous task of searching for the bodies of the missing men inside the tiny wheelhouse – but there were no bodies inside and he concluded that the two men must have been carried away in the heavy seas as the boat sank.

William Lewis tells me that he has had a long and varied experience in all aspects of divining. He found the fishing boat by map dowsing with a pendulum. He worked over a chart of the bay and the pendulum swung steadily back and forth when it passed over the spot where the boat was subsequently found – as it did so William Lewis experienced a definite physical reaction.

Kevin McCauley was anxious to find the bodies of the three drowned men, Timothy Butler and his nineteen-year-old son, Vincent, who came from West Bromwich, and Graham Angel of Wednesbury, but the dowser William Lewis thought this might be more difficult than finding the boat: 'Bodies are not static objects like the boat was and they may well move with the tide,' he pointed out when Kevin McCauley asked him what the chances were of being able to locate the bodies. 'Furthermore,' said the dowser, 'by the time the divers reach any spot I mark, the bodies could well have moved again ....'

The fishing boat, dramatically located by a dowser when normal and usual methods had failed and the search had been called off, looks like staying at the bottom of the Haven since Tim Butler's widow has said she has no wish for it to be recovered and at a depth of around 100 feet it is no hazard to other ships using the waterway.

In 1972 reports circulated in America and elsewhere about a truck driver and dowser named Frederick Fell who apparently succeeded in locating an old sewer with his divining rod after searches with electronic equipment and a mine detector had failed.

A team of engineers, under manager Graham Peatty, reportedly spent hours trying to find the whereabouts of an old sewer underneath the streets of a town. The workmen were required to install manholes into the sewer so that it could be periodically inspected from street level, but the plans showing the location of the sewer were lost and the engineers spent many hours looking for the sewer with their sophisticated equipment before truck driver Fred Fell located it within moments with the aid of his divining rod.

Graham Peatty is reported to have said afterwards:

It was amazing. Our modern equipment had done nothing, but he was able to pinpoint the sewer effortlessly. I've never seen anything quite like it. . . . . We were getting nowhere. We had a full team of engineers out trying to figure out where it was and we had a mine detector trying to trace metal rods we had pushed along the sewer from a point a couple of hundred feet away. But for some reason the detector could not guide us and we were nowhere near it. We dug four holes in the street but none of them hit the sewer. We decided the only thing to do was to cut a trench, six feet deep, across the whole width of the street and so be sure of hitting the sewer. Then someone suggested asking Fell, one of our truck drivers, to try his hand with a divining rod.

Fred Fell produced a forked branch of a hazel tree; he held it carefully with a hand at the end of each branch, balanced it delicately, and walked across the road about a dozen times. Suddenly the rod shuddered and twisted at a certain spot, he did it again and announced that he had found the sewer. We dug there and he had found the exact spot where the sewer crossed the road and he was able to show the engineers the exact route of the sewer under the street. We are very grateful, but don't ask me to explain it!

In 1979 I endeavoured to contact Mr Frederick Fell for a first-hand account of his experiences but my letter was returned by the postal authorities.

Anyone who studies the subject of dowsing and divining soon becomes aware of the discrepancy between statements and claims made by the dowsing fraternity and official pronouncements by scientific organizations.

When a scholarly British scientific journal comes up with a study (as happens from time to time) announcing that the results of tests between dowsers and non-dowsers attempting to find water or buried objects suggest that dowsing appears to be no more reliable than a series of guesses, or a United States Geological Official Survey reports, as it did in 1972, that controlled experiments have shown conclusively that 'water witching is not a reliable method of locating ground water', the dowsing societies usually come back with a statement something on the lines of: 'Never mind what anyone says. If you believe that dowsing works, then it usually will work; if you approach it in a doubting frame of mind, then often you'll get a negative result.' It is the kind of remark that opens the whole question once again and leaves nobody satisfied. Yet, oddly enough, it is often true.

There are scores of unconfirmed and enthusiastic stories and accounts of wonderful achievements by dowsers – stories that may well be true but have never been confirmed and so remain in the limbo of unsubstantiated folk tales. For example, American dowsers assert that in Vietnam soldiers repeatedly dowsed with wire coat-hangers and other makeshift divining rods to clear the tracks and pathways of enemy mines and booby traps but there does not appear to be any photographic evidence or official statements that this ever happened.

American dowsing societies also frequently claim that dowsing for these and similar purposes is or was actually taught at several marine corps bases but again there does not appear to be any official confirmation that this is so.

Dowsers the world over refer to Albert Einstein (1879-1955), propounder of the theory of relativity (that all motion is relative and that space and time are mutually inseparable), as a lifelong devotee of the practice of dowsing, but again there is no indisputable proof for this widely held belief.

The dowsers, when confronted with such dilemmas, reply that dowsing has been used for centuries and in fact almost all the fresh water in the western world has been found by dowsers, but nobody – or hardly anybody – admits to the fact for fear of being laughed at.

Dowsers are therefore understandably delighted when there is any kind of 'official' confirmation of successful dowsing, such as the published fact that an American electricity corporation, the Southern California Edison Company, employs a dowser full time. In 1972 it was stated that Jerry Smith, whose official title is Agricultural Sales Representative, works from the company's San Bernardino office and that, with his slightly curved, 2 foot rod, he has located no less than 8000 wells in the last forty years. The Edison Company supports Smith because the owners of the wells he discovers usually employ electricity to pump and work the wells.

Vast untapped supplies of water beneath parks and inside mountains are the kind of subjects that dowsers talk about and inevitably there are stories of great discoveries of water by means of divining rods but dowsing rarely gets the credit. A case in point is the bringing back to life of a waterless Lake Elsinore in Southern California. Here, Vernon L. Cameron of Elsinore, a lifelong dowser, both privately and professionally, will always be credited by the dowsing fraternity because it was his persistent conviction that his divining rod showed the presence of water that resulted in the continued drilling and eventual discovery of the lake's present water supply. Sadly Vernon L. Cameron died in 1971.

Then there is Mount Gleason, 10 miles north of La Canada, also in Southern California. Dowsers maintain that the mountain could yield enough good fresh water to meet the needs of Southern California for the rest of this century. A group of dowsers from the American Society of Dowsers believe they have discovered a vast network of underground rivers, streams and springs beneath the mountain that extend into the surrounding area, with a major tributary extending under Griffith Park that exists as a giant reservoir of untapped water. Armed with this information, they prepared to inform state officials in 1972 that this meant that the state had wasted nearly $2½ billion in building canals and pumping stations to bring water into the area from Northern California.

The dowsers knew that they would have to supply convincing evidence before their case would be seriously considered, and they formed a committee to collate the various findings, backed up with maps and geological and topographical information that would be irrefutable and enable them to pinpoint a spot where drilling would yield all the water the area would be likely to need for years to come.

Unfortunately, personality clashes developed within the dowsing organization and then the deaths of two prominent dowsers in the Southern California Chapter, Vernon L. Cameron and E. P. McMillen of La Verne, virtually brought the project to a halt. But other dowsers, including Jack Burgan of Tujunga, strove to get the scheme revived, and today the idea of a thoroughly researched, documented and workable presentation of the project is by no means dead. Jack Burgan, who is an instructor in Los Angeles schools, is still determined to present the facts about the Mount Gleason water to the world, based on the techniques of dowsing.

And it is in the techniques employed in the apparent location of water under Mount Gleason that much of the difficulty lies. Many people are prepared to accept, albeit reluctantly, that the traditional dowser with his forked twig may have something – be it an undefined affinity with underground water, a sixth sense or just good luck; anyway they are prepared to concede the occasional oddity of a man finding water with a forked stick or even a pair of divining rods, but the dowsers who claim to have located water under Mount Gleason used map dowsing. While many veteran dowsers consider this method of dowsing to be just as reliable and valid as the traditional use of the twig or metal rods, few modern, scientific and rational human beings are prepared even to consider the possibility of map dowsing or dowsing at a distance. It is of no use the dowsers explaining their conviction that vibrations and other forces not fully understood or recordable to known science make distance no barrier to the dowser's art, and that he can work equally well from a plan or map or photograph as he can from the actual location itself. So the now long-standing claims by American dowsers that great untapped veins of water extend for miles under and around Mount Gleason remain unproved and unsubstantiated by orthodox scientists – which is a pity, for sometimes dowsers have proved their usefulness in unexpected ways.

There is no doubt that existing case histories and some demonstrations of water divining are unconvincing; unquestionably it sometimes works but the why and how has yet to be completely established. To be fair to government and scientific organizations, they would probably be only too pleased to adopt any single technique that would consistently and unfailingly find water but no such single technique has yet been demonstrated to exist.

The sceptic points out that while there may be many cases of dowsers finding water that was not known to exist, it is indisputable that in some areas where this has happened the existence of natural features would make the presence of underground water extremely likely; in other places where dowsers have demonstrated their ability to find water, it would be extremely difficult *not* to find water and if a dowser fails to find water for someone who has asked him to dowse, his failure is unlikely to attract much attention while his successes will quickly enhance his reputation so it may be that a completely false picture is being presented by the evidence brought forward by dowsers.

An American dowser at Dover-Foxcroft, Maine, according to Joseph J. Weed in his *Psychic Energy,* succeeded in locating the missing bodies of two teenagers under the ice of a frozen river after they had been missing for days and other methods of finding the boys' bodies had failed. It seems that no one had any idea of what had happened to the boys, although it was thought they may have been the victims of an accident of some kind. Then a dowser suggested the possibility of a tragic casualty on the frozen river and with the co-operation of the police he searched for the bodies with his divining rods.

At the first position on the ice where he had obtained an indication, the dowser said he had found the bodies and after making the necessary arrangements the police broke the ice and immediately found the body of one drowned boy wedged under a rock, exactly at the place indicated by the dowser. There was, however, no sign of the other body and the dowser tried again and after a while decided on a spot some distance downstream from where the first body had been found. It was thought by everyone present, except the dowser himself, that he had made a bad mistake but when the ice was broken the body was found, having apparently been carried along by the flow of the river after the original position had been found.

An Austrian dowser can justly claim a unique service to humanity for it would appear that his divining ability has cut the accident rate on the Vienna-Salzburg autobahn.

The road is fairly straight and seems safe enough near Linz, Austria, but at one particular spot which is marked by a kilometre stone no less than twenty-six mysterious and unexplained accidents took place between 1960 and 1966. One motorist was killed and, in the majority of the incidents – nearly 70 per cent – the police were completely baffled as to why there had been an accident at all.

Then Rudolf Wenger, a retired chemist and amateur dowser, heard about the crop of strange and inexplicable accidents and he visited the spot and went over the ground with his divining rod. He quickly located three underground streams that converged at that precise point and he is reported to have said at the time: 'These streams send out rays that affect some people and make them react without realizing that they are being affected.'

Wenger approached the autobahn department and talked to George Hofer. He explained that he believed he had found the reason for the occurrence of the accidents that seemed to happen without cause or reason and he requested permission to bury three loops composed of 'special metal' at the accident black spot. George Hofer reportedly told him: 'Go ahead – after all we know the metal loops can do no harm . . . .' Another autobahn official present added, somewhat acidly, 'We would bury dead dogs there if we thought it would help to cut down the accident rate!'

Rudolf Wenger duly buried his three loops near the 120.5 kilometre marking stone and, between 1966 and 1969, only eight accidents took place in the vicinity, and every one of them was explained in terms of bad driving, so either Wenger's 'special metal' loops did help and the underground streams were indeed affecting motorists in some unknown and frightening manner, or the autobahn maintenance crews and possibly the police were doing their work better than before. Like so many instances of the apparent ability of dowsers, it is simply impossible to come to a watertight and final conclusion on the effect of the dowser's performance.

Another unusual example of dowsing skill was published in the *Saturday Evening Mercury* of Hobart, Tasmania, in August 1978. It related the success of Ralph Thomas, an early member of the British Society of Dowsers who now lives at Leith in the north-west of Tasmania.

A farmer in Cheshire, England, told Thomas that he was having considerable trouble with crops on his farm where nothing seemed to grow satisfactorily. Ralph Thomas asked him to send a scale plan of his farm out to Australia.

When he received the plan, the dowser, at his coastal home, spread out the map and set to work with his divining rod, passing it over and over the plan in an effort to discover exactly what was wrong with the ground it represented. Thomas believes that he can discover the particular needs of any soil and, after working over every part of the plan of the Cheshire farm, he relayed his findings back to the English farmer, drawing his attention to some paddocks. His advice proved to be sound and later the farm was reported to be flourishing.

Ralph Thomas also diagnoses human ailments by using a whalebone divining rod in combination with a wall chart depicting human anatomy. All he needs to 'tune in' to the 'patient' is a snippet of hair which is pressed against the rod as Thomas moves it across the chart. He has been doing this 'health divining' – he refuses to call it 'curing' – for nearly forty-five years and freely admits that he does not know how or why it works. He simply accepts that it does work and therein perhaps lies a clue to his success.

There are other equally unexpected success stories that stem from dowsing and divining. The Yorkshire Television production, 'When the Sun Turns Red, it's Pay Day', a programme in the *Once in a Lifetime* series broadcast in February 1979, told the story of Walter Polglase, a Cornishman who found a valuable mine with the help of old maps and plans left to him by his father, a natural miner who had collected a wealth of information about dead mines.

Using every means available, including map and surface dowsing, Walter Polglase and his son eventually found and worked a mine that had not been entered in two generations, and in this long-abandoned mine they found a valuable source of mineral ore. Dowsing and other methods had enabled them to discover the seam of a lifetime.

The authoritative and respected journal *New Scientist* carried a three-page article on dowsing in the issue dated 8 February 1979, an article contributed by Tom Williamson, a geologist with an interest in mineral prospecting. The article was headed 'Dowsing Achieves New Credence – Reports from the Soviet Union of successful scientific experiments in the ancient arts of water and mineral divining have forced a fresh look at possible practical applications of the technique'. Towards the end of the article Tom Williamson refers to a study of dowsing at Utah State University where two scientists at the Water Research Laboratory discovered that more than 99 per cent of the people tested obtained dowsing reactions and he reasoned that, if dowsing reaction really is as general as this, and if claims by Soviet scientists are taken at face value, 'there would seem to be every reason for making water and mineral divining the subject of a concerted research effort'.

Earlier in the article Williamson had mentioned a report from the Moscow-based All-Union Scientific Research Institute of Hydrogeology and Engineering Geology on the results of mineral surveys in Karelia, the Ukraine and Tadzikistan in 1974 (tests that involved the use of a variety of photo-geological, geophysical and geochemical methods). The two scientists involved, N. N. Sochevanov and V. S. Matveev, drew attention to one particular method, 'recently developed in the Soviet Union, known as BPM'.

Used in conjunction with other methods and techniques, BPM, it seemed, had proved extremely useful in pinpointing several worthwhile metal ore deposits. In a later paper, says Williamson, Sochevanov and three other Russian geologists list many other uses of BPM, especially in the successful location of water wells. BPM

The Divining-rod in mines in the sixteenth century. Sebastian Munster, *Cosmographia universalis* (Basel, 1544).

Exploration of a mining area by means of the Divining-rod in the
sixteenth century. Georg Agricola, *De Re metallica* (Basel, 1571).

Exploration of a mining area by means of the Divining-rod in the seventeenth century. S.E. Lohneyss, *Bericht vom Bergkwerck* (Zellerfeldt, 1617).

A river scene such as some dowsers visualise as they walk across a barren track of land; actually the River Severn near Gloucester.

prospecting equipment is described as 'extraordinarily cheap, lightweight and simple in design' so it is understandable that Williamson should regard it as 'astonishing that such an important new method should have been so ignored in the West ....' Ignored by the scientific community perhaps, for it transpires that the letters BPM stand for 'biophysical method' and BPM is nothing more than a new name for an old technique – dowsing!

There has always existed a certain abhorrence or hostility to, or at least distaste of, dowsing among the hydrologists and other engineers who work in the water authorities and in scientific water geology; certainly, when I approached all the water authorities in Britain during the course of research for this book, the majority replied in terms such as, 'although our hydrologists would not doubt that dowsing and divining for water is possible, they prefer to use methods which are rather more scientific'. So Tom Williamson hits the nail on the head when he says in the *New Scientist* article that, since water diviners have not been prepared to master the rudiments of ground water geology and other relevant sciences, preferring to elaborate naive theories about dowsing, they have never been able to present their claims in a form acceptable to scientists.

He suggests an ingenious way out of this impasse: shift attention away from the claims of practising water diviners towards a study of the dowsing reactions of ordinary people. This seems a useful and practical suggestion for, if an appreciable volume of independent evidence could be collected and presented in a scientific manner, there is every reason to believe that it would be treated with respect and lead to a serious appraisal of the merits of dowsing and divining for water.

He admits that the sceptic will still maintain that the small hand movements that result in the reaction that dowsers accept as evidence of their powers are entirely psychological in origin and do not bear any relation to external stimuli, but he suggests that the possibility should also be considered that some dowsing reactions are direct physiological responses to small changes in the environment. After all, researches at universities as far apart as Illinois and Moscow have suggested that some biological systems may have evolved a remarkable sensitivity to minute changes in ambient magnetic and electromagnetic fields.

It is acepted by science that mineral veins and flowing ground water are both associated with geological faults, fractures, cavities, channels and so forth and, since these 'discontinuities' cause small geophysical irregulations in magnetic strength, this could account for the reaction obtained by dowsers. At all events this appears to be the belief of Soviet geologists who have studied the subject for more than a decade.

Indeed conferences devoted to BPM were held in Moscow in 1968 and again in 1971, the latter attracting more than 100 scientists from forty research institutes throughout the Soviet Union. By this time it was clear to everyone involved that the subject was a far more formidable undertaking than it had seemed to be at first sight, and it would appear that research into several different areas will be necessary before the problem of whether or not a physical mechanism is operating can be definitely decided.

In the meantime Sochevanov and Matveev continued with their studies into the subject, and in 1974 they conducted a combined photogeological survey by helicopter with a dowser over a plot of land, several hundred kilometres in area, where it was known that rare minerals were to be found. The dowser's reactions were continuously monitored and it was found that he obtained positive reactions that corresponded with the conclusions of the hydrologists, and subsequent exploration drilling proved the effectiveness of the combined survey.

Other examples of the useful applicatiion of dowsing techniques in the Soviet Union include the location of other ore bodies and water wells, and help in certain engineering problems. In 1973, in a region near Cheliabinsk, 1120 fruitful wells were dug with the help of four dowsers, while 158 wells were located by geophysical methods. The proportions of wells found to be dry ranged from 6 to 8.5 per cent for the BPM and 12.7 per cent for the geophysically sited wells.

Not that dowsing has achieved complete recognition in the Soviet Union. There, just as much as in the West, there is considerable opposition to the practice, and on similar grounds to those put forward by British and American scientists: the unscientific nature of the practice, the lack of theoretical basis, alleged or apparent links with the occult and, perhaps the largest and at the same time most puzzling weakness, the repeated failure of experienced dowsers to demonstrate their abilities under test conditions. Of course there have been successful tests (as we shall see in a later chapter in this book) but there have also been many instances of unsuccessful tests.

Often the dowser will make excuses or give his reasons for failure after the experiment and it may be that his reasons are valid, but the dowser knows the conditions before the test and he agrees to them in the same way that he agrees to undergo the tests; it does seem likely that there is a psychological element in dowsing which simply is not sympathetic to test conditions. Or perhaps there is something in the make-up of most dowsers that prohibits their giving of their best under certain conditions. If so, this is a pity, and it is to be hoped that it will be possible to find some way in which to overcome this hurdle for otherwise it is difficult to see how dowsing can be used scientifically.

British experiments in dowsing and divining do not appear to correspond with the findings of the Russians. Experiments conducted by R. A. Foulkes of the Institute for Industrial Research and Standards, Dublin, and organized by the British Army and Ministry of Defence, are summed up in the report published in *Nature* 15 January 1971 as 'no more reliable than a series of guesses'.

To return to Tom Williamson's refreshingly unprejudiced article: he says that there are few facts in a subject 'as controversial and ill-defined as dowsing', not marked by 'unbridled speculation and volumes of dubious literature' (I hope I am not adding to it!), but the recent work in the Soviet Union and some research by scientists Duane Chadwick and Larry Jensen at the Water Research Laboratory of Utah State University have added considerably to our knowledge.

Foulkes tested a few established and experienced dowsers, but the Utah investigators concentrated on testing the abilities of 150 students and staff of the university – people without any previous experience or special knowledge of the subject – and they found that 99 per cent of the people they tested revealed some kind of dowsing reaction.

Tom Williamson rightly points out that, if the dowsing reaction or ability really is as general as this, and if the Russian claims of the effectiveness of BPM as a prospecting technique are to be taken at their face value, there would seem to be every reason for making a concerted effort to research the apparent ability. He adds that the Soviet geologists have repeatedly pressed for the setting up of a research institute devoted to the study of BPM. They have no doubt, it seems, that dowsing reactions are related to weak electromagnetic fields; now they want to prove it.

There are obvious benefits to be obtained from such a cheap water prospecting technique as would appear to be possible, even likely, in view of the implications of different tests in different parts of the world and under different conditions and supervision. It could be the means of bringing water to many arid areas in underdeveloped countries, to mention only one aspect; but, if dowsing should after all be shown to have a psychological element and to be impracticable as a working method of finding water, the exploration of the subject would still be a valuable exercise and demonstration of the value of scientific method.

Notwithstanding the fact that the value of dowsing and divining has yet to be established scientifically and statistically, the art or science or gift or ability of dowsing is firmly established in the modern world. Dr Lyall Watson tells us that 'every major water and pipeline company in the United States has a dowser on its payroll'.[1] The Canadian Ministry of Agriculture, we are told, employs a permanent dowser; UNESCO has engaged a Dutch dowser and geologist to pursue official investigations for them. Engineers of the US Marines were trained to locate booby traps and buried mortar shells in Vietnam with the use of divining rods; and the Czechoslovakian Army has a special corp of permanent dowsers.

Lyall Watson also recounts some interesting Russian experiments in biophysical method. In 1966 the already referred to scientist and Leningrad mineralogist, Nikolai Sochevanov, carried out survey operations near the Russian border with China. Special equipment carried on the aeroplane included a magnetometer of the kind that is commonly used by mining companies while carrying out aerial prospecting; a less expected feature of the expedition were several dowsers who stood with their dowsing rods ready for use as the plane flew over the River Chu in the Kirghiz region.

Sochevanov observed with interest that the vast amount of water over which they were flying – the centre of the river – had no apparent effect on the divining rods but all the dowsers could feel an immediate reaction on the rods whenever the plane was flown near either shore of the river. This curious effect has occurred in other tests in other parts of the world, and it does seem that a large mass of water moving at speed affects dowsers far less than slow-moving water in friction with the soil, particularly where the surface of the soil is in contact with water over a large area, as it is in ground saturated with water moving slowly through very small crevices or capillaries. When he arranged for the aeroplane to fly over an area which was known to contain mineral deposits, Sochevanov noticed and recorded definite and marked reactions from the dowsers and, in ground tests, following up the aerial dowsing responses, his investigators located, among other deposits, a seam of lead no more than 3 inches thick at a depth of almost 500 feet. Larger deposits, nearer to the surface, had

[1]*Supernature* (Hodder and Stoughton, 1973).

caused such violent reactions that some of the wooden rods had been jerked out of the dowsers' hands – an event which prompted the Russian scientist to design a steel, U-shaped divining instrument that had roller-bearing handles and rotated freely.

Another fascinating experiment, also detailed by Dr Lyall Watson in *Supernature,* concerned a survey that took place in October 1966 over an area near Alma-Ata where 3 million cubic metres of rock were about to be blown up as part of a development scheme. The team of dowsers were flown over the area just before the rock was dynamited and then again immediately afterwards.

The dowsers stated that their rods indicated enormous changes in underground patterns caused by the dynamiting and, for no less than four hours after the explosion, the shape of the remaining rock continued to change and settle. The dowsers continued to plot the various changes until at last the pattern and shape settled down and seismographs confirmed that all tremors had subsided. By this time the dowsers found that the pattern of the rock strata had almost returned to its original design and lay-out – almost but not quite. Later, the small differences between the rock patterns before the explosion and those afterwards were found to be due to underground fractures that were the result of the explosion – and this was confirmed by actual excavation.

In his book *Mysterious Powers*[1] Colin Wilson reproduces a photograph of a resident site engineer demonstrating a sophisticated set of divining rods that a large building construction firm has considered a worthwhile investment. The apparatus – it is in fact the Revealer we have examined in a previous chapter – consists of two extending L-shaped rods and a small metal frame with strings and containers to take samples of different material that may be encountered during dowsing operations: copper, lead, cast iron, plastic. When he is looking for an article or deposit of a particular material, the operator holds the appropriate string in his fingers and the rods are said to react if they pass over that material.

[1]Aldus Books, 1975.

It seems that anyone can use the rods, although the reaction obtained by some people is stronger and more definite than with others. This particular firm uses the rods as an easy means of locating pipes carrying water underground, buried pipes that carry high-voltage wiring and other obstructions likely to be found on building sites. With such an example of the practical use of dowsing and divining in the modern world, let us have a look at how it may be possible for practically anyone to acquire the art or skill of dowsing.

9. How to Acquire the Art of Dowsing

There are those who believe that it is impossible to acquire the art: you either possess the ability or you do not and there the matter ends. Colonel Merrylees, a much respected dowser of many years standing told me, as recently as April 1979: 'I do not believe that dowsing can be taught beyond testing the novice for sensitivity and suggesting what he should do next.' Tom Graves, an educational graphic designer who teaches dowsing in London and is author of the successful *Dowsing Techniques and Applications*[1] opens his book with the bald statement: 'Anyone can dowse.'

Perhaps the truth lies somewhere between the two and, with the conviction that anyone with sensitivity and a certain inherent ability can indeed learn to dowse, let us look at the best ways of acquiring a skill which, as Tom Graves puts it, 'like any other, can be learnt with patience, awareness and a working knowledge of its basic principals and mechanics' – a skill which can be used as and whenever it is needed, or simply for the pleasure of dowsing, anywhere and at any time. Certainly the overwhelming majority of people, perhaps as many as 99 per cent, and almost certainly 80 per cent, do obtain some reaction when they are shown how to hold and use a divining rod.

Since it is abundantly clear that most people are potential dowsers – with some help, guidance, encouragement and example – it seems certain, in spite of the conviction to the contrary of some dowsers, that invol-

[1] Turnstone Books, 1976.

untary and unconscious muscular movement is responsible for making the dowsing instrument begin to move.
After that a great deal depends on the sensitivity and
experience of the dowser.

The great Wiltshire dowser John Mullins was quite
certain at one stage of his life that he was exceptional in
his family in this respect, and the only one of them who
could find water, but as the years passed his sons became
sufficiently proficient to carry on his dowsing business
after their father's death.

There are several simple experiments that will quickly
convince almost anyone that there is something odd and
not yet fully understood about the practice of dowsing.

The archaeologist and writer, Tom C. Lethbridge, was
an enthusiastic dowser and his books are full of remarkable examples of his techniques.[1] His straightforward
experiment for non-believers was simple in the extreme.
He suggested that the enquirer should equip himself
with a makeshift pendulum: simply a fairly light weight
attached to a short length of thread or twine; anything
will do for the weight – a key, a medal, a piece of wood,
a screw, a pen – anything that has enough weight to
hold the supporting thread or twine taut, and the thread
should be pinched securely between the thumb and
forefinger a few inches above the weight so that the
'pendulum' hangs freely. Any spare line can be hooked
round the fingers to keep it out of the way.

Hold the pendulum thread so that it hangs freely; it
makes no difference whether you are sitting down or
standing up, but it will be found most convenient if the
arm is bent at the elbow so that the forearm holding the
pendulum is approximately parallel with the ground.
Swing the weight gently and get it to move forwards
and backwards and in circles both clockwise and anti-
clockwise, using only just sufficient movement of the
thumb and forefinger and the arm to get the pendulum
to move. Adjust the length of the string or twine a little
from time to time.

[1]*Ghost and Ghoul*, (1961), *Ghost and Divining Rod* (1963), *ESP: Beyond Time and Distance* (1965), *A Step in the Dark* (1967), *The Monkey's Tail* (1969) and *The Power of the Pendulum* (1976). (All published by Routledge and Kegan Paul.)

As you get used to the feel of the pendulum moving in your fingers you will discover your best and most natural length of twine – which will be when the pendulum swings almost naturally – and you will soon find that at the right length for you the pendulum will swing almost unconsciously or at any rate with very little effort on your part.

The next step is to take three coins, two of which should be of the same value and ideally the same date – say, two two-pence pieces and a third coin of a different date and a different denomination, say a five-pence piece. Put the latter on one side for a moment (at least 1 foot away) and place the two two-pence pieces in front of you, one ahead of the other, about 4 inches apart.

Take up the pendulum again, holding the thread at the ideal distance that you have discovered and with the weighted end a little above the coins and between them. Watch the pendulum and allow it to oscillate from one coin to the other; gradually the rhythm will become apparent and it would seem that the pendulum is attracted first to one coin and then to the other. When this rhythm is clearly established, have someone replace the two-pence piece further away from you, with the third coin that you have kept in reserve, the five-pence piece.

You may be able to manage moving it yourself with your spare hand, but it is rather tricky to do so without upsetting the rhythm of the pendulum.

You will of course endeavour to hold the pendulum exactly as you have been holding it, and without becoming tense or concentrating too much; just watch the pendulum and you will see the swing completely change. It is almost as though the different coin repels the pendulum. Perhaps the movement will change to a diagonal swing or it may rotate; at all events it will be quite different from the oscillation or swing observed when the pendulum was held above the two coins that are identical or very similar.

Do not attempt to affect the pendulum, simply watch it carefully and, once it has set up the totally different rhythm in respect of the third coin, change that coin back for the original two-pence piece. Again, without any conscious movement on your part – in fact you should endeavour to keep your hand and arm quite motionless but without creating any tension for a relaxed and quiet concentration seems most beneficial – you will see the pendulum revert to the original rhythm and oscillation that it had settled down to between the two two-pence pieces.

Tom Lethbridge did not make any real attempt to explain this phenomenon, but simply stated that it works for practically everyone, and it does. If you do not believe it, try it. Unconscious muscular action it may be, or is it? Get someone to change the coins without your knowledge while your eyes are closed or when you are blindfolded and then changed again – you may get a surprise.

In one of his books[1] Lethbridge likens the force that is present in dowsing to poltergeist phenomena and psychokinesis – a form of force or power that might be called resonance, and the most ordinary example of resonance, he says, with which many people are familiar, is water divining. Resonance, Lethbridge states, 'appears to be akin to electromagnetics, but [it] is not able to work without the linkage of a human mechanism to it'.

Lethbridge became fascinated with dowsing and taught himself to be quite efficient at water divining; he believed that he was able to study fields of force 'with nothing more elaborate than a hazel fork' in his hand. And we must remember that Tom Lethbridge was a Cambridge University don, yet his pursuit of the art of dowsing 'opened his scholar's vision to unimagined horizons' (as the *Washington Post* put it in their issue of 24 December 1978). 'From living a normal life in a three-dimensional world,' Lethbridge says in one of his books, 'I seem to have suddenly fallen through into one where there are more dimensions. The three-dimensional world goes on as usual but one has to adjust one's thinking to the other.'

It is possible to look forward to a time when the

[1]*Ghost and Ghoul* (Routledge and Kegan Paul, 1961).

dowsing ability, whatever it may be, will be employed automatically and by everyone as naturally as by Tom Lethbridge.

Another simple experiment that anyone can try is outlined in *Water Witching U.S.A.*[1] The authors assert that anyone who has tried his hand with a divining rod or a pendulum will know how convincing and mysterious the experience can be; and anyone who has not had personal acquaintance with such methods may like to try the following experiment.

Attach a small weight (such as a key or a ring or a coin) to about ½ metre of twine, string or tape, or even a light chain. Now hold the loose end of the suspending material between the tips of two fingers of one hand and stand upright so that the weighted end swings back and forth like a pendulum. If you now forget all about the hand and arm holding the twine or string and concentrate instead on the object acting as a pendulum and try to imagine or think of the weight as gyrating in a clockwise circle; almost certainly the pendulum will soon begin to revolve in a circular movement without any conscious effort on the part of the person holding the pendulum. With very little practice most people will find that they can get the pendulum to reverse its circular movement and swing in a line back and forth, or swing from side to side, all without any conscious effort on their part; and the emphasis is on the word 'conscious' for, whether you like it or not, you are unconsciously influencing the movement of the pendulum by your hold on the supporting twine or cord.

It is also true that dowsing works for most people and, while it may be accepted that it is unconscious muscular energy that is affecting the pendulum, what is it that affects the muscles or the mind so to affect the pendulum that it *correctly* locates water or some mineral or whatever may be sought by the experienced dowser? Perhaps he is not right 100 per cent of the time, but the available evidence suggests that he is right far in excess of chance expectation.

[1] Evon Z. Vogt and Ray Hyman, (University of Chicago Press, 1959).

Legory H. O'Loughlin, the president of the Southern California Chapter of the American Society of Dowsers, tells me that in his experience the best way to start dowsing is with simple L-rods and, when that has been mastered, it is an easy matter to learn to dowse with Y-rods or forked twigs or a pendulum. 'So far,' 'Gory' O'Loughlin informed me in January 1979, '*every* person who has tried with me has felt the pull of the rod.' So, justifiably it would seem, he feels that, '*everyone* has the ability to dowse; one needs only the desire to learn, and then practice, practice and still more persistent practice creates the dowser'.

Now what exactly are L-rods? A very simple pair can be made by anyone and the rods described and illustrated on the BBC television programme 'Now You See It, Now You Don't' in December 1977 are an excellent example. To recapitulate, simply take a plain wire coat-hanger, snip off the handle, cut in half, straighten the two wires, bend them at right angles about 2 inches from each end, insert the short ends into the barrels of old ball-point pens and you have a pair of L-rods.

L-rods or angle-rods are generally considered to be the most sensitive of the four main types of dowsing tools, the other three being the traditional forked twig, a straight pliable wand, and a pendulum.

You can use a pair of L-rods by holding them steadily in front of you, one in each hand, by the plastic handles, so that the long straight rods are approximately parallel with the ground. Hold them lightly, about the width of your body apart, with your thumbs uppermost and with your elbows tucked into your sides, but not unnaturally stiff or uncomfortable. As you stand still so the rods will remain motionless but, when you move forwards, backwards or side-ways, the rods are liable to move in one of three ways: either inwards (so that they cross), outwards (so that they point in opposite directions), or sideways (keeping parallel). You can try these movements consciously by turning your wrists vertically towards each other, by turning your wrists vertically outwards, and by turning your wrists together in the same direction. This will give you the feel of the movements for all three may be experienced in actual dowsing, although each movement can be interpreted as supplying the user with different information.

Of course, you may prefer the more traditional forked twig and if you happen to live in the country there is nothing wrong with making a start with a Y-rod, or indeed with a straight, pliable wand cut from a growing bush, but neither are quite as easy for a beginner as L-rods. And you will probably need to find live, springy wood for either a forked or straight dowsing twig.

There is a lot to be said for hazel and many experienced dowsers will tell you that there is a special 'feel' to hazel wood, a feel which is almost independent of life, something that is not found in any other wood; and it keeps its spring and tension longer than most twigs which soon become dry and brittle and easily break under tension. Willow is good too, and hawthorn, rowan, apple, cherry and several other trees and shrubs; indeed some dowsers will assure you that the wood makes not the slightest difference: it is knowing the joined twig to cut that is important.

Look carefully for a Y-shaped fork where the arms are about the same thickness, about ½ metre long, and it is best if the angle is not too wide. The length of the arms in the final divining rod may be in accordance with individual requirements or personal inclination and so may the thickness of the rod, but most people will find that a fairly thin twig is the easiest and most convenient to handle. Once the twig has been chosen, it should be cut fairly close to the fork but far enough away to avoid any possibility of the forked twig splitting when it is held in tension. It should be cut cleanly and then stripped of any odd spikes or leaves, trimmed down to the desired size and the rod is then ready for use. It is quite likely that several rods will be cut before you decide on the most suitable and comfortable one. There is much to be said for a traditional live wood divining rod; it has a satisfaction and a feeling that is not to be found in artificial rods. On the other hand all natural cut rods dry out and become brittle, some even snap and so become unusable. Experienced dowsers will often continue using their rods long after they are dry and brittle until they actually break in use. Hawthorn dries out in a matter of hours and even hazel often lasts only a few days.

So let us take a look at the Y-rod that is an artificial forked rod made of plastic, metal or bone. If the size and feel suits you, it is a rod that you can become thoroughly familiar with and which will last you for years. If you wish to make your own artificial Y-rod you can do so by taking two equal strips or lengths of any springy and resilient material – a pair of long plastic knitting needles for example, or strips of plastic curtain rod, or whalebone. Fasten them together at one end, say by gluing two ends into a convenient plastic cup or even by sticking them into a cork.

However you make your Y-shaped rod, it is in effect a spring rod, inasmuch as you hold it, opening the branches outwards, one end of each leg in each hand, in such a way that you create an unstable tension so that any small movement of the hands will cause the rod to spring sharply up or down. To achieve the right position of the rod – pointing straight in front of you – and the right tension will take a little practice and many a rod has sprung clean out of the hands of a novice as he attempts to obtain the right tension but, once the knack has been found, many dowsers find the forked rod to be a highly sensitive indicator that is second to none.

In use the forked twig or circular rod is held firmly by the centre of the palms with the fingers closed over it and either with the joined end pointing away from the dowser or with the joined end pointing towards him. Some dowsers prefer the thumbs to run along the ends of the twigs or rod while others prefer the thumbs on the inside; it is purely a matter of personal preference and the way in which the dowser can best obtain and hold a tension in the rod is the right way for him. Probably the best way for a beginner is for him to start with a longish rod, where the branches are maybe ⅓ metre long. With the elbows close to the body and the forearms parallel with the ground and level with each other, he should clench the branches in the hands with the palms uppermost, leaving any excess branch on the outside of the hands, and by pulling backwards and outwards he should be able to adjust the tension so that the rod balances steady and horizontal, with the joined end pointing away from the dowser.

The method of holding a flat-strip type of Y-rod is rather different, inasmuch as the rod is flexed and held by the ends between the thumbs and fore-fingers, again in such a way that it is delicately balanced; but again there are dowsers who have individual ways of holding the flexible flat spring rods. The method of holding any dowsing instrument seems to be completely immaterial to the result; the idea is to hold the instrument in equilibrium so that the slightest movement of the hands will cause it to move. For some people the rod moves up and for others it dips down; almost invariably dowsers need to be moving in some way for the rod to move at all. Usually they walk, or turn, or sway back and forth while remaining on the same spot.

Finally, among the more common divining tools, there is the single, straight stick, or 'wand' as it is sometimes called, which is the least common and least popular, although some experienced dowsers will use no other. It is usually a stick of living wood, cut from a hedgerow, about 1 metre in length and springy and resilient, but it can also be a pliable rod such as a car radio aerial. The wand is held by the thin end (if there is one) and the dowser lets the other end (usually the thick end) vibrate gently up and down without consciously causing it to do so.

The dowser will then walk in a straight line or in circles or turn slowly round and round; when the rod reacts it will move in a circular motion. There are no special advantages for the beginner in using a wand, although some experienced dowsers say it is less tiring than a conventional forked twig when dowsing over a long period or a large area.

Obviously there are variations on dowsing implements, and we have looked at some of them in an earlier chapter. Here it is only necessary to describe the commonest instruments and the easiest for the novice to obtain or make to enable him to acquire the art of dowsing. And, while practically anyone can achieve some degree of reaction from whatever dowsing instrument he or she may choose to use, some authorities assert that, just as one cannot make scientific judgements without scientific training, so too one cannot always sense the subtle vibrations (if such exist) without having first received proper training.

We have already remarked on the advisability of being as relaxed as possible and keeping the eyes on the dowsing instrument and, it is interesting that the 'scientist yogi', Christopher Hills, who looks at the subject in a somewhat different light, says the operator of what he calls 'supersensonics' is always influenced by what he happens to be looking at. 'The eye as a specialized part of the body's sensing apparatus, appears to send out a carrier wave upon which the waves of the object under observation travel. Best results are achieved when the operator keeps looking at the instrument in his hands.'[1] In passing it may be relevant to mention that some students of poltergeist phenomena maintain that the human eye is a deterrent to such activity, and in fact poltergeist projected objects in flight frequently fall to the floor when they are observed by the human eye.

Christopher Hills also describes the making and testing of a simple pendulum and he suggests a wooden cotton reel suspended by its own thread. But while this may make a perfectly suitable pendulum, Hills stresses the importance of the following: the colour of the cotton reel (contradicted on successive pages in my copy); the colour of the cotton; the colour of the table cover; the necessity of having any table drawers open 'since cavities have a remarkable effect on magnetic vibrational fields and may suppress the influence you are going to detect through your nerves'; the use of a piece of stick, 'preferably unpainted but white or black or dark green as a second choice'; the use of a pocket compass and quite involved measuring of thread lengths for different oscillations and movement of the pendulum to different positions of the

[1]*Supersensonics* (University of the Trees Press, California, 1975).

compass; clockwise and anti-clockwise gyrations 'depending on a person's Shakti/Shiva balance of consciousness' until, 'having mastered this you have become sensitive to the invisible magnetic fields which pass through all of creation'.

All this may seem rather a long way from basic dowsing for the amateur so perhaps we should part company with Christopher Hills but before we do so we may note with interest that he, in common with most experienced dowsers, extols the virtues of positive thought: '... the feeling "this is going to work", will enable thought energy to manifest in the physical world. Consequently, human thought energy emitted with absolute belief seems to be the casual force for much that occurs in the phenomenal world'. While I remain unconvinced concerning Hills's reasons for positive thought in these regions, I am quite prepared to believe that it is a contributory factor to successful dowsing and indeed I doubt whether many of my fellow members of The British Society of Dowsers would disagree.

Hills's reference to 'invisible magnetic fields' passing through all creation is echoed by Herbert Weaver in his book on divining.[1] Herbert Weaver, a rationalist who takes a physiological view of divining, conducted a number of experiments with the Revealer Field Detector, which we looked at in the last chapter, and these experiments led him to conclude that the faculty of divining is due to unconscious sensitivity to electromagnetic fields and he asserts that every organism, down to single blades of grass, has its own unique chemical signal and it is these signals that dowsers detect, whether they realize it or not.

We can still obtain some hints on acquiring the right forked stick from the 200-year-old issue of the *Gentleman's Magazine* (referred to in Chapter 2, page 45) where it is stated:

A shoot that terminates equally forked is to be preferred, about two feet and a half long; but as such a forked rod is rarely to be met with, two single ones, of a length and size,

[1]*Divining, the Primary Sense* (Routledge and Kegan Paul, 1978).

may be tied together with thread, and will answer as well as the other.

In fact many variations of divining rods are used and a Yorkshire dowser finds that he can work best with a coin in the palm of his hand! When he is in the immediate vicinity of an underground stream, the coin turns over in his hand. Other dowsers use a pliable looped rod that is held upright between the hands, and for some practitioners it seems to be more sensitive than any other type of rod. Still others do their best work with a single stick, ranging in size from a matchstick to a beanpole!

Although the wand is now the least popular of all divining instruments, it is probably the most ancient type of rod and arguably the best rod for a beginner. Divination by the rod or wand is mentioned in the prophecy of Ezekiel; Hosea, too, reproaches the Jews as 'being infected with the same superstition': 'My people ask counsel at their stocks and their staff declareth unto them.' Thomas Pennant (1726-1798), the zoologist and traveller, mentions that the divining rod, as we have seen (Chapter 2, page 45) and says the forked rod had 'been cut in a planetary hour, Saturn's day and hour, because Saturn was the significator of lead'. Jupiter, Venus, Sol and Mercury also participated (says Pennant) in the operation 'according to their reputed several attributes and powers'.

Is this attribute 'psychic power'? It may well be linked with the mind in some way for experts tell the beginner that to be successful dowsers they must clearly know what they want to find; they must plainly visualize what it is they are looking for, and they must want to find it very, very much.

Having decided on the type of rod to use, the potential dowser will want exact instructions on how to hold it. Let us assume that he has found for himself a forked twig or has purchased an angle-rod.

The most popular method of holding the twig or divining rod has remained virtually unchanged for centuries, although there are a few dowsers who have developed their own individual methods of grasping the rod. As we have seen the palms of the hand should always face upwards and the rod is usually gripped lightly with both hands in the palms, one hand at each end of the forked twig or rod, or as near the end as may be convenient with the elbows comfortably close to the body and the arms bent. The rod is then usually held in such a way that the neck or base of the fork points forwards, and sometimes upwards, at an angle of about 45 degrees.

Once the beginner has so grasped the rod and achieved something like this position without straining and with as little tension as possible, it is the work of a few seconds to adjust the position of the hands and the angle at which the rod is held to a point where the slightest movement of the wrists or forearms will cause the rod to dip towards the ground or rise towards the sky. Once this delicate balance has been achieved with the rod held as lightly as possible the dowser is ready to traverse slowly the prescribed area, and he should do this in a methodical manner so that the whole area is covered.

Assuming that the plot of ground to be tested is roughly square or rectangular, an experienced dowser will often begin at one corner and walk slowly across the area diagonally to the opposite corner and then he will do exactly the same between the other two corners and, if he is unsuccessful in obtaining any dowsing response, he will then divide the plot into small areas and thoroughly explore each part until the whole plot has been covered. If at any time he receives an indication that there is something below ground that is affecting his rod, he will mark the place by driving a stick into the ground before resuming his search. In this way he will, if there is anything to find (and always providing that he is a competent dowser), eventually pinpoint the place where he receives the strongest indication and the route of any underground stream or seam of mineral.

When straight objects are used – sticks or wands, metal bars, brooms, agricultural implements or whatever it may be – they must be held in such a manner that they can swing or revolve, or bob up and down, or freely move in some way in the diviner's hands so that he can appreciate any indication that may present itself. Just about anything remotely suitable can be used for divining but there is no doubt that a forked implement resembling a branched twig is the most popular, probably the most successful, and almost certainly the best for the beginner.

Many dowsers suggest beginning with a pendulum and, while a small cotton reel makes a good 'bob', an ivory or plastic item on the end of a piece of thread makes an even better one. As a beginner hold the pendulum in one hand by squeezing the thread between the thumb and forefinger, and hold it over the other hand. Hand the 'bob' by a fairly short lead at first and gradually increase it and there will come a point when the 'bob' or pendulum will begin to gyrate or move backwards and forwards.

The length of thread that you have released to obtain a reaction in the pendulum is probably the best length for you in the general practice of pendulum work. Most people will find this to be in the region of about 4½ inches.

A prominent member of The Society of Dowsers, V. D. Wethered, B.Sc., has been among those who maintain that it is possible and indeed desirable, at this stage, to 'tune in' the pendulum to whatever may be the subject of the test.[1] He suggests that this can easily be accomplished by holding the pendulum over a sample of the object of the search and gradually letting the thread run through the fingers until gyration occurs. For instance (to quote Mr Wethered):

If your subject wanted to know whether sherry suited him, you could tune your pendulum in to the sherry until the pendulum was gyrating strongly and then transfer it to a point above the palm of your subject's hand. If the pendulum continued gyrating strongly your subject could drink sherry (in moderate amounts) with impunity.

Such tests, it is stated, can be satisfactorily made with standard pendulum suspension but the 'tuning in' pro-

[1] See *Practical Dowsing: A Symposium* (Bell, 1965).

cess can often add substantially to the dependability of such a specific test.

The reader who wishes to acquire the art of dowsing will need to know what to use, where to obtain the necessary instruments, how to hold and use the apparatus, where to make the first attempts at dowsing and how to develop. All these questions can be answered fairly briefly and I hope precisely. Let us take them in order.

What to use: As I have tried to show in this chapter, and as will be evident from passages throughout this book, there are any number of things that can be used for dowsing. There are two main types of instruments – rods and pendulums. There are two main types of rod – metal L-shaped rods or angle-rods that react to a static neutral balance, and the more traditional forked twig or artificial 'spring' rod that is used by holding it in an unstable tension. As we have seen, the angle-rods, held in both hands, respond by swinging inwards or crossing or swinging outwards to left or right, more or less parallel. The forked twig or traditional divining rod, also held in both hands, responds by dipping or lifting or moving to left or right. The pendulum is a weight on a thread or length of twine that is held in one hand between the thumb and forefinger and gyrates or swings to show response. The beginner cannot do better than make himself a simple pendulum and see for himself that it is possible to get a response that he is not consciously responsible for; then he can make himself a simple pair of angle rods and experiment with that before progressing to a forked twig or a manufactured rod.

Where to obtain the necessary instruments: Well, as we have seen any type of dowsing instrument need cost nothing: a simple weight on a length of twine forms a pendulum, a wire coat-hanger is quickly transformed into a pair of angle-rods or a forked twig can be found in almost any garden or hedgerow. If, however, the budding dowser prefers to buy apparatus, the Metaphysical Research Group, Archer's Court, Stonestile Lane, The Ridge, Has-

tings, Sussex, supply a variety of pendulums and divining rods or a complete dowser's kit, comprising one clear
plastic pendulum, one forked divining rod, one pair of
angle-rods and one long pendulum with spindle,
together with a forty-page elementary instruction book-
let. The pendulums available separately include: beech-
wood 'bobs' with cavities; a chromed brass pendulum
with cavity (as originally designed by the Abbé Mermet);
hollow perspex; solid wood (black and waxed). Long,
square, clear pendulums are also available, as are amplifying pendulums (a cross between a pendulum and a
divining rod) with single or double cavity in the handle
and a spring between the pendulum end and the handle
for greater sensitivity, and an 'aurameter' described as
'one of the world's most sensitive radiesthetic detectors'.
These and other dowsing aids are fully described in the
equipment catalogue that is obtainable from the Metaphysical Research Group. The British Society of Dowsers,
Secretary Mr M. D. Rust, Court Lodge Farm, Hastin-
gleigh, Ashford, Kent, can also supply rods and
pendulums.

How to hold and use the apparatus: Angle-rods are held by
the short ends in such a way that the long ends can
rotate easily; the grip should be that of a loosely clenched
fist. The long ends should be roughly parallel with the
ground and, with the help of relaxed concentration and
quiet confidence, the aforementioned reactions will be
obtained. Forked twigs and manufactured divining rods
are held with the palms upwards so that the rod is
balanced between springing upwards or downwards by
the slightest movement of the wrists. The joined end is
usually held so that it points away from the dowser and
it can be held at any height but about hip-height will be
found most comfortable for most people. The metal
spring rods can be held between the fingers and thumbs
but again with the palms facing upwards. The main
thing to remember regarding holding any type of divining rod is to hold it in the way that is most comfortable
and relaxed for you and where the necessary tension is
achieved with the minimum of effort.

Pendulums, irrespective of whether they are home-made – a cotton reel, a key, a coin or medal, a heavy needle, practically anything in fact – or whether they are manufactured in plastic, wood or metal, are all held between the finger and thumb of one hand with suffi-cient thread as may be convenient or has been found by trial and error to be the correct length for you.

Where to make the first attempts at dowsing and how to develop: Angle-rods and divining rods in general are best used in the open air, as far as beginners are concerned, but you can try them anywhere. It is a good idea to walk across your lawn where you know there must be water pipes and see whether you can trace the line of the pipes; afterwards, you can check to see whether you are right by finding out where in fact the water pipes do enter the house. Friends will usually be pleased to help in burying bottles of water or pieces of metal and before long you will feel confident enough to go on to more exciting adventures in dowsing and divining, here and abroad and in fact wherever you may find yourself.

Pendulums are best tried out indoors first of all and the simple tests already detailed in this chapter will quickly transform a passing interest into something that can become a lifelong and absorbing habit: dowsing for pleasure and profit, indoors and out of doors, in company and alone – there is always something different to try, always more to learn. And the more you practise dows-ing, in whatever form, the more proficient you will become. Aspiring dowsers cannot do better than join The British Society of Dowsers, which is discussed in Chapter 12.

Dowsers are friendly people; dowsing is a harmless, fascinating and unexplained phenomenon. It is some-thing that you can almost certainly do – try, and you will see.

10. Adventures in Dowsing and Divining

Ever since man found that he could dowse there have been strange and exciting adventures to be encountered while practising the still little understood art. We have already looked at some of these adventures in the chapter on 'Dowsers of the Past' and now we will take a look at some recent experiences, mentioning in passing that it is not only water, metal, minerals, medical diagnosis and cure, or even lost property and missing persons, that come under the scrutiny and surveillance of the dowsing fraternity and the thousands of amateur dowsers all over the world. Dowsing has been used in ghost hunting and at haunted locations, in archaeology, finding ancient burial grounds, treasure hunting and even in seeking the whereabouts of the Loch Ness Monster.

There is a lady, long resident near the shores of Loch Ness, who has become interested in the long search for the elusive monster. In common with many local people and those who have studied the evidence, she has no doubt that there is something in the loch that has given rise to all the reports over the years. I have heard of her useful activities in dowsing for 'Nessie' and her success in this and other fields, including work for the police on occasions, from two members of The Loch Ness Association of Explorers, but the lady in question is very much averse to publicity so I merely mention this private interest in passing and add that the idea of 'animal dowsing' for 'Nessie', 'Big Foot' and other yet to be located missing creatures is very much in the minds of British and American monster hunters. What a boost for dowsing if the divining rod or pendulum succeeds in locating these creatures where all modern methods of science have failed!

Robert Leftwich described to me many of his dowsing adventures in Britain, America and elsewhere. He told me about one occasion when he was approached by a big American concern who were engaged in industrial mining in the Middle East. When he heard this even Robert had doubts about his ability in view of the enormous areas involved – a rare thing, it must be said, for Robert was known for his supreme confidence, justified where his dowsing was concerned.

He thought it might prove to be very difficult to pinpoint accurately the best regions for mining and he explained to his prospective employers that while it should, in principle, be possible to dowse from the air, he had certainly had no experience of actually doing so, but he was quite prepared to take part in such a test if they thought it was likely to be worth while.

On a 'no result – no fee' basis he was flown out to the Middle East and a certain area was selected where there were no obvious geographical indications that could be regarded as giving him any clue as to the possible ore-bearing value of the terrain. A mountainous region was chosen in which, unknown to Robert, the company had already selected eight likely sites for exploration mining. When his report was eventually handed in and had been scrutinized, he was told that he had selected seven sites out of the eight pre-selected by the company and the site he had not selected later proved to be abortive. After that Robert Leftwich enjoyed a considerable reputation as a dowser in the Middle East and elsewhere, a reputation he thoroughly deserved and enjoyed.

During the course of a Ghost Club Annual Dinner speech Robert Leftwich referred to his conviction that many more people are gifted with potential powers that are at their command than is generally supposed but, due to the 'destructive influences of conventional life', these powers have become largely dormant but they can be revived and used as he had done with the ability to dowse, an ability which, he was certain, practically everyone had.

Leftwich went on to relate one of the most interesting finds he had ever had as a practising dowser. He had discovered some old buried walls located beneath the lawns of the garden of his home in Sussex and consultation with the deeds of the house indicated that there had probably been a building on the site as early as the sixteenth century.

Soon after Robert and his wife moved into the house, they began to hear stories of a ghostly 'white lady' who was reputed to walk down their garden periodically and, although they met a number of people who maintained that they had actually seen the ghost, the new occupants were not too concerned about the matter.

However, after a while, odd things began to happen inside the house. Mrs Leftwich would suddenly be aware that a hand was resting on one of her shoulders while she was working alone in the kitchen, perhaps at the sink or attending to something in the oven, and many times, when their two boys were much younger, both Robert and his wife would hear noisy disturbances from the upper part of their home. Thinking that the boys were up to some games Robert would set off upstairs to investigate but halfway up the stairs the noises always ceased and when Robert entered the boys' bedroom they were invariably found to be fast asleep.

Other disturbances included the distinct impression that something or somebody passed by Robert's open study door; there were innumerable instances when a peculiar aroma resembling rotten fish pervaded the kitchen, always followed by the presence of a cold vertical column of air that defied all normal physical laws by not being instantly dispersed by the surrounding warm air or the movement of objects.

One evening, Robert believed he located the exact position of the haunting entity in the kitchen with the help of his divining rods, and he put his rods on one side and boldly addressed the 'ghost'. He said that, while 'it' obviously had an older and possibly greater right to be there than he and his family, the house had now become their home and some of the present occupants and especially the children could not understand such activity and therefore if any future manifestations could be restricted to non-materialistic activity, it would be greatly appreciated.

In addition, and to prove to his satisfaction that 'it' had understood his request, Robert suggested that the entity should move a large oil painting that hung above the fireplace in the sitting room during the night and he would accept any change of position the following morning as an indication that all would be well in the future.

Next morning the elder son of the family was first up and he came running into his parents' bedroom exclaiming that burglars must have broken in during the night and the sitting room was in a terrible mess; he also mentioned that the large oil painting had been removed from its position over the fireplace and was on the floor on the other side of the room. Investigation proved that a considerable disturbance had indeed taken place in the sitting room and in addition to the movement of the oil painting a number of delicate porcelain ornaments had been removed from their places on the mantelpiece and lay broken on the floor.

After that incident the Leftwich family was only occasionally aware of an intangible force in the house, and they were certainly never again bothered to any serious degree. Once or twice Robert took his divining rod and went through the house from top to bottom but he could find no trace of the 'ghost' and he firmly believed that, with the help of his rods and a practical and positive approach, he had 'laid the ghost'.

Robert Leftwich ended his address to The Ghost Club on that occasion by reiterating his conviction that there were many people gifted with unusual powers and he added a warning that their development could be misused:

For example, apart from the location of subterranean matter, most competent dowsers also possess the ability to heal and this, together with an inner sense of orientation, enables them to 'tune in' and recover lost objects and if this ability is applied to the location of personally desired objects and backed by additional extra-sensory powers and extreme faith and confidence, the misuse of such a powerful combination can be very frightening indeed for most of our desires can then become reality . . . .

There are several interesting examples of ghosts being apparently located by the dowsing faculty in Tom Lethbridge's appropriately entitled *Ghosts and Divining Rod*.[1] In one incident, when he and his wife were waiting for the possible re-appearance of a ghost, they had both experienced a tingling sensation. Lethbridge, recalling that dowsers often experienced a similar sensation in their hands as they approached water, took his divining rod to the spot where the ghost had been seen. He found that a stream ran close by and vanished into the grass. He lost no time in tracing the course of the little stream with his divining rod and he found that it curved and passed directly below the spot where he had seen the ghost.[2]

So *water* seemed to be a possible element in ghost sighting . . . a tingling sensation suggested a field of force . . . . Can a stone somehow record the emotions of a person associated with that stone (as seems likely in view of recent theories and the occasional phenomenon of bricks from a haunted building used elsewhere resulting in the appearance of the ghost in the new vicinity of the bricks)? Lethbridge asked himself whether water too might not be able to retain human emotions, perhaps like a magnetic tape . . . . As a dowser he was sensitive to the force field of water, and might that be why he was able to pick up a recording that was invisible to others, he pondered.

Tom Lethbridge, much-travelled explorer, archaeologist and occult theorist, for thirty years Director of Excavations for the Cambridge Antiquarian Society and for the University Museum of Archaeology and Ethnology, seems to have developed into an expert dowser, and one fascinating example of his skill in the dowsing art is

[1] Routledge and Kegan Paul, 1963.
[2] See also Colin Wilson's *Mysteries* (Hodder and Stoughton, 1978).

quoted in his book, *Witches: Investigating an Ancient Religion.*[1]

During the course of investigating Viking graves on Lundy Island – an investigation that proved abortive – it was suggested that Tom Lethbridge, with his undoubted dowsing ability, should see whether he could find any buried volcanic dykes. Lethbridge readily agreed to try and insisted that he be blindfolded as an added precaution against his picking up any clues visually. He was led along the cliff tops and every now and then the divining twig in his hands would turn violently. Afterwards he learned that he had accurately located every one of the known buried volcanic dykes.

In a book published posthumously fourteeen years later, *The Power of the Pendulum,*[2] Tom Lethbridge (1901-1971) refers to the fact that, although he had known for many years that he could find hidden water movements and had even found a lost Anglo-Saxon cemetery by the dowsing method, he took no great interest in the subject until he and his wife Mina moved to Cornwall in 1957.

Soon they experienced a long summer drought resulting in insufficient water to drive the hydraulic ram. They had an alternative water supply but needed the ram to start, and clearing the spring outlets leading to it proved to be quite a problem since there was no plan of the whereabouts of these outlets and it looked as if they would have to search a 5 acre field.

Recalling his experiments in water divining years previously, Lethbridge cut himself some forked twigs of hazel wood and soon found four sources of water where there was absolutely no surface indications of the underground water, although pipes from two of the springs did run through a medieval fish pond – long dry.

His interest in dowsing thoroughly revived, Tom Lethbridge realized that the hazel twig, efficient as it undoubtedly could be, is hardly an instrument of precision, since you cannot discover within a hand's breadth where the movement takes place, and then he remembered something that he had read long ago. It was a

[1]Routledge and Kegan Paul, 1962.
[2]Routledge and Kegan Paul, 1976.

pamphlet by a French soldier, a brigadier, who claimed
to have located German mines in the sea during the First
World War with the aid of a pendulum. Lethbridge soon
made himself a pendulum and so began one more
adventure for this enterprising and original man. His
books, all of them, reflect a refreshingly open mind and
independence of thought and well repay study and
examination; furthermore, they are a pleasure to read.

In several of his books Tom Lethbridge explores the
possibility that there are various types of field forces
connected with water, woods, mountains, open spaces;
and he suggests that if this were so it would explain
many previously mysterious appearances, feelings, emotions and experiences. It may well be that the dowser
and the ghost hunter should walk hand in hand.

Dowsing has of course been used at haunted places for
many years but usually in association with some aspect
of the case other than the ghosts; for example, at Borley,
on the site of 'the most haunted house in England',
dowsing was employed in a search for the missing
church plate as long ago as 1947 – the year I first visited
Borley and spent a night on the allegedly haunted site.

The late rector of Borley-cum-Liston, the Reverend
Alfred Henning, told me about several attempts at
dowsing and divining that had taken place at Borley. A
local water diviner had spent a lot of time in the old
rectory garden looking for water and he had found a
curious reaction at a certain spot. Time and again he
found himself drawn to that particular place, yet he
knew from the reaction that he obtained, that it was not
subterranean water that attracted his twig and after
considerable testing and deliberation he told Mr Henning that he thought there might be treasure buried
there.

It was an opinion that interested the rector considerably, for some years previously he and his wife had
spent time in the same vicinity of the rectory ruins with
a dowser, searching for the lost church treasure which,
according to popular belief, was buried there. The reactions of the water diviner renewed the interest of the
Hennings in the possibility of locating this missing

treasure and they approached a friend, Mrs Parker of Long Melford, who made a speciality of dowsing for various metals, and she agreed to see whether she could obtain any interesting reaction with her divining rods.

After a while Mrs Parker became convinced that there was buried treasure somewhere in the old rectory garden. She was trying to find a water supply for Tom Gooch, who then owned the lower part of the property, when her stick acted very strangely and bent over with such force and in such a singular manner that both she and Tom Gooch could hardly force it up again. Mrs Parker was very puzzled by the curious reactions that she obtained and told Tom Gooch that such a definite movement could well indicate treasure.

In fact a great deal of digging was carried out at her suggestion in the rectory garden and eventually three workmen dug a hole 9 feet deep, but nothing was found. As a test, silver was hidden under the ploughed-up lawn, unknown to the diviner, who however immediately found it.[1] The digging continued and another large hole was dug beneath one of the old walnut trees in the garden but again nothing of interest was found. Oddly enough, soon after the hole had been filled in, a terrific storm in the area (the spire of nearby Foxearth church was just one casualty) tore down the walnut tree which fell exactly on the spot where the digging had taken place.

Alfred Henning was always very interested in every incident that took place at haunted Borley that might have a paranormal origin and he was fascinated by the 'strange behaviour of the hazel twig', as he put it.[2] During the period that Mrs Parker was exploring the rectory grounds, each evening as she finished for the day, she would place the twig in a tree on the site close to where digging was taking place, so that it was convenient and ready for the next day's work.

By this time Tom Gooch was building a bungalow for himself and his wife on the lower part of the old rectory

[1]Peter Underwood, 'The Borley Haunting, 1947-1952' (unpublished manuscript).

[2]See A. C. Henning, *Haunted Borley*(privately published, 1949).

he Tower Lieutenant's official residence. The missing Barkstead
reasure is likely to be buried somewhere nearby.

Opposite: The Tower of London where several dowsers have attempted
o locate hidden treasure.

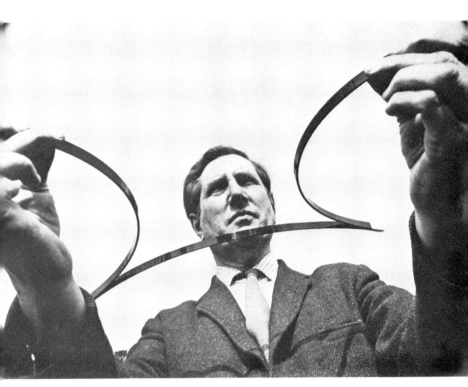
Mr Robert Leftwich.

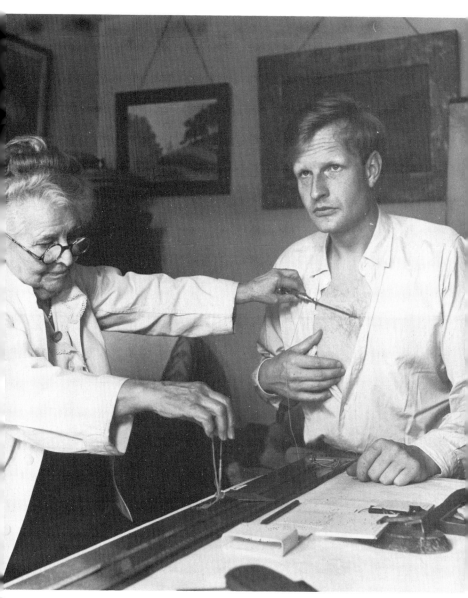

reating a patient by radiosthesia. (Radio Times Hulton Picture
ibrary).

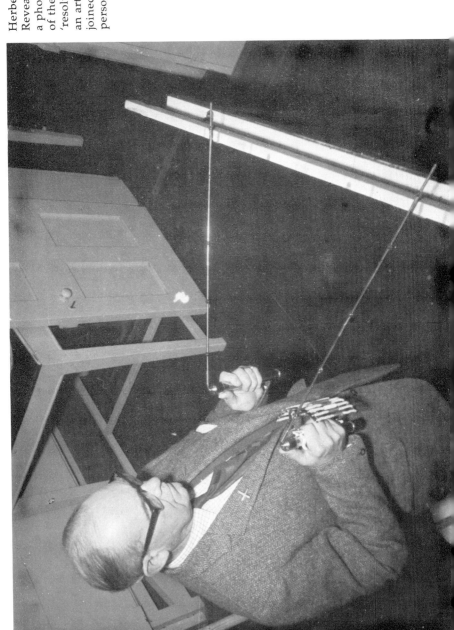

Herbert Weaver using the Revealer Field Detector; a photographic record of the first attempt at 'resolving the centre of an artificial ray-path joined to a missing person', 1967.

garden, a bungalow where they eventually lived for many years until they both died in the 1970s. In fact it was on Tom Gooch's land that the walnut tree stood where the digging was taking place at that particular time. One morning Tom Gooch found Mrs Parker's forked divining twig thrown down on the ground outside his house some little distance from the site of the haunted rectory. Thinking that some local boys might have come across the twig that was a divining rod and dropped it outside his house, Tom Gooch picked it up, walked up the road and restored it to its place in the tree. Next morning he was astonished to find the divining twig again in the road outside his house, only a yard from the spot where he had previously picked it up.

Years later there was more dowsing at Borley. During the course of research for his volume on haunted churches[1] Marc Alexander visited Borley church where a wealth of apparently paranormal activity had been reported over the years.[2]

In 1975, during the course of a BBC programme, Michael Bentine, the famous comedian and ex-Goon who has psychic powers and has always been interested in the paranormal, went to Borley and had a curious experience inside the church.

Viewers of the television programme saw Michael Bentine walk slowly up the nave of the church towards the massive Waldegrave tomb that dominates the church and suddenly he declared that the tomb seemed to be emitting an 'uncanny aura'. Michael stopped a few feet from the tomb, opposite the pulpit. His late father, Adam Bentine, also once visited Borley for purposes of investigation and sensed 'something' in this area. Michael felt that he was encountering something inexplicable and was on the edge of 'a zone of extreme coldness'. Moving backwards he found that he moved out of the 'cold spot' and into the normal temperature of the church. Stepping forward again, he apparently crossed the invisible div-

[1]Marc Alexander, *Haunted Churches and Abbeys of Britain* (Arthur Barker, 1978).
[2]Peter Underwood and Paul Tabori, *The Ghosts of Borley* (David and Charles, 1973).

iding line and found himself again inside the area of icy coldness. By means of experimentation, stepping backwards and forwards in a circular manner, he succeeded in establishing to his satisfaction the periphery or boundary of the strange, clinging coldness that seemed to permeate the area in the immediate vicinity of the oppressive Waldegrave monument, which many people believe may be the centre of much of the paranormal activity that has been experienced within this little church.

A Ghost Club member from Norwich tells me that when he was at Borley Michael Bentine talked with Tom Gooch's widow who had recently found a nun's rosary near the old main gate to Borley Rectory.[1] Michael seemed fascinated by the rosary and, exercising his gift of psychometry, he handled the object for some time and then told Mrs Gooch that he had the distinct impression that it dated from the seventeenth century. This is interesting in view of information obtained at various seances and by other psychometrists and the theorizing of Canon Phythian-Adams, which suggests that the ghost nun at Borley may have been murdered in 1667. My informant, an enthusiastic photographer, wanted to take a photograph of Mrs Gooch and the rosary but she declined; being of a somewhat superstitious nature she thought it might bring her bad luck. Mrs Gooch died in December 1976 and I have no knowledge of the present whereabouts of the rosary.

Mrs Gooch often talked about unexplained nocturnal diggings that took place in the old rectory garden and mysterious noises that were heard by her and by other local people when she lived at Borley, and she often wondered whether the missing church plate was in fact unearthed and recovered by some person or persons unknown, possibly acting on the reactions that dowsers have obtained in the vicinity.

Another area that might usefully be explored at Borley by those with dowsing ability is the search for the

[1]Useful plans of Borley Rectory site and of Borley church are included in my volume *Hauntings, New Light on the Greatest True Ghost Stories of the World* (Dent, 1977).

church crypt. I well recall Miss Ethel Bull, one of the daughters of the Reverend H. D. E. Bull who built Borley Rectory, telling me that she knew nothing of a crypt at Borley – a statement that is at variance with that attributed to her by Harry Price, who said she told him of coffins in the crypt having been unaccountably moved and also later evidence which suggests that she may have been down the crypt herself. But where is the entrance? Could the answer to some of the mysteries at Borley reside within the elusive crypt? Perhaps an efficient dowser could establish whether or not there is a crypt at Borley, and if so where the entrance might be. I have often wondered whether it is in the vicinity of the Waldegrave tomb . . . .

When Marc Alexander went to Borley in August 1977 – the last visit he made to a church in connection with his book on haunted churches – he took with him Cheryl Carter, a young lady with powers of a medium who had no knowledge of the ghostly associations of Borley Church. Marc Alexander's main purpose was to take some photographs of the interior of the church for his book and as he was setting up his camera Cheryl, who had followed him into the church, suddenly exclaimed, 'I'm sorry but I can't stay here. There are negative forces coming from that tomb . . . it's so overpowering that I must get outside . . . .' The tomb she indicated was the Waldegrave monument.

Alone inside the church Marc Alexander approached the enormous tomb that seems massively out of propor-tion in the tiny church. He was not conscious of Michael Bentine's 'cold zone' or Cheryl's 'negative force' but then he does not profess to have any psychic powers or to be particularly sensitive to psychic atmospheres. But it occurred to him that there was one way in which he might test the reactions of many people to this tomb.

Some time before his visit to Borley a water board inspector had used a pair of copper angle-rods to locate a broken pipe at Marc's Cumbrian home and, when he had expressed interest in the faculty, the inspector had readily instructed him in the rudiments of the art of dowsing. In fact, Marc Alexander had become quite proficient with the rods in finding water and he carried them about with him in his car. Now, he thought, he would see whether he obtained any reaction to a very different kind of force.

With the rods held lightly in either hand he approached the Waldegrave tomb; he held the rods some 18 inches apart and pointed them directly in front of him. I cannot do better than quote from his published account of the incident.

I continued to walk slowly until I was about four feet from it [the tomb] when I felt the rods twist in my hands and the two pointers swing inwards and touch as they do when a 'find' has been made. There was no doubt about it, there was *something* at that spot which had activated the copper. Normally the rods swing slowly towards one another as one approaches underground water, but in this case they literally jumped together as though they had struck a sharply defined margin of influence. I stepped back and the rods swung apart. I stepped forward and they immediately made contact.

By moving round the memorial tomb and stepping backwards and forwards I found that the area of influence surrounded the monument like an invisible square.[1] I must confess that this experiment delighted me although, as with so many other symptoms of unseen forces, it did nothing to explain what it was that emanated from the monument. All I can say is that to my own satisfaction I proved that there was something outside our ordinary experience there.

When I described my dowsing experience at Borley to Colin Wilson, he immediately declared: 'I'd like to bet that that monument lies on the intersection of two ley lines!' To illustrate the point he took me to a megalith on the edge of a cliff close to his home in Cornwall, explaining that he believed it stands where ley lines cross. He then approached it with his own dowsing instrument, which consisted of two pieces of whalebone bound together at one end so that they resembled the letter Y. When he was close to the ancient stone the stem of the Y twisted upwards despite the obvious strength he was using to hold it straight. When held so that it almost touched the surface of the megalith the whalebone appeared to take on a will of its own as it writhed in his hands .... Many people

[1] Of course he could only circumnavigate two sides of the tomb as the monument is set into the corner of the north wall of the church.

believe that ley lines are old straight tracks of ancient Britain
which follow so-called 'magnetic' lines of force within the
earth's surface ... and it is an interesting conjecture that
Borley Church may well stand at a junction of ley lines and
the mysterious force which they channel could be the catalyst
which heightens the psychic activity there.[1]

Adventures in dowsing and divining by proficient
exponents of the art are virtually limitless; from the past
with people like Evelyn Penrose[2] who was employed by
the Government of British Columbia in 1931 as an official
water and mineral diviner and whose success rate in
finding water, copper, silver, lead, gold and oil was
calculated to be above 90 per cent, and Henry Gross and
his discovery of Bermuda's first natural wells[3] to present
day dowsers such as Mr Leslie Palmer of Plymouth. I
wrote to Mr Palmer at the kind suggestion of the South
West Water Authority and I quote his reply in full:

Thinking that perhaps you will receive plenty of information on the more usual aspects of dowsing and divining, I will
confine what I have to say to something rather different . . . .

Some time ago an accident at work resulted in my sustaining
a broken ankle, fractured in three places while under extreme
tension ... the general opinion of the doctors being that I had
made a real job of it!

When the plaster came off for the last time, the ankle had
'seized up' and was very swollen and painful. My doctor
arranged for me to attend Plymouth's Physiotherapy Department in Dale Road where I was put into the capable hands of
Miss R. Hackworthy, a brilliant young lady who exuded
professionalism and confidence. Some of the manipulatory
treatment tended to be rather painful and Miss Hackworthy
encouraged me to talk about any subject I chose, to help to
take my mind off the work she had to do.

Early on in the eighty or so sessions of treatment I received,
I talked about water divining. This happened to be in the
March of the year of the great drought. By the end of August
I was able to walk on level surfaces and with the aid of a stick

[1]Marc Alexander, *Haunted Churches and Abbeys of Britain* (Arthur Barker,
1978).
[2]See E. M. Penrose, *Adventure Unlimited* (London, 1958).
[3]See Kenneth Roberts, *Henry Gross and his Dowsing Rod* (Doubleday, New
York, 1952).

I could just about manage to walk on the roadway; other than this it was a pretty painful business to move.

It was during my last treatment that my young physiotherapist suddenly put me 'on the spot'. She told me that a natural spring supplying the reservoir that watered a dairy herd and was also used for domestic purposes had dried up – could I help her friends since I was a dowser . . . .

When she said that she would be present herself, to see that I didn't undo all the good work she had done on my ankle, I somewhat reluctantly agreed. Frankly I was very frightened of damaging my ankle again and I knew that the walking involved would be a painful business.

On the appointed day we met at the farmer's residence and he took all of us to the site in his ancient Land-Rover. As soon as we had walked down to our first site the heavens opened and the rain poured down in torrents. Nevertheless within a few minutes I had 'found' water; and then of course, as always happens, everyone present wanted to try their hand at dowsing. So there we were: three men divining for water while the ladies did their best to keep us dry with umbrellas. The farmer's sister and her husband were staying at the farm on holiday and he proved to be an excellent dowser, with very little help from me. And then the rain stopped.

From then on we worked as a team, tracing parallel streams, getting the directions of flow and so on. Miss Hackworthy kept a professional eye on me and carried my walking stick when I was not using it while the others supplied the divining twigs and saw to the markers. Finding water was no problem but deciding which was the best source was more difficult. Another problem soon became apparent: the area is potentially rich in various minerals and these can easily be wrongly identified as water by the inexperienced. Realizing how plentiful the potential water sources were, the farmer said he would prefer a gravity feed if we could find a suitable source.

We decided to follow two strong streams uphill to the plateaux some way above. This meant climbing through a natural forest with an incline like a railway embankment – and of course it was littered with rotting wood and loose shale and this had to be traversed for about half a mile.

We eventually succeeded in climbing up and everyone was feeling very pleased with themselves; but what about my ankle, you may be asking; well my ankle is the real reason for relating this true experience. Immediately I found water, all the pain and stiffness in my damaged ankle completely vanished! Not only did this last all the time I worked with the divining rods but there were no ill effects from all the tough exercise. I am not saying that it was a cure but it is a fact that for me the act of divining never fails to bring me relief from pain.

This particular water seeking session being over, Miss Hackworthy's fertile and enquiring mind suggested that we try a few experiments. Feeling far better than I had expected, I set to work and soon found a weak response spot in the lane. I kept the 'sticks' responding while she tried unsuccessfully to interrupt the response by using heavy and large rubber car mats. Then we tried again while I used copper rods and again the mats made no difference at all and it is quite clear that it does not matter whether I am bare-footed or wear rubber boots, as far as divining is concerned. But dowsing and divining is a fascinating subject and practically all comments and statements concerning it are subject to challenge and qualification. In my experience, given elementary tuition, about two in ten people can dowse to some degree (including very small children); some do it better than others certainly, and some do it better with sticks or twigs, others with L-rods or angle irons, a few with a single stick or wand; some people are equally good with both the traditional divining twig and angle irons.

The conventional dowsing twigs, when held some ten to fifteen degrees above horizontal will rise on 'contact' and can give a nasty smack on the nose or mouth; likewise when held ten to fifteen degrees below the horizontal it will descend and can prove painful and embarrassing unless you walk with your knees rubbing, or wear a heavy raincoat – or a sporran!

Dowsing rods, on the other hand, are held at shoulder width, about body width apart, and they cross on 'contact' (horizontally) and there is no danger to one's person.

Anyone can try divining at home. It is an easy matter to arrange for someone to place some ten-pence pieces under the carpet and let you find them. Or you can trace power cables under the bedroom floor, or the mains cable, or water mains, where they enter the house – there is no end to experiments that can be traced without any expense and no preparation. I prefer to use sticks to find anything and then rods to give me the final 'spot on' analysis.

It really doesn't seem to matter very much what variety of bush or tree you obtain the divining stick from; personally I prefer hazel, withy or poplar as they are smooth-skinned and less likely to blister or skin the user's palms and fingers. For rods I use ten millimetre copper tubing: it's handy, very light, the right size (for me anyway) and it fits the hand comfortably. Rub any rods with your bare hands and swish them a few times immediately before use on each occasion.

I get more 'feel' from wooden rods although it is far more tiring to use them because divining can be very tiring. Most theorists say we receive something through the rods: I believe we 'give out' something because contacts are so debilitating. It is hard to explain but to a woman its probably something like the physical feeling immediately after the birth of her baby; to a man, perhaps endeavouring to emulate Casanova three times in an hour! It is not ordinary fatigue or tiredness, but a general sapping of something – a vital something – from the body. Recuperating, I have worked out, is of the order of about four to one: four hours rest for every hour of divining. Fatigue can be tolerated for about three hours, after which rest and nourishment becomes a necessity.

Incidentally, I cannot catch fish . . . I have only caught two in the whole of my life: both brown trout on the same fishing trip on the Hudson River in the United States years ago. I've spent hours trying to fish. At Gibraltar I have seen brit or whitebait come to within an inch or two of my bait, hesitate and then immediately dash across and take my neighbour's bait! Yet on occasions it has been his rod and line that I am borrowing and he has baited it with his own bait – and I was fishing under his tuition.

I have noticed that I generate a lot of static electricity and frequently I give little shudders which I have always assumed mark the discharge of the really considerable amount of electricity generated; my short, cropped hair attracts dust like a vacuum cleaner. I think that this static probably has something to do with divining as I have noticed that after driving a car for some hours I don't get good dowsing results for half an hour or so.

I also believe that divining and so-called faith healing have a very close affinity. In other words I believe it to be the same gift with a different application. To this end I was extremely disappointed that Miss Hackworthy could not 'divine' water.

If you find that you *are* a dowser, then try this harmless little bit of fun – all in the cause of science, of course . . . . Find a spot of high response and persuade your partner to stand on it. Moisten your lips and give him, or her, the gentlest of gentle kisses. Be prepared for him, or her, to swoon at your feet. If it doesn't work, reverse the situation. Scientific experiments can be so exciting sometimes and the results so satisfying . . . .

In 1975 I took a leading part in the BBC television documentary 'The Ghost Hunters', screened in December 1975 and subsequently for three succeeding Christmases. Also in the programme Andrew M. Green of Robertsbridge, Sussex, talked about a skeleton underneath the flooring of his 'haunted home' – a skeleton that had been located by 'a water diviner'.

Viewers were told that some months previously, when a water diviner had been at the cottage, Andrew had asked him whether he could find bones and the diviner had said that he could, providing he had a bone to work with, so he was given a cat's jawbone that had been dug up in the garden(!) and the diviner went all over the cottage and Andrew stated on the programme that he saw the hazel twig vibrate at a certain spot and the diviner said, ' You've got a six-foot body along there under the floor . . . .' Since then, Andrew said, about twenty-seven people had fainted at that spot.

During the course of knocking down a baking oven Andrew found a carving knife and during the broadcast he remarked that two or three people had told him that the knife was 'a murder weapon that had killed somebody there . . . .' The diviner had no doubt about there being a body under the flooring and even indicated the location of the head and feet.

When I came to research this book I thought it would be rather interesting to look a little closer into this story and I telephoned Andrew and he promised to let me have the name and address of the diviner and a full account of the incident, but instead he wrote to say, 'I would point out that there is not a shred of evidence to support the belief of the dowser involved and any suggestion that the skeleton, if any exists, might be human is completely unfounded.'

I must confess to being a little puzzled by the latter observation since Andrew goes on to say, 'a complete exploration of the foundations of the area might prove positive or negative'; however I can appreciate the situation when he adds that the present owner of the house could hardly be expected to dig through several inches of concrete to find out whether or not a skeleton is buried beneath his flooring.

Many seemingly fascinating stories of dowsing claims and alleged hauntings prove on the very slightest investigation to be very different from what they appear to be at first sight and this story, so graphically related on the television screen, seems to be no exception. But there are also many equally curious and well-authenticated instances of dowsing ability in widely different circumstances and involving all sorts of people in varying walks of life that must convince any open-minded person that some truly remarkable and very strange adventures in dowsing and divining do exist that defy normal explanation in the light of our present knowledge.

11. Dowsing Tests and their Problems

Some years ago a Dutch geologist set out to expose water divining as a fraud but after ten years of study Professor Solco W. Tromp became convinced that there was something in the subject and said, 'while we may not completely understand the mechanics of the matter' – a slight understatement, I would think – 'the plain fact is that it works'.

His lengthy report[1] contained three basic conclusions: the existence of a human sensitivity to underground water can be demonstrated by experiments; most people have this sensitivity developed to some degree; and the sensitivity can be explained scientifically without invoking 'second sight'. His experiments, he said, would prove his claims if they were confirmed by other workers in the field undertaking the same experiments.

During the course of his experiments Professor Tromp took a professional diviner, blindfolded him, and plugged his ears with cotton wool. He then led the diviner towards an electric apparatus while the man was holding his divining twig in a working position. When enough current was switched on to set up a weak magnetic field, the tip of the diviner's twig jerked sharply downwards. This suggested to Professor Tromp that the diviner had some hitherto unrecorded sensitivity.

The professor then proceeded to carry out tests with other diviners, using bent wires instead of the traditional twigs, and these showed that the diviners could also

[1] *Psychical Physics* (Elsevier, Houston, 1949).

detect minute changes in the strength of the magnetic field around them. Professor Tromp also claimed that similar results were obtained when minute electric currents were applied to a diviner's skin, and he went on to produce charts, made by a portable heart-beat recorder, of a diviner's reactions when passing over underground water, showing that the human body unconsciously detects some sensation whether a divining rod is carried or not.

Professor Tromp came to the conclusion that some physical force related to the presence of water influences the body through the skin and this in turn affects the nervous system which, in turn again, makes the muscles twitch and results in the movement of the divining rod.

The rod, he thought, serves to magnify this movement and puts the forearm muscles under tension. Professor Tromp regarded the human skin as the most likely detector because a diviner's sensitivity seems to depend on the electrical resistance of his skin. Any diviner, he claimed, could increase his sensitivity by rinsing his hands in salt water or weak sulphuric acid before attempting to dowse.

The diviners he tested did better in his tests when their skin was well insulated from the soil by thick-soled boots and they put up a poor show when they were tested barefoot. This latter fact presents problems when the dowsing ability is compared with the curious detecting sense proved to be present in some dogs. At one time the British War Office conducted tests that proved beyond any doubt that dogs can detect hidden land-mines by some mysterious means which does not involve sight, sound or scent . . . so perhaps it would be as well to conduct any tests on human dowsers and diviners with complete disregard of the undoubted and little understood faculties of our canine friends.

The results of an interesting series of tests appeared a few years ago in the *New Zealand Journal of Science and Technology*. A series of seventy-five divining tests were conducted under the auspices of Mr P. A. Ongley, each diviner being tested according to his claims. Of the diviners claiming to be able to find water (fifty-eight) not one showed in the tests a result that was significantly better than chance.

The results of the tests carried out on the remaining diviners showed no better achievements and Ongley concluded, perhaps a little hastily and unfairly, that 'divining reactions are due not to earthly radiations but to suggestion'.[1] He might, I think, have mentioned the difficulty of conducting dowsing tests in such a way that every possible aspect of the subject is taken into account. It is a difficulty that many investigators have encountered and not a few have sought to overcome.

Interesting laboratory experiments in dowsing have included those conducted by Paul Williamson and detailed in *Water Witching U.S.A.*[2] A consulting geologist who specialized in finding oil, Williamson originated a test for oil diviners (or 'doodlebuggers' as they are known in America) which consisted of ten cigar boxes, each filled with sand but one box also containing a bottle of oil.

Since the oil diviners claim they can locate oil hundreds of feet below ground Williamson argued that they should have no difficulty in finding the box containing the oil. Each diviner was given ten opportunities to find the box containing the oil with the cigar boxes being shuffled after each attempt. With correct shuffling the diviner's chance of finding the oil was one in ten and therefore in the complete experiment of ten runs, the chance expectation was one correct out of the whole trial.

The highest score obtained out of the whole fifty diviners was three. It has to be realized that rare events do occur and given sufficient opportunity they will occur; over fifty runs of ten trials one would have to expect three or four diviners to get a score of three or more correct. So, again in Williamson's tests, the diviners did not do more than might be expected by chance and

[1] New Zealand Diviners, *New Zealand Journal of Science and Technology*, volume 30, pp. 30-54.
[2] Evon Z. Vogt and Ray Hyman (University of Chicago Press, 1959).

the dowsing faculty has still to be proved to the satisfaction of scientists.

It cannot be over-emphasized that this simple fact must always be remembered when carrying out any scientific test, especially those that involve human beings. *If sufficient opportunity is given for a rare event to take place, it will eventually occur.* However stringent the conditions and however difficult the circumstances, if a sufficient number of tests are carried out, the unlikeliest occurrence will ultimately occur; and unfortunately it is human nature to neglect the large number of unsuccessful or common results and emphasize out of all proportion the rare but statistically normal result.

For example, if you or I were to run 50,000 tests and one is 100 per cent accurate, that is the one we would remember and quote but the odds may well show that such a result is by that time overdue, and in fact is only to be expected, and has no significance whatever. Human nature being what it is, such a result will always be remembered by the person taking the test and by the person supervising it, with possibly unfortunate results years later when the full details of the whole test are forgotten. On the other hand, well thought out investigation and carefully controlled tests are never a waste of time.

As early as the beginning of this century Sir William Barrett had acquired some interesting facts about dowsers and dowsing that hold good to this day. He found that early dowsers tended to think the answer to their gift or instinct was electricity – then little understood and often used to account for any mysterious occurrence, but Barrett shrewdly noticed:

If the dowser knows that he himself or his forked twig is insulated from the ground, it is true the rod will not work, but if he *doesn't* know it, although good insulation has secretly been effected, the rod works as well as ever, and *vice versa*. Precisely the same effect of suggestion occurs if the dowser be tried with radio-active substances and is disposed to believe that is the cause, or if he believes the rod moves upwards for approaching underground water and downwards on receding from it, or if it turns for minerals when he holds a piece of ore in his hand, or for water if he holds a wet rag, or just the reverse of this, as is actually the case in some parts. All these are well-known effects of suggestion, and the dowser is a very suggestible subject.

The explanation, I believe, is not physical but *psychical*. All the evidence points to the fact that the good dowser subconsciously possesses the faculty of clairvoyance, a supersensuous perceptive power ... this gives rise to an instinctive, but not conscious, detection of the hidden objects for which he is in search. This obscure and hitherto unrecognized human faculty reveals itself by creating an automatic or involuntary muscular spasm that twists the forked rod. Sometimes it produces a curious *malaise* or transient discomfort, which furnishes some dowsers with a sufficient indication to enable them to dispense with the use of a forked twig, or loop of wire, used by some.

This hypothesis I have put to the test of experiment with a good amateur dowser and found he really possessed this kind of second sight. If so dowsers ought to be able to find other hidden things, besides water and minerals, and this is the case. Long ago the divining rod was used in the search for buried treasure and hidden coins, and although we may smile at such credulity, nevertheless there is in recent times good evidence of the dowser John Mullins repeatedly finding carefully hidden coins.

With two amateur dowsers, Mr J. F. Young and Miss Miles, I have made numerous experiments to ascertain their powers in this respect. The experiments were in all cases arranged so as to exclude the possibility of their gaining any knowledge, from unconscious indications given by myself, of the position of the coins, hidden in their absence. To get rid of possible telepathy was more difficult; the person who alone knew where the coin was hidden was excluded from the room and unaware when the trial was begun; this made no difference in the results, which, though not invariably successful, were far beyond any success that could be achieved by mere chance.

There is therefore, very strong presumptive evidence that a good dowser is one who possesses a supernormal perceptive power, seeing as it were without eyes. Like other supernormal faculties it resides in the subliminal self and usually reveals itself through some involuntary muscular action. Possibly a like faculty of discernment beyond the power of vision may exist in certain animals and birds, and afford an explanation of the mystery of many otherwise inexplicable cases of homing and migratory instincts.[1]

[1]W. F. Barrett, *Psychical Research* (Williams and Norgate, 1911).

Presumptive evidence in the early days of this century is one thing, practical and statistical evidence that would be acceptable to science today is a very different matter.

To obtain scientific evidence for dowsing it is necessary to institute a method of testing that involves not only a dowser – or preferably a score of dowsers – but also a similar number of non-dowsers, and then compare the findings. It is also necessary to discover whether a professional geologist or hydrologist can obtain a similar result by simple observation and experience, based on the geology of the area and the likely places where water will be found, for it seems highly probable that some dowsers, if not all, rely on geological observation, either consciously or unconsciously.

For a scientific laboratory test, therefore, it would be desirable, even necessary, so to construct a completely level and plain platform that it is divided into identical small squares, and hidden and unknown to any of those taking part in the experiment would be identical containers under each square, some containing water and some empty (the selection being decided by a system of random selection) resulting in an arrangement of a fifty-fifty chance throughout.

After the dowsers have made their reports, a similar number of non-dowsers should also take the test and, if the dowsers were able to show a substantial and consistent higher-than-average result and the non-dowsers no more than chance expectation, then science would be justified in looking further into the subject, but it has to be said that to date all scientific and semi-scientific experiments into the alleged dowsing faculty have resulted – for whatever reason – in not establishing the claims of the dowsing fraternity.

An excellent example of a scientific field test – in fact probably the only one where an adequate number of test wells were sunk – was instituted by the American Society for Psychical Research in 1949 in the state of Maine, where a reasonably satisfactory tract of land was selected after careful scrutiny, consideration and research. The tests took place in the month of August when relative drought ensured the absence of any surface water.[1]

The test area, a field, was finally chosen because it represented a complete absence of any surface clues to the presence or otherwise of underground water, such as dampness. Each dowser who was included in the experiment (there were twenty-seven in all) spent as long as he liked in the field and gave his verdict; then he selected the best place to sink a well and stated his opinion as to the depth at which water would be found and the approximate volume of water. He then repeated the procedure blindfolded. Two professional people, a geologist and a water engineer, also took their time, independently, to inspect the area and also made estimates of the depth and rate of flow of underground water at sixteen points in the field, both relying on normal and known facts about subterranean water.

Test wells were sunk at each of the places designated by the dowsers and by the experts and the depth and amount of water measured. The end product showed that the experts had achieved good results in estimating the depth of water at specific points and the total amount of water but neither did well in their assessment of the amount of water to be found at specific points, although the engineer was quite close to the estimated total rate of flow.

The dowsers completely failed in their estimates of depth and amounts of water to be found, both collectively and individually, and the Society's report states: 'Not one of our diviners could for any moment be mistaken for an expert ... we saw nothing to challenge the prevailing view that we are dealing with unconscious muscular activity ....'

Colonel A. H. Bell, then president of the British Society of Dowsers, commented on this report in the British Society for Psychical Research *Journal* (volume 36, number 664). He pointed out that there are numerous cases on record where the dowser has located underground water in an area where a geologist has failed to do so. He went on to criticize the site selected for the test which

[1] L. A. Dale *et al.* 'Dowsing: A Field Experiment in Water Divining', *Journal of the American SPR*, vol. 45, 1951.

was 'practically waterlogged' and in such conditions a geologist would be *certain* of finding water. It was not apparent that any of the twenty-seven dowsers were possessed of dowsing skill and experience, the organizers had not allowed them to work freely – they were blindfolded and manhandled. Colonel Bell ends his letter by saying: 'This test adds one more to a list of many others carried out by uninformed experimenters under unsuitable conditions and from a scientific point of view is misleading and quite without value.'

On the national BBC television programme 'Pebble Mill', on Thursday, 8 March 1979, two scientists and a number of lay people showed reactions when they walked over the ground at the rear of the television studios holding divining rods. One of the scientists, Tom Williamson, admitted that there exist other devices for discovering water wells and mineral deposits but suggested that the use of the dowsing stick or divining rod could provide a cheap way of doing the same thing.

The problem now was to prove beyond any doubt that dowsing could produce results. This would entail exhaustive tests over a measured plot of ground with those taking part not seeing each other or being aware of other reactions. It was important that the tests should be independent and carefully controlled and analysed. Tom Williamson, incidentally, became a dowser himself after his father taught him to recognize the reactions. His father had been a full-time dowser and had repeatedly found water for farmers in East Africa.

A fascinating and scientific exploration of a dowser's faculties was most carefully and thoroughly carried out by a member of the British Society for Psychical Research in 1958, and to Denys Parsons I will leave the last word on this difficult and demanding, but absorbing and worthwhile, subject of dowsing tests. In doing so I gratefully acknowledge the generous permission of Denys Parsons and the Society in granting me permission to reproduce this article from the Society's *Journal* dated March 1959, volume 40, number 669:

EXAMINATION OF A DOWSER

by Denys Parsons

Mr D. claims to be able to detect the course of underground fuel pipelines and to locate static underground fuel deposits, to find buried metals, archaeological remains and coins, and so on. I arranged to see him on the afternoon of 22 March 1958, at my home. He is a quiet earnest Canadian, who works for an engineering contractor, but he is not himself qualified.

His apparatus consists of steel rods of diameter one-sixteenth to one-quarter of an inch, coated with kraft paper. Such rods or lengths of wire are available commercially in the paper-coated form and some are of brass, some of copper and some of steel. Mr D. bends these rods to an L-shape about eighteen inches by five inches for the thicker ones, and ten inches by four inches for the thinnest. He uses them in pairs.

Detection of oil: Mr D. had brought some small bottles of mineral oil with him and proceeded to show me his method for detecting underground oil. He placed a small cylindrical aluminium canister containing oil on the floor. Then he took a pair of his L-shaped rods, and starting about three yards away from the container, he walked slowly towards it and over it. The rods were held lightly in his hands, which were stretched forward in front of him. The short side or handle of the L was supported vertically, at its upper end by the distal joints of his first and second fingers, and at its lower end by the fleshy part of his palm below the base of the little finger. As his body moved directly over the canister of oil the rods, which until that moment had been pointing away from him, parallel to each other, swung inwards so that they crossed at about the mid-points, then swung further, so that the rod in his left hand pointed towards his right hand and *vice versa*. Mr D. illustrated this effect several times and then invited me to try it. I obtained no reaction, the rods remaining parallel. I noticed, however, that the slightest muscular movement was sufficient to cause the rods to swing.

Mr D. then indicated a pair of slippers and suggested that I should put a drop of oil on the sole of one slipper and he would tell me which was the treated slipper. I retired behind a curtain and drew a coin from my pocket, having first decided that tails meant left and heads meant right. The coin showed tails, so I put the drop of oil on the sole of the left slipper. I then put the two slippers a yard apart on the floor and Mr D. proceeded to walk over them with his rods repeating the walk two or three times over each. He obtained no reaction from the left slipper, and a positive reaction from the right slipper, which he indicated must be the one with the oil on it. I then showed him that the oil was on the left slipper. Mr D. was puzzled: he replaced the slippers and walked over them again with his parallel rods; this time he got the reaction from the left slipper.

In fairness to Mr D. I pointed out that since I used these slippers for various activities they might possibly have become contaminated with oil. Mr D. expressed the wish to repeat the test with a pair of rubber boots which were handy, so I suggested that we should first make sure these had a negative reaction before we put oil on one of them. We confirmed that neither boot gave a reaction. I then retired again behind a curtain and allowed the draw of a coin to decide that the oil would be on the left boot. Once more Mr D. got a reaction from the right boot. This puzzled him still further and he suggested we should take the boots out into the garden. He now got a reaction only from the left boot; i.e. that which he knew to have a drop of oil on the sole.

Detection of buried objects: At Mr D.'s request, I had before his arrival buried a few inches below the surface in the garden, the following objects: two small glass bottles of mineral oil, two boxes of coins, a steel chisel and a steel trowel. One member of each of these pairs of objects was buried for me by a third party to ensure that I did not know their location. In addition I buried a gold ring. The locations of the four objects I myself had buried were chosen by a random method, (by supposing the garden to be divided up into square areas and by tossing a coin to narrow the choice down to a given square). When an object was buried in a flower-bed care was taken to disturb the soil over the whole area of the bed.

The method used by Mr D. for the location of hidden objects was as follows: He placed one of a pair of rods on the ground at some arbitrary point, he then retreated to a distance of about twenty yards and walked down the garden carrying the other rod of the pair outstretched before him, and keeping the grounded rod to his right or left. Sometimes in the course of this manoeuvre, the rod he was holding would swing over to one side to point at the grounded rod; Mr D. would then say that the buried object lay on a line between himself and the grounded rod; he would then proceed to narrow this down by walking along this line with both rods, or sometimes taking another pair or rods, and finding the spot at which the rods crossed in the usual way. In this manner Mr D. indicated successively four incorrect sites at the top end of the garden, where the steel trowel and the gold ring happened to be buried, known to myself. I had to dig at the sites indicated by Mr D. as I did not know the location of three of the other objects, although I knew they were buried not more than two inches below the surface.

I then conducted Mr D. to the bottom end of the garden and told him that at least two objects were buried there. Mr D. could not get any firm reaction until I told him that a box of coins was buried at the right end of a certain flower bed. He then obtained a reaction on a spot five feet to the left of the correct one, but he obtained a reaction over the coins when I pointed out the exact spot.

Mr D. by this time was coming to the conclusion that the wire fences surrounding the garden were interfering with his detection methods. (But it must be pointed out that his preliminary successful demonstrations with the canister of oil did not appear to be interfered with by two cast iron radiators within a few feet.)

Attempts to locate the gold ring: I took Mr D. back to the top of the garden and told him that a gold ring was buried along a certain line. He did not seem able to get any firm reactions, so I narrowed it down to a space of about four yards, but the site finally indicated was over a yard away from the correct one. Mr D. indicated possible interference from the lead fountain of the fishpond nearby. (But the same lead fountain caused no interference with the detection reaction when the rubber boots were taken into that part of the garden.)

Other demonstrations: Mr D. then said that an empty glass could be placed next to an oil canister and would not inhibit a positive reaction from the oil, but if the glass was full of water the reaction would be inhibited. He proceeded to demonstrate that this was true by walking over a canister and adjacent glass which was either full or empty of water. I then asked what would happen if we covered the canister and glass with a cardboard box so that he could not see the state of affairs. He readily agreed to this condition, and turned his back while I arranged the oil canister next to a full glass of water and covered both vessels with a cardboard box. Mr D. walked over the box and obtained no reaction, this being the correct response. He then turned his back again and I substituted an empty glass for the full one, and replaced the cardboard box. This time he obtained no reaction where he should have obtained a reaction, and it puzzled him greatly.

The oil canister had, by the time we came to do this test, been wrapped up in brown paper in preparation for his departure. Mr D. removed the brown paper and showed that he now obtained the correct reaction. He attributed his previous failure somewhat hesitantly to the presence of the brown paper wrapping.

Mr D. took a 4-foot galvanized water pipe and showed that he got no reaction when walking over it with a pair of copper-coated rods, and that his lightest rods, steel ones, would not react to the metal pipe, unless a drop of oil was put on the pipe. I did not make any tests upon this effect.

Elimination of unconscious muscular action: At the outset, Mr D. had emphasized that the rods swung of their own accord and that he exerted no force on them. This is very commonly claimed by diviners, but it is not a claim which can be substantiated. I produced two short cardboard tubes which made convenient sleeves for his rods, and asked him to hold the sleeves with the rods free to turn within them, and to walk over the oil canister in the usual way. I did not say what result I expected. There was no reaction, and the inference could be drawn that all the movements of the rods when held directly in the hands, were produced by unconscious muscular action.

Discussion: Mr D. was puzzled and depressed at the general failure of almost all the tests during the afternoon, although he said I had only seen a fraction of what he was able to do in other circumstances; he said that the wire fences and lead fountain had constituted interfering factors and that he had seldom known the tests with the oil on the shoes to fail. (The odds, of course, are evens.)

It is of some interest to enquire why diviners are commonly so successful on occasions other than the occasion of tests by an experienced investigator. The failure of scientific tests is so common that it has led to the belief on the part of many diviners that scientific investigators give off 'hostile radiations' which inhibit the reactions. (It is to Mr D.'s great credit that he at no time complained that my tests were unfair.) The apparent success of demonstrations to an audience of laymen is due to the layman's ignorance of the pitfalls. First of all he is probably conditioned to an acceptance of the phenomena by an erroneous belief that *water*-divining is a well-established fact. He is inclined to accept the assurance of the diviner that he is not exerting any force on the rods because he has not heard of unconscious muscular action, and because the diviner is obviously sincere. Moreover the diviner will be unlucky if he cannot find at least one member of his audience who is able to get the same reactions as he does, and this, for most people, clinches the genuineness of the diviner's claims.

A diviner may make unconscious use of sensory clues. If a person has hidden an object it is not easy for him to conceal that knowledge, and he may give information away in various ways; either by careless or involuntary glances towards the hiding place, by a studied avoidance of looking at or walking near the hiding place, by an almost imperceptible change of breathing when the diviner is 'getting warm', and so on. Experiments conducted by S. G. Soal with the medium 'Fred Marion', who was very sensitive to such sensory clues, showed that if the medium could see even only one-fifth of the body area (not necessarily the head) of the person who had hidden the object, he could obtain enough information to locate the hiding-place.[1] Hence the advisability of having a number of objects hidden by an assistant who will not be present during the experiment.

Another source of inflation of the scoring rate of certain dowsers, cloud-busters, and the like, lies in the compliance of some observers with their habit of discounting failures. 'That was just a rehearsal; we'll start with the next one.' 'Don't write that one down; I was put off by that lorry passing.' 'We'll have to start all over again. I forgot to make such-and-such adjustment', and so on. The impropriety of expunging such trials from the mind or from the record is seldom appreciated by the untrained observer.

I was particularly careful to treat Mr D. as a welcome guest in my home, and to be sympathetic rather than critical when the tests failed. We parted on the best of terms. But after intermittent experience of dowsers and dowsing literature over seventeen years I cannot pretend that I still have an open mind on the subject.

[1] S. G. Soal, *Preliminary Studies of a Vaudeville Telepathist* (London, 1937).

On this basis it might be argued that the hostile ray hypothesis is plausible. The difficulty confronting those who adopt this hypothesis is to explain how, in the face of the investigator's supposed hostile emanations, the dowser is able to achieve 100 per cent success – whenever he knows the answer.

12. The British Society of Dowsers

The British Society of Dowsers, in common with similar organizations in America and many other countries, not only seeks to present good evidence for the dowsing faculty to the world at large and to provide a convenient and lively centre for dowsers; it also welcomes outsiders and people who are interested in any aspect of the subject. It holds meetings, organizes lectures and conferences, publishes a quarterly journal, and possesses an excellent library of books, pamphlets and journals for the use of members – and some dowsing intruments are available for purchase.

The British Society was founded by Colonel A. H. Bell, who became the first President, in May 1933. The objects of the society were 'to spread information amongst its members by means of a journal, lectures and other means, about the use of dowsing for geophysical, medical, agricultural and other purposes'; it also keeps a register of dowsers for water, mineral, oil and for other purposes. The present secretary, M. D. Rust, tells me that the present (1979) membership is a little short of 1000, with approximately one third overseas and most of those coming from the Commonwealth and English-speaking countries. Twenty-five volumes of the journal have been published without a break, three times a year, since the formation of the society forty-six years ago. There are several offshoots of the society in various parts of the British Isles and eleven independent local dowsing groups throughout Britain are listed in the journal.

Colonel Bell, who I understand was not a dowser, ran

the society as president and secretary from its inception until 1963 when P. Bernard Smithett became secretary and he continued to serve the society in that capacity until his sudden death in December 1978. In 1964 Colonel K. W. Merrylees was appointed president and he was succeeded in 1966 by Major-General J. Scott Elliot. In 1976, Dr Arthur Bailey, after a number of years as scientific adviser to the society, was elected president and remains so to the present time. A university lecturer of electronics, he presides over the present society with its three vice-presidents: Dr A. T. Westlake, C. B. Thompson and Edwin Taylor, and its seven council members: Sir Charles Jessel, Major-General R. W. T. Britten, Major Bruce MacManaway, Wing-Commander Clive V. Beadon, L. Locker and Tom Graves.

Editor of the journal is I. G. Gretton and some idea of the variety of dowsing aspects covered by the society can be gained by some of the contents in *one* recent journal. They included: records of talks by a practising dowser, Edwin Taylor (a vice-president of the society), who has at least seventy-six wells in the north of England and south of Scotland to his credit – or, as he puts it, 'as a result of this little piece of whalebone'; a talk on wells and well drilling; another on proxy dowsing; and another called 'Dowsing: Tissue Salts' – an examination of substances which are essential to maintain health and alleviate minor illnesses. Other articles included such topics as: dowsing for Roman roads; underground streams and noxious radiations; weather prediction by dowsing and ionization over underground water veins. In addition there are reports on a recent congress held at the south coast, notes and news of items appearing in newspapers and periodicals that are of interest to members of the society, letters to the editor and book reviews.

The present (July 1980) entrance fee to become a member of the British Society of Dowsers is £1.00 the annual subscription, payable on 1 July, is £8.00 for members in Great Britain, and for overseas members (not North America) it is £7.00 annually. Subscription rates for North America are $18.00 per year. Members under 18 are admitted at half the above rates.

The British Society of Dowsers is not only well-intentioned and enthusiastic, it is also efficient and provides a unique service for the growing number of dowsing aspirants and for the increasing number of former sceptics who realize that overwhelming evidence suggests some ability is possessed by some people that defies explanation in the light of present knowledge. Long may the Society of Dowsers continue on its present path; anyone interested in exploring this subject cannot do better than join the society and the first step to do that is to contact the helpful secretary, Mr M. D. Rust.

Epilogue: a last word on how dowsing works

In any dispassionate examination of the divining rod it becomes very clear that suggestion plays a part in triggering off unconscious muscular action. Practically every dowser will admit that he began by imitating another dowser – who probably passed over his twig or rod with some such comment as: 'Here, you try; anyone can do it ... .' The idea is planted in the subconscious that the rod will move and as every psychic investigator and medical practitioner knows suggestion is a very powerful influence.

Taking the rod for the first time into his hands, the would-be dowser grips the rod exactly as he is instructed by the experienced dowser (more suggestion, for he is told that by so holding it the rod will work) and then he concentrates with his eyes fixed on the tip of the rod, thereby focusing all his conscious attention and opening the gates of his subconscious. Some aspiring dowsers become almost entranced – more often they become totally oblivious to everything else at this particular time and they are likely to grip the rod with considerable concentration if not actual force or strength as they seek to maintain the required equilibrium for as long as it takes before the rod moves. Gradually and imperceptibly over a period of time the grip of the would-be dowser either increases or slackens, or so it would seem, and the inevitable reaction is seen in the movement of the rod.

Suggestion comes into play yet again when he is reminded that the ability to dowse improves with practice and, if there is no initial reaction to a spot where he knows or is told that underground water exists, the novice will often remark that he did experience a tingling sensation – a subconscious manifestation of the fact that something ought to happen. Perhaps it is not stretching the imagination too far to say that with repeated attempts at dowsing this tingling sensation becomes an overt movement with a corresponding reaction in the movement of the rod. Yet, in spite of everything one may say about suggestion, the fact remains: *dowsing does work*. This is a simple statement of fact that practically anyone can prove for himself and, in all probability, in doing so he will find an interest for life in a strange and curious mystery, as have so many dowsers over the years.

Select Bibliography

Agricola, Georgius, *De re metallica* (trans. Hoover), 1950.
Alexander, Marc, *Haunted Churches and Abbeys of Britain*, 1978.
Baring-Gould, S., *Curious Myths of the Middle Ages*, 1897.
Barrett, Sir William, *Psychical Research*, 1911.
Barrett, Sir William, and Besterman, Theodore, *The Divining Rod*, 1926.
Bell, A. H. (editor), *Practical Dowsing: A Symposium*, 1965.
Besterman, Theodore, *Water Divining*, 1938.
Carpenter, W. B., *Mental Physiology*, 1874.
Colvill, Helen Hester, *Saint Teresa of Spain*, 1909.
Copen, Bruce, *Dowsing for You*, 1975.
Eadie, John, *A Biblical Cyclopaedia*, 1855.
Elliot, J. Scott, *Dowsing One Man's Way*, 1977.
Evans, Dr Christopher, *Cults of Unreason*, 1973.
Gardner, Martin, *Fads and Fancies in the Name of Science*, 1957.
Graves, Robert, and Hodge, Alan, *The Long Week-end*, 1941.
Graves, Tom, *Dowsing Techniques and Applications*, 1977.
Hazlitt, W. Carew, *Faiths and Folklore*, 1905.
Henning, A. C., *Haunted Borley*, 1949.
Hills, Christopher, *Supersensonics*, 1975.
Hitching, Francis, *Pendulum: The Psi Connection*, 1977.
Inglis, Brian, *Fringe Medicine*, 1964.
Jastrow, Joseph, *Wish and Wisdom*, 1935.
Jones, William, *Credulities Past and Present*, 1880.
Jurion, Jean, *La Radiesthésie techniques et applications*, 1976.
Leftwich, Robert, *Dowsing: the Ancient Art of Rhabdomancy*, 1976.

Lethbridge, Tom C., *Witches: Investigating an Ancient Religion*, 1962, *Ghost and Divining Rod*, 1963, *Ghost and Ghoul*, 1966, *ESP Beyond Time and Distance*, 1965, *A Step in the Dark*, 1967, *The Monkey's Tail*, 1969, *The Power of the Pendulum*, 1976.
Maeterlinck, Maurice, *The Unknown Guest*, 1914.
Mitchell, John, *The View Over Atlantis*, 1969.
Pennant, Thomas, *Tours in Wales*, 1778-81.
Penrose, E. M., *Adventure Unlimited*, 1958.
Price, Harry, *Fifty Years of Psychical Research*, 1939.
Quarrell, Charles, *Buried Treasure*, 1955.
Rawcliffe, D. H., *The Psychology of the Occult*, 1952.
Roberts, Kenneth, *Henry Gross and his Dowsing Rod*, 1952.
Tabori, Cornelius, *My Occult Diary*, 1966.
Taylor, Professor John, *Superminds*, 1975.
Tromp, Solco W., *Psychical Physics*, 1949.
Tyrrell, G. N. M., *Science and Psychical Phenomena*, 1938.
Underwood, Guy, *Pattern of the Past*, 1969.
Underwood, Peter, 'The Borley Haunting 1947-1952' (unpublished MS), *Deeper Into the Occult*, 1975, *Hauntings*, 1977, *Dictionary of the Supernatural*, 1978.
Vogt, Evon Z., and Hyman, Ray, *Water Witching USA*, 1959.
Watkins, Alfred, *The Old Straight Track*, 1925.
Watson, Dr Lyall, *Supernature*, 1973.
Weaver, Herbert, *Divining, the Primary Sense*, 1978.
Wendt, Herbert, *The Romance of Water*, 1963.
Wethered, V. D., *Practical Dowsing*, 1965.
Wheatley, Dennis, *Drink and Ink 1919-1977*, 1979.
Wilson, Colin, *The Occult*, 1973, *Strange Powers*, 1973, *Mysterious Powers*, 1975, *Mysteries*, 1978.
Also: Journals of the British Society of Dowsers; Journals and Proceedings of The Society for Psychical Research; the New Zealand Journal of Science and Technology; Proceedings of the Scientific and Technical Congress of Radionics and Radiesthesia; Proceedings of the International Conferences of Parapsychological Studies, etc.

Index

Abbot, Geoffrey, 119
Abrams, Albert, 100–1
Adventure Unlimited, 196n
aerial rod, 92
Agricola, Georgius, 16, 17–18, 43
Alani nation, 43
Alexander, Marc, 193, 195–7, 197n
ambient magnetic and
  electromagnetic fields, 83
American Society for Psychical
  Research, 54, 54n, 208–9
American Society of Dowsers, 130,
  132, 133, 155–6
American University of the Trees,
  67–8
amplifying pendulum, 92–3
Angel, Graham, 152, 182–4
angle-rod, 91–2, 173, 179–80
animals, 38–40, 94–7, 207
ankh, 89
archaeology, 185, 189
Arrianus, Flavius, 14
L'Association des Amis de la
  Radiesthésie, 36
aurameter, 93
auto-suggestion, 55–6, 205, 206–7
Autrigue, M., 79–80
Aymar, Jacques, 20–5, 80

baguette, 28–29
Bailey, Dr Arthur, 218
Barkstead, John, 119–24
Barkstead treasure, 119–26
Barnothey, Madeleine, 83
Barrett, Sir William, 15, 18, 27–8,
  31–5, 55–7, 91–2, 206–7
Beadon, Wing-Commander Clive V.,
  218
Beausoleil, Baroness de, 26–7
Bell, Colonel A.H., 75, 209–10, 217–18

Bentine, Adam, 193
Bentine, Michael, 193–4, 195
Besterman, Theodore, 15, 18, 85, 85n,
  112
Biblical Cyclopaedia, A, 16n
Biblical references, 16, 40, 41–2, 179
biophysical method, *see* BPM
'black-box', 93–4, 100–4
Bleton, 29–30
Blyth-Praeger, Major J.F.F., 97n
Boothby, Captain Robert, 59–60
Borley church, 191–7
Borley Haunting, The, 192n
Bovis, A., 79
Bown, David, 49–50, 52
BPM (biophysical method), 160–1,
  162–3, 164, 165
British Congress on Radionics and
  Radiesthesia, 53–4
British Society for Psychical
  Research, 105–7, 209–216
British Society of Dowsers, 36, 53,
  159, 178, 184, 209, 217–19
Britten, Major-General R.W.T., 218
Brown, Hugh A., 50–1, 52
Bull, Ethel, 195
Burgan, Jack, 156
Burgoyne, W.H., 81–2
Buried Treasure, 121n, 123
Burridge, Gaston, 15n
Butler, Timothy and Vincent, 152

cable divining, 143
Cameron, Vernon L., 155
Camus, Cardinal, 29
Canada, 165
Carpenter, W.B., 65–66, 65n, 66n
Carter, Cheryl, 195
Castle of the Soul, The, 26
Centre International d'Étude de la
  Radiesthésie, 36

Chadwick, Duane, 164
channel of communication, 148–9
Chantereine, Mlle, 98
Charles II, King, 119, 120, 122
Chevreul, Michel Eugène, 64n, 65, 65n, 98
children, determining sex of, 63, 76
Christian Science Monitor, 45
Cicero, Marcus Tullius, 14
clairvoyancy, *see* extrasensory perception
Clarke, John, 80–1
Clever Hans, 63
colour and emanation of consciousness, 57–8
Congrés de Souriers, 72
Cooper, Dr C.M., 54–5
Copen, Bruce, 88n
Cosmography, 16
Credulities Past and Present, 111n
criminals, location of, 20–6, 29, 63, 67–9, 80
Cromwell, Oliver, 119, 122
Csucsek, Father Anthony, 126–7
Culme-Seymour, Lady, 137
Cults of Unreason, 101n
Czechoslovakia, 165

De Officiis, 14
De Quincey, Thomas, 30
De re metallica, 17
Deeper Into the Occult, 20n, 140–3
divining rod, history of: Greeks and Romans, 14–17; Biblical references, 16, 40, 41–2, 179; early English references, 18; 16th-century Germany, 18–19, 27–8, 29, 43; association with the Devil, 19–20; 127; Jacques Aymar, 20–5; St Theresa of Avila, 25–6; Baroness de Beausoleil, 26–7; worldwide use, 27; Cornish mines, 28; Southern France, 28–9; Bleton, 29–30; American 'water witching', 30–1; John Mullins, 31–3; J.H. Jones, 33–4; Barrett's tests, 34–5; metallurgic gods, 40–1; fairy tales, mythology, 127, 128; *see also* dowsing instruments
Divining Rod, The, 15, 18
Divining, the Primary Sense, 107–8, 178n
dowsing, aspects of: metals and minerals, 17–18, 27–8, 29, 55, 63, 111–12, 113, 125, 159–60, 165–6,
185, 197, 212–13; water, 25–7, 29–36, 44–6, 50, 63, 82–3, 91–2, 113–19, 126–7, 130, 131–2, 135, 136–7, 138–9, 140–3, 154–7, 160–3, 164, 196, 197–9; map, 63, 67–76, 117, 131, 132–3, 156; pendulum, 63, 64–6, 67, 68, 69–73, 74, 75–80, 82–3, 88–91; 97–8, 99–100, 151–2; sexing eggs and children, 63, 76; radiesthesia, 63, 76, 77–80, 96–104; locating criminals and missing people, 29, 63, 67–9, 72–3, 76, 80–2, 128, 151–2, 157; 'talking horses', 63–4; table turning, 66–7; ouija board, 67; treasure-hunting, 109–12, 119–26, 185, 191–2, 207, 211–13; passages and tunnels, 137–8, 150, 152–3; mine detecting, 154, 165, 191; prevention of accidents, 158; ghost-hunting, 185, 187–8, 189, 191–7, 201–2; archaeology, 185, 190; monsters, 185–6
dowsing, authenticity of: 37, 40; vibratory resonance, 38–9, 47–8; comparisons with animals, 38–40; historical viewpoint, 40–4; extrasensory perception, 44
dowsing instruments: 84; forked twig, 84–6, 87–8, 174, 179–80, 182, 183; other forked implements, 86, 174–76, 183; hands, 86, 96–7; straight rod, 86–7, 176, 179, 182; aluminium or wire rod, 88, 90; polyethylene rod, 88; pendulums, 88–91, 97–8, 99–100, 181; angle-rods, 91–2, 173, 179–80 183; aerial rod, 92; 'motorscope', 92; amplifying pendulum, 92–3; aurameter, 93; 'black box', 93–4, 100–4; Revealer, 105–6, 166–7, 178; where to obtain instruments, 182–3; *see also* divining rod, history of
dowsing techniques: teaching, 168–9, 199–200; experiments for non-believers, 169–72, 199; using L-rods, 173–4, 179–80, 182, 183, 184; using forked twig, 174, 178, 179–80, 182, 183, 199–200; using forked implement, 174–6, 182, 183; using straight rod, 176, 179, 180–81, 200; using a pendulum, 177, 181, 182, 183, 184; positive

thought, 178; where to try dowsing, 184
dowsing, theories of: electromagnetic disturbance, 47, 178; vibratory resonance, 47–8; attraction between like substances, 48; power of conviction, 48–9; inheritance, 49; radiant energy, 51–2; radiation, 53, 145, 146; extrasensory perception, 53–4, 56–7, 116–18, 205–6; anatomy and gait of dowser, 54–5; auto-suggestion, 55–6, 205; colour and emanations of consciousness, 57–8; magnetic currents, 58–9, 162, 164; ley lines, 59–62; physical impression, 117–18, 145–8, 204; channel of communication, 148–9; resonance, 171
'Dowsing: A Field Experiment in Water Divining', 209n
Dowsing for You, 88n
Dowsing Techniques and Applications, 168
Dowsing: the Ancient Art of Rhabdomancy, 84n
Drown, Dr Ruth, 101

Eadie, John, 16n
eggs, sexing of, 63, 76, 97
Einstein, Albert, 154
Elberfeld Horses, 63
electrical effects, 39–40
electromagnetic disturbances, 47
Elliot, Major-General J. Scott, 73–5, 218
Evans, Dr Christopher, 101

fairy tales, 128
Faraday, Michael, 66–7
Fate, 50–1
Fell, Frederick, 152–3
Fifty Years of Psychical Research, 135n
Fludd, Robert, 18
forked twig, 84–6, 87–8, 174, 178–9, 179–80, 182, 183
Foulkes, R.A., 163–4
Franks, Sir John, 33–4
fruit and vegetable testing, 133–4
Fry, Catherine, 143

Galvani, 127
Gentleman's Magazine, 43, 178
Germania, 14

Germany, 18–19, 27, 28
Gesellschaft für Wissenschaftliche Pendelferschung, 36
Ghost and Ghoul, 169n, 171n
'Ghost Hunters, The', 201
ghost hunting, 185, 186–9, 191–7, 201–2
Ghosts and Divining Rod, 189
Ghosts of Borley, The, 193n
Goddard, Sir Victor, 104
Gooch, Tom, 192–3, 194
Gooch, Mrs T., 194
Gramenis, François, 72–3
Graves, Robert, 69, 69n
Graves, Tom, 168, 218
Greeks, 14–17, 76
Green, Andrew M., 201–2
Gretton, I.G., 218
Gross, Henry, 197

Hackworthy, R., 197–200
Harben, Sir Henry, 31
Harris, Captain Ralph W., 131–3
Harrison, Dr Vernon, 52–3
Haunted Borley, 192n
Haunted Churches and Abbeys of Britain, 193n, 195–6, 196n
Hauntings, New Light on the Greatest True Stories of the World, 194n
Haynes, Renée, 143–4
Hazlitt, W. Carew, 19n
Henning, Rev. Alfred, 191–2, 192n
Henry Gross and his Dowsing Rod, 197n
Hephaestus, 40
Hermes, 14–15
Herodotus, 43
Hicks, Kirsten, 94–5
Hills, Christopher, 38n, 91n, 177–8
Hitching, Francis, 119n
Hodge, Alan, 69, 69n
Hyman, Ray, 63n, 64, 172, 172n, 205n

illness, diagnosis and treatment of, 63, 76, 77–80, 97–104, 159
India, 114–15, 118
indirect dowsing, *see* map dowsing
Indra, 40
inheritance, 49
instruments, *see* dowsing instruments
International Congress of Radiesthesia, 36

Jensen, Dr E.T., 79
Jensen, Larry, 164

Jessel, Sir Charles, 218
Joad, Dr C.E.M., 76
Johnson, Dr, 43
Jones, J.H., 33–4
Jones, William, 111n

Kalahari desert, 139
Keck, George, 45–6
Kelly, Sapper, 91–2
King family, 70–2
Kingfisher, 151–2
Kirchner, Athanasis, 127

L-rods, *see* angle-rods
La Restitution de Pluton, 26
La signal de Sourcier, 59
Lady Wonder, 63
Lambert, Abbé Gabriel, 135
Lancet, The, 65
Latham, L.J., 40, 69–70
Leftwich, Robert, 48–9, 84n, 90, 143,
    186–9
Lethbridge, T.C., 44, 169–72, 189–91
Lewis, William A., 151–2
ley lines, 59–62
Lilly, William, 29, 109–11
Linnaeus, Carl von Linné, 111–12
location of criminals and missing
    people, 63, 67–9, 72–3, 76, 80–2,
    128, 151–2, 157
Loch Ness monster, 185–6
Locke, John, 28
Locker, L., 218
Luther, Martin, 18–19

McCauley, Kevin, 151–2
MacManaway, Major Bruce, 218
McMillen, E.P., 155
Madden, Dr H., 65–6
magnetic currents, 58–9, 99
map dowsing, 63, 67–8, 68–75, 118,
    131, 134–5, 156
Marcellinus, Ammianus, 43, 64
Martin, Dr Ernest, 78–9
Matacia, Louis, 131
Matveev, V.S., 160–1, 162
Max Planck Institute, 96
Medhurst, Dr George, 105–7
Meier, Henri, 82–3
Mermet, Abbé, 68–9, 76
Merrylees, Colonel K.W., 143–9, 168,
    218
metal and mineral divining, 17–18,
    27–8, 29, 55, 63, 111–12, 113, 125,
    159–60, 165–6, 185, 197, 212–3

metallurgic gods, 40–1
migrating birds, 39–40, 94
Miles, Miss, 57, 207
mine detecting, 154, 165, 191
missing people, location of, 29, 63,
    67–9, 72–3, 76, 80–2, 128, 151–2,
    157
mnemonic charts, 104
Moses, 16, 40, 41–2
'motorscope', 92
Mount Gleason, 155–6
Mullins, John, 31–3, 169, 207
Munster, Sebastian, 16
My Occult Diary, 128n, 129n
Mysteries, 189n
Mysterious Powers, 166–7

Nature, 96, 163
nervous tension, 129
New Scientist, 160–2, 163–4
*New Zealand Journal of Science and
    Technology*, 204–5
'Now You See It, Now You Don't',
    88, 91, 173

O'Loughlin, Legory H., 130–3, 173
Old Straight Track, The, 61
Oliver, J.C., 105, 106
Ongley, P.A., 204–5
oscilloclast, 100–1
ouija board, 67

Palmer, Leslie, 197–201
Parker, Mrs, 192–3
Parsons, Denys, 210–16
Pasquini, Signor Elio, 93
passages and tunnels, 137–8, 150,
    152–3
Patton, General George, 132
Peatty, Graham, 152–3
'Pebble Mill', 210
pendulum, 63, 64–6, 67, 68, 69–73,
    74, 75–80, 82–3, 88–91, 97–8,
    99–100, 151–2, 169–73, 177–8,
    181–2, 183, 184
Pendulum: the Psi Connection, 119n
Pennant, Thomas, 43, 179
Penrose, Evelyn, 46, 197
Pepys, Samuel, 120–4
Phillips, Catherine, 103–4
Philosophia Moysaica, 18
Pliny the Elder, 17
Phythian-Adams, Canon, 194
Pogson, Major C.A., 92, 112–119,
    124–6, 129, 135

Pogson, W.N., 113
Polglase, Walter, 159-60
Power of the Pendulum, 190
Practical Dowsing: A Symposium, 74, 75, 78, 79n, 81, 97n, 181n
prevention of accidents, 158
Price, Harry, 76, 135, 135n, 138, 195
Psychic Energy, 157
Psychical Physics, 15n, 203n
Psychical Research, 18, 29n, 33n, 55-7, 207n
Psychology of the Occult, The, 73, 91n, 118n
Psychosomatic Research Association, 53

Quarrell, Charles, 121-4

radiant energy, 51-2
radiation, 53, 94, 96, 100
'radiational paraphysics', 67-8
radiesthesia, 37-8, 47, 53, 63, 76, 77-80, 93-4, 96-104
Radiesthetic Approach to Health and Homoeopathy, A, 79
Radionic Association, 53
radionic box *see* 'black box'
radionics, 53
Rawcliffe, D.H., 73, 91n, 118n
ray-paths, 107-8
research and experiments, 160-7, 203-16
resonance, 171
Reuter, Dr Camillo, 126-8, 129
Revealer, 105-8, 166-7, 178
Rey, Colonel, 138-9
rhabdomancy, 16-17, 29, 37
Rhine, Prof J.B., 44, 63
Rivers-Moore, Colonel, 138
Roberts, Kenneth, 197n
Robertson, Dr A.J.B., 54
Rocard, Yves, 58-9, 99
Rockingham Castle, 137-8
Roessler, 127
Romans, 14, 16, 17, 76
Rust, M.D., 217-9
Rutter, 65-6

sceptre, as emblem of power, 40
schlag-ruthe, 28
Schott, Gaspard, 29, 89
Scythians, 43
serpents, 15, 40-1
Seward, Percival, 97-8

sexing children and eggs, 63, 76
Shepherd's Calendar and Countryman's Companion, 85
sixth sense *see* extrasensory perception
Smith, Jerry, 154
Smith, Reginald, 59-60
Smithett, P. Bernard, 218
Sochevanov, N.N., 160-1, 162, 165-6
societies, 36, 217-19
Southern California Edison Company, 154
Soviet Union, 160-1, 162-3, 164, 165-6
Spain, 35
Spary, Major Harold, 143
Speculum metallurgiae, 127
Speleological Society, 124
spiritualist session, 66-7
Stone, W., 34-5
Stonehenge, 62
Superminds, 99
Supernature, 96-7, 165n, 166
Supersensonics, 38n, 91n, 177, 177n
Swift, Jonathan, 30

table turning, 66-7
Tabori, Cornelius, 126-8, 128n, 129, 129n
Tabori, Dr Paul, 126, 128, 128n, 193n
Tacitus, Publius Cornelius, 14, 43, 64
'talking horses', 63-4
Taylor, Edwin, 218
Taylor, Prof John, 99
Thomas, Ralph, 159
Thompson, C.B., 218
Thor, 40
Thouvénel, Dr, 29
Tower of London, 119-26
treasure-hunting, 29, 109-12, 119-26, 185, 191-2, 207, 211-13
Tributsch, Dr Helmeut, 96
Trinder, Captain W.H., 76-7, 135-40
Tristan, Count de, 87
Tromp, Prof Solco W., 15n, 203-4
Turenne, Louis, 47
Tyler, Major F.C., 59

Underwood, Guy, 59-62
Underwood, Peter, 192n, 193n
UNESCO, 165
United States, 30-1, 44-5, 130, 164-5
Utah State University, 164

Vallemant, Abbé de, 87
Van Jaarsveld, Pieter, 86

Veale, L.J., 105, 107–8
Vedic, 40
'vertical magnetic tuners', 104
vibratory resonance, 38, 47, 48
Vogt, Evon Z., 64, 172, 172n, 205n
Volta, 127

Walker, Mrs Ellie, 133–5
Warr, George de la, 101, 102–4
'Water Diviners of India', 116
water divining, 25–7, 29–36, 44–6, 50,
   63, 82–3, 91–2, 113–19, 126–7, 130,
   131–2, 135, 136–7, 138–9, 140–3,
   154–7, 160–3, 164, 196, 197–9
Water Divining, 85n
'water witching', 39, 45, 153
Water Witching, U.S.A., 63, 64, 66, 172,
   205
Watkins, Alfred, 60–1
Watson, Dr Lyall, 96–7, 164–6

Watson, Dr T.T.B., 98, 101–2
Weaver, Herbert, 107–8, 178
Weed, Joseph J., 157
Wenger, Rudolph, 158
Westlake, Dr A.T., 218
Wethered, V.D., 78–9, 79n, 181
Wetherhead, Dr Leslie, 104
Wheatley, Dennis, 19
'When the Sun Turns Red, it's Pay
   Day', 159–60
Williamson, Paul, 205
Williamson, Tom, 160–2, 163–4, 210
Wilson, Colin, 166–7, 189n, 196–7
'wire treatment', 79
witchcraft, 30
*Witches: Investigating an Ancient
   Religion*, 190
Wright Rain, 150

Young, J.F., 57, 207
Young, William, 143, 150